Excel® 2007 PivotTables and PivotCharts

Peter G. Aitken

Excel® 2007 PivotTables and PivotCharts

Published by
Wiley Publishing, Inc.
10475 Crosspoint Boulevard
Indianapolis, IN 46256
www.wiley.com

Copyright © 2007 by Wiley Publishing, Inc., Indianapolis, Indiana

Published by Wiley Publishing, Inc., Indianapolis, Indiana

Published simultaneously in Canada

Library of Congress Control Number: 2007006577

ISBN: 978-0-470-10487-3

Manufactured in the United States of America

10 9 8 7 6 5 4 3 2 1

For general information on our other products and services or to obtain technical support, please contact our Customer Care Department within the U.S. at (800) 762-2974, outside the U.S. at (317) 572-3993 or fax (317) 572-4002.

Library of Congress Cataloging-in-Publication Data

Aitken, Peter G.
    Excel 2007 PivotTables and PivotCharts / Peter Aitken.
        p. cm.
    Includes index.
    ISBN 978-0-470-10487-3 (paper/website)
    1. Microsoft Excel (Computer file) 2. Business—Computer programs. 3. Electronic spreadsheets. 4. Charts, diagrams, etc.—Computer programs. I. Title.
    HF5548.4.M523A456 2007
    005.54—dc22

                                    2007006577

WILEY is a trademark of Wiley Publishing, Inc.

About the Author

Peter Aitken has been writing about computers and programming for over 15 years. He has more than 45 books to his credit with over 1.5 million copies in print, as well as hundreds of magazine and trade publication articles. His areas of special interest include Microsoft Office programs, digital imaging, and Visual Basic programming. Aitken is the proprietor of PGA Consulting, providing custom application development and technical writing services to business, academia, and government since 1994. For 18 years, Aitken was a member of the faculty at Duke University Medical Center. He left Duke in 2000 to devote full time to his writing and consulting.

Acknowledgments

Many people are involved in the creation of a book such as this one. Although I can't name everyone, there are three people who stand out as having made significant contributions: Ed Ferrero, Technical Editor; Sydney Jones, Development Editor; and Katie Mohr, Acquisitions Editor. Thanks everyone!

Contents at a Glance

Table of Contents

Part II: PivotTables and Charts: Going Beyond the Basics

Part III: Getting the Most out of PivotTables and Charts

Introduction

Microsoft Excel is a powerful and popular program for organizing and analyzing data. One of its most powerful capabilities is PivotTables, which enable you to pull meaningful information from huge masses of seemingly meaningless data. The name PivotTable comes from one of the most powerful features of Excel—the ability to quickly and easily "pivot" the data to view them in different ways.

Given all their power, PivotTables (and the related PivotCharts) are necessarily somewhat complex. You can't get something for nothing, after all, and in order to make the most of these powerful tools you need a good understanding of what they are and how they work. That's where this book comes in. Excel PivotTables and Charts covers the topic from A to Z, starting with the basics and moving on to the most advanced and sophisticated aspects of PivotTables. The book uses a lot of illustrations and real-world examples to make it easier for you to relate the information to your own work.

Who Should Read This Book

This book does not assume that the reader has any prior experience with PivotTables. It starts at square one and moves on from there. However, even those who do have previous PivotTable experience may well find the book useful for dealing with the more arcane aspects of PivotTables or with the many changes that are present in the latest version of Excel. The book is written specifically for Excel 2007.

How This Book Is Organized

The book is divided into chapters, with each chapter providing a number of sections that cover some specific aspect of PivotTables or PivotCharts.

- **Chapter 1** explains the principles behind PivotTables and shows you the steps required to create a simple PivotTable and chart from your worksheet data.

- **Chapter 2** explains the various data sources that you use to create a PivotTable.

- **Chapters 3–5** get into the nitty-gritty details of PivotTables including formatting, filtering, grouping, and custom calculations.

- **Chapter 6** is devoted to creating PivotCharts from the data in your PivotTables.

- **Chapter 7** explores the advanced topic of using PivotCharts with multidimensional data.

- **Chapter 8** shows you how to extract hard data from a PivotTable for further analysis in your worksheet.

- **Chapter 9** explores some other Excel analysis methods, such as subtotals and database functions, that may be preferable to PivotTables for some data analysis needs.

- **Chapter 10** covers the use of the VBA programming language to create and manipulate PivotTables.

The book includes three appendixes:

- **Appendix A** discusses troubleshooting some common PivotTable problems.

- **Appendix B** details the PivotTable-related differences between Excel 2007 and the previous version of Excel.

- **Appendix C** provides a primer of Excel charts for those who need to brush up their knowledge.

The workbooks that you'll need for many of the book's exercises are available for download at www.wiley.com/go/excel07pivottables.

Part I

PivotTable Fundamentals

Chapter 1
Understanding PivotTables and Charts

Chapter 2
Understanding Data Sources for PivotTables

Chapter 3
Using PivotTable Tools and Formatting

Chapter **1**

Understanding PivotTables and Charts

In this chapter, you learn about PivotTables and PivotCharts, which are powerful data-analysis tools in Excel. They are invaluable for pulling meaning from huge masses of seemingly meaningless data. Given their power, PivotTables and PivotCharts are surprisingly easy to use, but using them still involves many unavoidable complexities. This book teaches you how to use PivotTables and PivotCharts efficiently and effectively. As the first step, you need to understand what these tools are and when you might want to use them.

In This Chapter

- ◆ Understanding how PivotTables work
- ◆ Working with PivotTables
- ◆ Creating a PivotTable report
- ◆ Creating a PivotTable report with multiple columns
- ◆ Using the PivotTable and PivotChart Wizard
- ◆ Creating a PivotChart

Understanding How PivotTables Work

PivotTables enable you to extract meaning from large amounts of data. This description is deceptively simple because in fact PivotTables are powerful and sophisticated tools that enable you to do things that would be impossible or difficult to do any other way. A PivotTable enables you to take what seems to be an indecipherable mass of facts and extract any trends and patterns buried in the data. You can organize and summarize your data, perform comparisons, and extract meaningful information that can be invaluable to you and your organization. A PivotTable can work with data that is located in an Excel workbook and also with data from an external database. This is an important factor because it enables you to analyze data sets that are much too large to be contained in a workbook. Now that Excel 2007 is here, this point seems less important than in the past. With a capability of one million rows, it seems probable that most data sets will fit into a workbook easily. A more compelling reason to work with an external database is that it ensures data integrity throughout an organization—not to mention that it is easier than importing the data into Excel just to create a PivotTable.

Why the term *pivot?* It comes from an analogy between the way PivotTables work and the way you investigate a physical object. Imagine that you have been handed a complex device and asked to figure out what it does. You don't just look at it from one angle; rather you turn it in your hands, examining it from all possible perspectives to be sure you do not miss any important clues. PivotTables work the same way, enabling you to turn or pivot the raw data and examine it from various perspectives to extract the information you need. Then you also have the option of creating a *PivotChart,* a graphical representation of the information in a PivotTable.

Suppose you work for a chain of sporting-goods stores. Every day you receive a report from each store that includes complete details on that day's activities, such as number of customers each hour, sales in each of 30 categories, items returned for refund or exchange, and number of employees on duty at different times of the day. It won't be long before your Excel workbook is chock-full of this raw data, but what good does it do you? You could stare at this information for hours without gaining any useful insights from it. But with a PivotTable you can quickly and easily answer the following types of questions:

- Which days of the week show the highest sales?
- Which categories of merchandise sell best at different times of the year?
- Are more employees scheduled to work during periods of the highest customer load?
- Do certain categories of merchandise suffer from unusually high rates of return or exchange?

These are the kinds of questions that a business needs to answer in order to operate efficiently. These are also the kinds of questions that PivotTables are designed to answer. The same kinds of analysis are appropriate for almost any kind of data you can imagine, from political surveys to weather patterns, from quality control in a manufacturing plant to test scores in a high school. That's the beauty of PivotTables—they are powerful *and* flexible.

Working with PivotTables

I could talk about PivotTables until I am blue in the face, but it's much better to actually show an example. By looking at the kind of data that PivotTables are used for, and seeing the resulting PivotTable in action, you will get a good understanding of the what and why of this powerful tool.

Figure 1-1 shows some data that are typical of the kind you would analyze using a PivotTable. These data are based on the sporting-goods store example I mentioned earlier. As with other examples in this book I have intentionally simplified the data to illustrate the points I am trying to make without confusing you with unnecessary details. You should not think that PivotTables are limited to relatively simple data such as these.

What questions might you want to ask about these data? Here are a few that come to mind:

- What are the sales for the Camping category for each region?
- In each store, which days of the week see the most customers?
- In each store, which category has the highest sales?
- Which day of the week has the lowest total sales?

In the following demonstration, you explore the first question. You create a PivotTable report that shows the total sales of goods in the Camping category subtotaled by region.

Changes to Excel PivotTables and Charts

If you worked with PivotTables and PivotCharts in earlier versions of Excel you will find lots of changes in the current program. The tables and charts have not themselves changed much, but the procedures you use to create and work with them have been streamlined and simplified. I think you'll find these changes to be great improvements—but some of the older techniques are still supported for those users who are accustomed to using them.

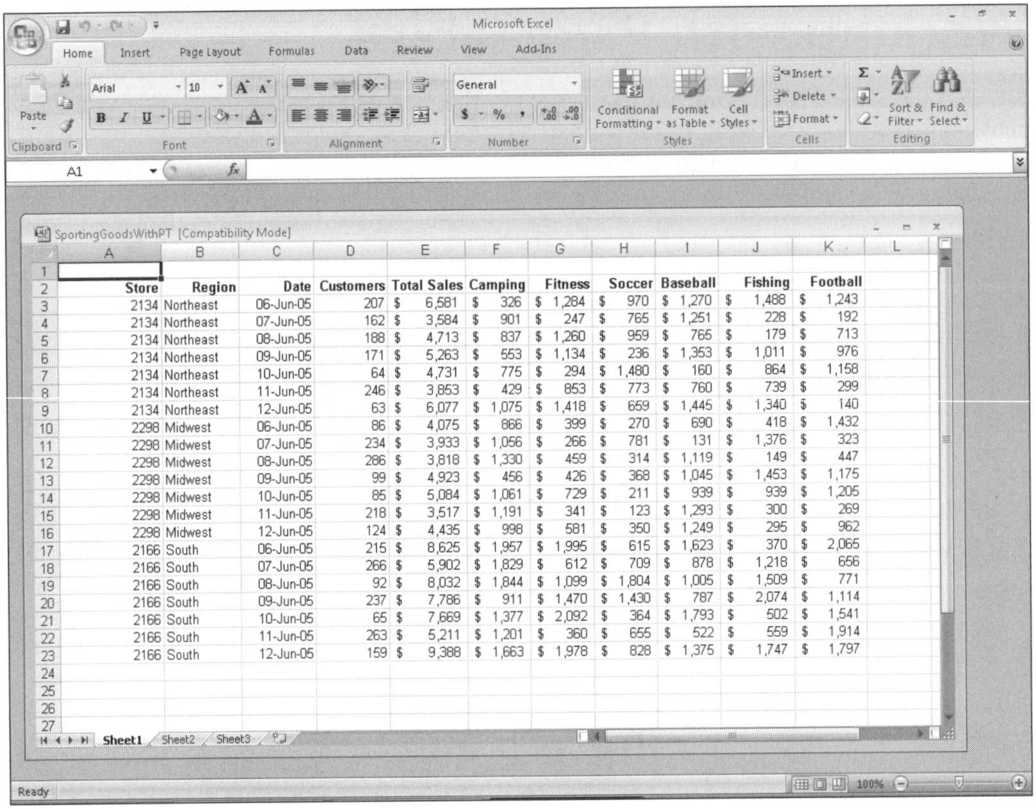

Store	Region	Date	Customers	Total Sales	Camping	Fitness	Soccer	Baseball	Fishing	Football
2134	Northeast	06-Jun-05	207	$ 6,581	$ 326	$ 1,284	$ 970	$ 1,270	$ 1,488	$ 1,243
2134	Northeast	07-Jun-05	162	$ 3,584	$ 901	$ 247	$ 765	$ 1,251	$ 228	$ 192
2134	Northeast	08-Jun-05	188	$ 4,713	$ 837	$ 1,260	$ 959	$ 765	$ 179	$ 713
2134	Northeast	09-Jun-05	171	$ 5,263	$ 553	$ 1,134	$ 236	$ 1,353	$ 1,011	$ 976
2134	Northeast	10-Jun-05	64	$ 4,731	$ 775	$ 294	$ 1,480	$ 160	$ 864	$ 1,158
2134	Northeast	11-Jun-05	246	$ 3,853	$ 429	$ 853	$ 773	$ 760	$ 739	$ 299
2134	Northeast	12-Jun-05	63	$ 6,077	$ 1,075	$ 1,418	$ 659	$ 1,445	$ 1,340	$ 140
2298	Midwest	06-Jun-05	86	$ 4,075	$ 866	$ 399	$ 270	$ 690	$ 418	$ 1,432
2298	Midwest	07-Jun-05	234	$ 3,933	$ 1,056	$ 266	$ 781	$ 131	$ 1,376	$ 323
2298	Midwest	08-Jun-05	286	$ 3,818	$ 1,330	$ 459	$ 314	$ 1,119	$ 149	$ 447
2298	Midwest	09-Jun-05	99	$ 4,923	$ 456	$ 426	$ 368	$ 1,045	$ 1,453	$ 1,175
2298	Midwest	10-Jun-05	85	$ 5,084	$ 1,061	$ 729	$ 211	$ 939	$ 939	$ 1,205
2298	Midwest	11-Jun-05	218	$ 3,517	$ 1,191	$ 341	$ 123	$ 1,293	$ 300	$ 269
2298	Midwest	12-Jun-05	124	$ 4,435	$ 998	$ 581	$ 350	$ 1,249	$ 295	$ 962
2166	South	06-Jun-05	215	$ 8,625	$ 1,957	$ 1,995	$ 615	$ 1,623	$ 370	$ 2,065
2166	South	07-Jun-05	266	$ 5,902	$ 1,829	$ 612	$ 709	$ 878	$ 1,218	$ 656
2166	South	08-Jun-05	92	$ 8,032	$ 1,844	$ 1,099	$ 1,804	$ 1,005	$ 1,509	$ 771
2166	South	09-Jun-05	237	$ 7,786	$ 911	$ 1,470	$ 1,430	$ 787	$ 2,074	$ 1,114
2166	South	10-Jun-05	65	$ 7,669	$ 1,377	$ 2,092	$ 364	$ 1,793	$ 502	$ 1,541
2166	South	11-Jun-05	263	$ 5,211	$ 1,201	$ 360	$ 655	$ 522	$ 559	$ 1,914
2166	South	12-Jun-05	159	$ 9,388	$ 1,663	$ 1,978	$ 828	$ 1,375	$ 1,747	$ 1,797

Figure 1-1: The sample data.

Creating a PivotTable Report

In this section I will guide you through the steps required to create a report that answers the question posed above: What are the sales for the Camping category for each region?

To begin, you must start Excel and open the workbook that contains the raw data, `SportingGoodsRawData.xlsx`. This workbook is provided for download from `www.wiley.com/go/excel07pivottables/`.

After you have opened the workbook, make sure that the cell pointer is on any cell in the table of data. Then, start by clicking the PivotTable button on the Insert ribbon. Excel displays the Create PivotTable dialog box as shown in Figure 1-2.

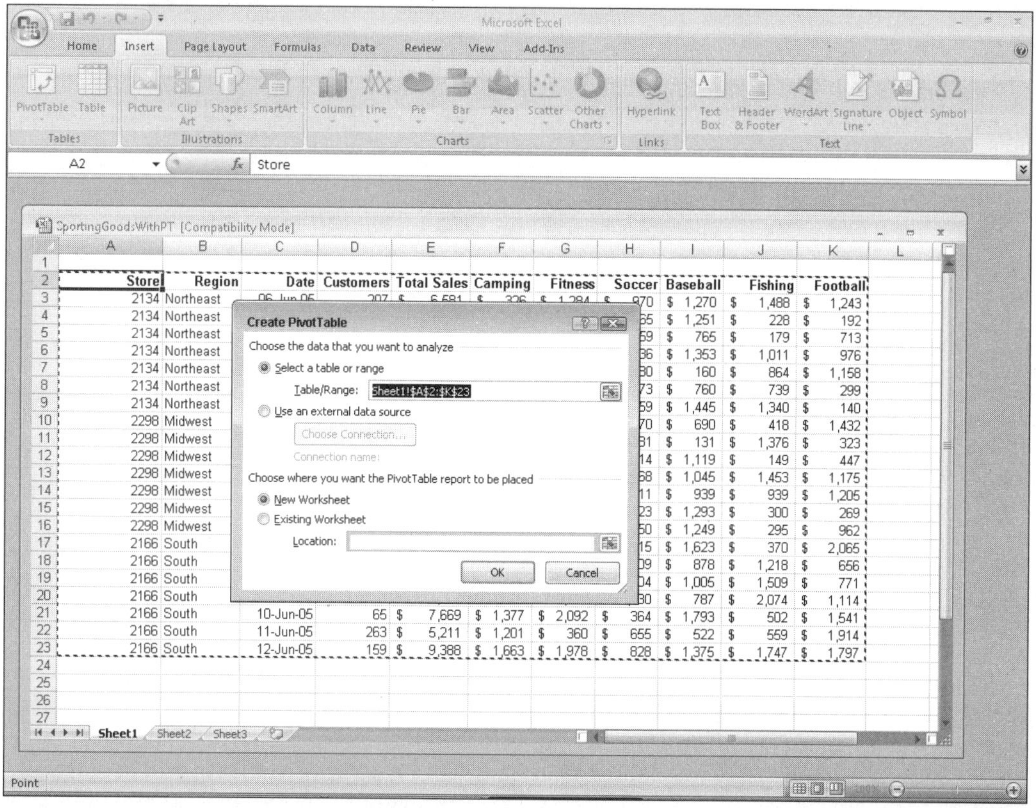

Figure 1-2: The Create PivotTable dialog box.

In this dialog box, you can see that the address of the data range—A2:K44 in this example—is already entered in the Table/Range box. Make sure that the options are selected as shown in Figure 1-2 and described here:

- Select a table or range
- New Worksheet

Then click the OK button to close the dialog box and create the PivotTable—or, to be more accurate, the shell of the PivotTable because there are a few more steps required. At this stage Excel will look as shown in Figure 1-3.

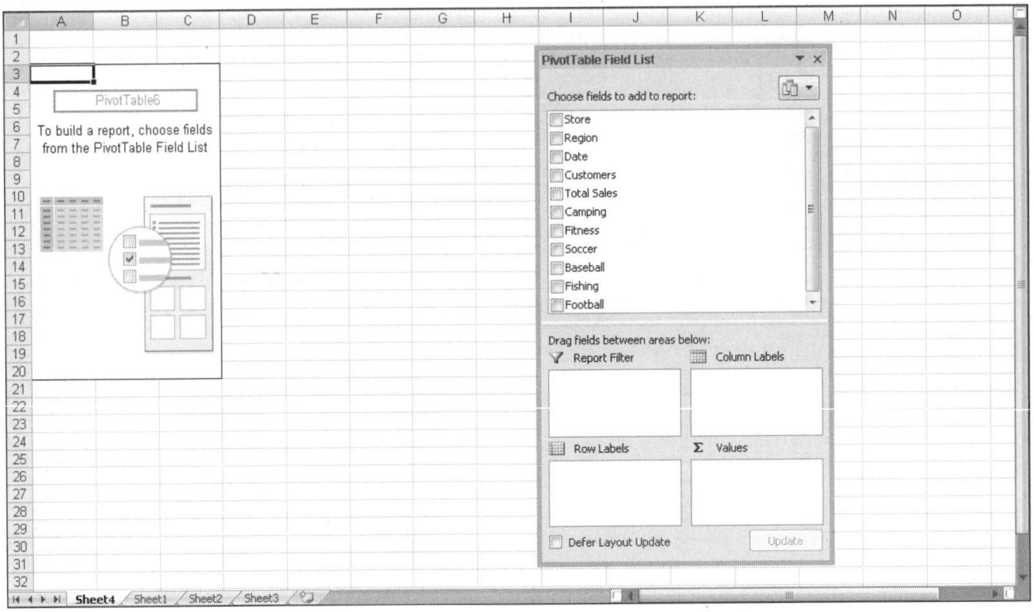

Figure 1-3: The shell of the PivotTable has been placed in a new worksheet.

Please note two things about Figure 1-3. On the left is the shell of the PivotTable; this is where it will be displayed after you have finished defining it. On the right is the PivotTable Field List, and it's here that you define what data will be in the PivotTable and how it will be arranged. Later in the book you'll learn all the details of using the PivotTable Field List, but for now just follow along.

In the PivotTable Field List, click the Region item to place a check mark next to it. You'll see that Region is displayed in the Row Labels section of the PivotTable Field List, and that the PivotTable itself changes to display the three regions—Midwest, Northeast, and South—in column A.

Next, click the Camping item to place a check mark next to it. Sum of Camping will be displayed in the Values box at the bottom of the dialog box, and the sums for the Camping category will be displayed in column B of the PivotTable, along with a grand total for all regions.

Finally, click the down arrow next to Sum of Camping in the Values box and then select Value Field Settings from the context menu. Excel displays the Data Field Settings dialog box. Click the Number Format button to open the Format Cells dialog box. Select the Currency format; then click OK twice to close all dialog boxes. At this point your PivotTable will look like Figure 1-4.

Region	Sum of Camping
Midwest	$6,958.00
Northeast	$4,896.00
South	$10,782.00
Grand Total	$22,636.00

Figure 1-4: The completed PivotTable report.

I hope that you are suitably impressed with how easy it is to create this PivotTable report. Yes, it's a simple one, but the same principles apply for more complex requirements. At this time, I want to point out a couple of other aspects of PivotTable reports.

When the report is active, the PivotTable Field List is displayed. Fields that are part of the report are displayed in boldface and with a check mark in this list. They are also displayed in the various boxes at the bottom of the dialog box showing what role they have in the report. To make the PivotTable active, click anywhere in it. To make it inactive, click somewhere else in the worksheet.

Note that the Region heading in the report has a drop-down arrow next to it. If you click this arrow, Excel displays a list of all the row values as shown in Figure 1-5—in this case, the names of the three regions, Midwest, Northeast, and South. By selecting or clearing individual items in this list, including the Select All option, you can change what the PivotTable displays. You can also perform other actions here, such as sorting—these will be covered in a later chapter.

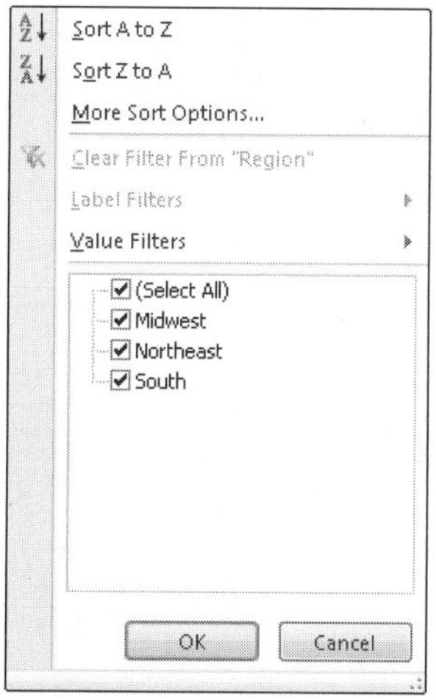

Figure 1-5: Selecting which rows to display in the PivotTable report.

For example, by selecting only the Midwest item and then clicking OK, you modify the report to show the Camping category sales for the Midwest region only, as shown in Figure 1-6.

Region ▼	Sum of Camping
Midwest	$6,958.00
Grand Total	$6,958.00

Figure 1-6: The PivotTable report customized to display only the Midwest region.

Creating a PivotTable Report with Multiple Columns

The example PivotTable presented in the previous section was just about the simplest PivotTable you can create. It will be useful to go through the process of creating a somewhat more sophisticated PivotTable report, one that has multiple columns as well as rows. The data you will use is shown in Figure 1-7. It is inventory data for a chain of video-rental stores.

VideoStoreRawData_WithPT_1

	A	B	C	D	E	F
1						
2	Popcorn Video Rentals					
3						
4	**Store**	**Category**	**Titles**			
5	Main Street	Action	374			
6	Main Street	Drama	180			
7	Main Street	Childrens	63			
8	Main Street	Sci-Fi	324			
9	Main Street	Classics	203			
10	Main Street	Comedy	145			
11	Northgate	Action	45			
12	Northgate	Drama	287			
13	Northgate	Childrens	320			
14	Northgate	Sci-Fi	36			
15	Northgate	Classics	79			
16	Northgate	Comedy	225			
17	Clarkville	Action	22			
18	Clarkville	Drama	172			
19	Clarkville	Childrens	203			
20	Clarkville	Sci-Fi	324			
21	Clarkville	Classics	251			
22	Clarkville	Comedy	345			
23	West End	Action	310			
24	West End	Drama	369			
25	West End	Childrens	220			

Figure 1-7: The video-rental store inventory data.

These raw data are organized differently from the data in the previous example. Each row in this table represents a specific category of video for a specific store. The number is the count of titles in stock for that category. The goal is to create a PivotTable report that presents this information in an easy-to-read form and to display summary information.

To begin, open the workbook VideoStoreRawData.xlsx. Make sure the cell pointer is on a cell in the table; it does not matter which one. Then click the PivotTable button on the

Insert ribbon to display the Create PivotTable dialog box (shown earlier in Figure 1-2). Make sure the following options are selected:

- Select a table or range (and verify that the correct range, A4:C28, is entered in the Table/Range box)
- New Worksheet

Click OK to create the shell of the PivotTable and display the PivotTable Field List. The list contains Store, Category, and Titles. Select all three field names. Excel will:

- Move Store and Category to the Row Labels box.
- Move Sum of Titles to the Values box.
- Create the PivotTable.

The results are shown in Figure 1-8.

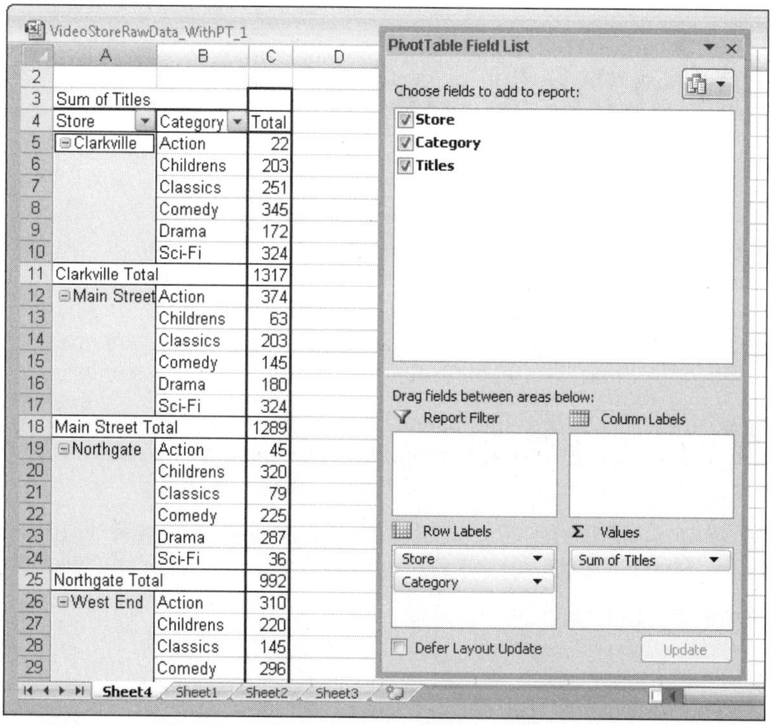

Figure 1-8: The initial PivotTable created for the video rental store data.

Although this is a perfectly legitimate PivotTable, it is not what you want. You can see that both the Store and Category fields are used as row headings—you want a report where Category is a column heading. This is easily fixed: In the PivotTable Field List, go to the

Row Labels box and click the down arrow next to Category. From the context menu, select Move To Column Labels. The field will move to the Column Labels box and the PivotTable will change to the desired format, as shown in Figure 1-9. This is an example of pivoting the table so the data is arranged differently.

If you are working along in Excel, be sure to save your workbook after creating the PivotTable and pivoting it. You'll use this PivotTable again later in this chapter.

Sum of Titles	Category						
Store	Action	Childrens	Classics	Comedy	Drama	Sci-Fi	Grand Total
Clarkville	22	203	251	345	172	324	1317
Main Street	374	63	203	145	180	324	1289
Northgate	45	320	79	225	287	36	992
West End	310	220	145	296	369	236	1576
Grand Total	751	806	678	1011	1008	920	5174

Figure 1-9: The final PivotTable has Store as a row field and Category as a column field.

In Figure 1-9, notice that Excel automatically creates totals for each category and each store, as well as an overall total.

Using the PivotTable and PivotChart Wizard

Before Excel 2007 (the current version of Excel), you used the PivotTable and PivotChart Wizard to create PivotTables. Even though Excel 2007 provides a new and simpler way to create PivotTable, as described in the previous sections, the PivotTable and PivotChart Wizard is still available. Some people may prefer the wizard, particularly those who have experience with it. For this reason, I have included it in this book. However, if you are happy with the new techniques for creating a PivotTable, you can ignore these sections.

If you want to work along with this walk-through, open the file SportingGoodsRawData. This worksheet contains data for a sporting goods chain and gives customer count and sales in various categories for three stores over a week. It is shown in Figure 1-10.

Make sure the cell pointer is on a cell in the table, and then press Alt+D followed by P to open the PivotTable and PivotChart Wizard. Figure 1-11 shows the first step of the wizard.

In this dialog box, make sure that the options are selected as shown in Figure 1-11:

- Select Microsoft Office Excel List or Database
- Select PivotTable

SportingGoods:RawData

Store	Region	Date	Customers	Total Sales	Camping	Fitness	Soccer	Baseball	Fishing	Football
2134	Northeast	01-Mar-07	207	$ 6,581	$ 326	$ 1,284	$ 970	$ 1,270	$ 1,488	$ 1,243
2134	Northeast	02-Mar-07	162	$ 3,584	$ 901	$ 247	$ 765	$ 1,251	$ 228	$ 192
2134	Northeast	03-Mar-07	188	$ 4,713	$ 837	$ 1,260	$ 959	$ 765	$ 179	$ 713
2134	Northeast	04-Mar-07	171	$ 5,263	$ 553	$ 1,134	$ 236	$ 1,353	$ 1,011	$ 976
2134	Northeast	05-Mar-07	64	$ 4,731	$ 775	$ 294	$ 1,480	$ 160	$ 864	$ 1,158
2134	Northeast	06-Mar-07	246	$ 3,853	$ 429	$ 853	$ 773	$ 760	$ 739	$ 299
2134	Northeast	07-Mar-07	63	$ 6,077	$ 1,075	$ 1,418	$ 659	$ 1,445	$ 1,340	$ 140
2918	Northeast	01-Mar-07	89	$ 775	$ 294	$ 1,480	$ 160	$ 864	$ 1,158	$ 990
2918	Northeast	02-Mar-07	132	$ 429	$ 853	$ 773	$ 760	$ 739	$ 299	$ 659
2918	Northeast	03-Mar-07	90	$ 1,075	$ 1,418	$ 659	$ 1,445	$ 1,340	$ 140	$ 325
2918	Northeast	04-Mar-07	145	$ 1,330	$ 459	$ 314	$ 1,119	$ 149	$ 447	$ 343
2918	Northeast	05-Mar-07	213	$ 456	$ 426	$ 368	$ 1,045	$ 1,453	$ 1,175	$ 254
2918	Northeast	06-Mar-07	98	$ 1,061	$ 729	$ 211	$ 939	$ 939	$ 1,205	$ 645
2918	Northeast	07-Mar-07	78	$ 1,191	$ 341	$ 123	$ 1,293	$ 300	$ 269	$ 126
2298	Midwest	01-Mar-07	86	$ 4,075	$ 866	$ 399	$ 270	$ 690	$ 418	$ 1,432
2298	Midwest	02-Mar-07	234	$ 3,933	$ 1,056	$ 266	$ 781	$ 131	$ 1,376	$ 323
2298	Midwest	03-Mar-07	286	$ 3,818	$ 1,330	$ 459	$ 314	$ 1,119	$ 149	$ 447
2298	Midwest	04-Mar-07	99	$ 4,923	$ 456	$ 426	$ 368	$ 1,045	$ 1,453	$ 1,175
2298	Midwest	05-Mar-07	85	$ 5,084	$ 1,061	$ 729	$ 211	$ 939	$ 939	$ 1,205
2298	Midwest	06-Mar-07	218	$ 3,517	$ 1,191	$ 341	$ 123	$ 1,293	$ 300	$ 269
2298	Midwest	07-Mar-07	124	$ 4,435	$ 998	$ 581	$ 350	$ 1,249	$ 295	$ 962
2300	Midwest	01-Mar-07	132	$ 1,995	$ 615	$ 1,623	$ 370	$ 2,065	$ 8,625	$ 1,957
2300	Midwest	02-Mar-07	90	$ 612	$ 709	$ 878	$ 1,218	$ 656	$ 5,902	$ 1,829
2300	Midwest	03-Mar-07	145	$ 1,099	$ 1,804	$ 1,005	$ 1,509	$ 771	$ 8,032	$ 1,844
2300	Midwest	04-Mar-07	213	$ 1,470	$ 1,430	$ 787	$ 2,074	$ 1,114	$ 7,786	$ 911
2300	Midwest	05-Mar-07	98	$ 2,092	$ 364	$ 1,793	$ 502	$ 1,541	$ 7,669	$ 1,377
2300	Midwest	06-Mar-07	78	$ 360	$ 655	$ 522	$ 559	$ 1,914	$ 5,211	$ 1,201
2300	Midwest	07-Mar-07	86	$ 1,978	$ 828	$ 1,375	$ 1,747	$ 1,797	$ 9,388	$ 1,663

Figure 1-10: The worksheet containing the sporting goods sales data.

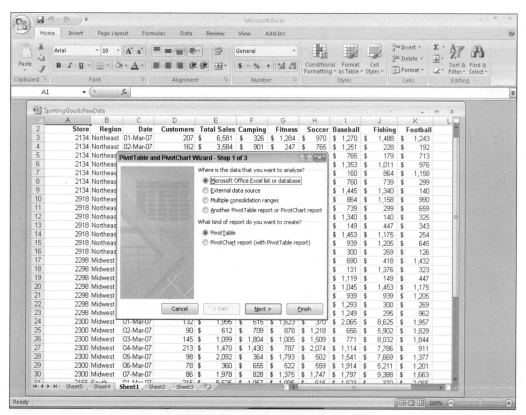

Figure 1-11: The first step of the PivotTable and PivotChart Wizard.

Then click the Next button to move to Step 2 of the wizard, shown in Figure 1-12. Here you specify the range where the data is located. If you placed the cell pointer in the table before starting the wizard, Excel will automatically select the range for you, A2:K44 in this example, as shown in Figure 1-11. Otherwise you can type the range into the Range box or select it with the mouse as follows:

1. Click the Select button (at the right end of the Range box). The dialog box collapses to a single line.

2. Drag the mouse over the desired data range. The range will be surrounded by an animated dashed border.

3. Click the Select button again. The dialog box expands to its normal size with the address of the selected data range entered in the Range field.

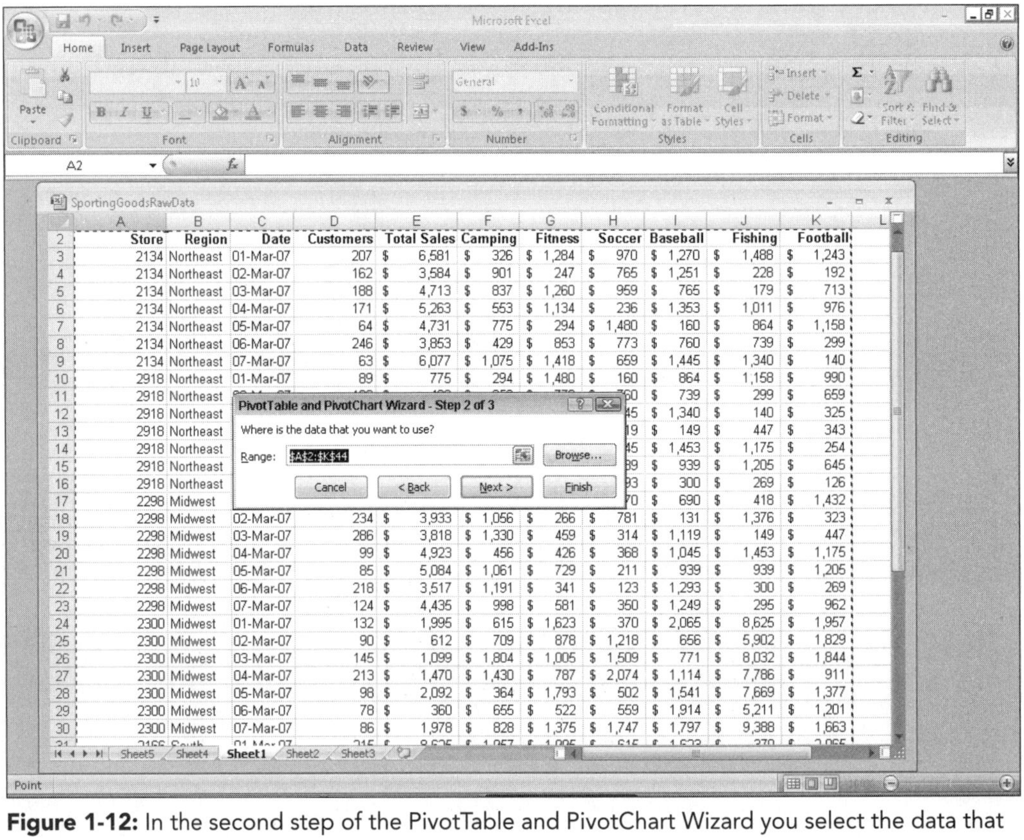

Figure 1-12: In the second step of the PivotTable and PivotChart Wizard you select the data that the PivotTable will be based on.

When you have the data range entered, click the Next button to move to the third and final step of the wizard, shown in Figure 1-13.

In this dialog box you specify where to place the PivotTable, either on a new worksheet or an existing worksheet. You can also specify the table layout and set some options using the Layout and Options buttons, but that's a topic for a future chapter. For now, just select the New Worksheet option, and then click Finish to create the PivotTable report (see Figure 1-14).

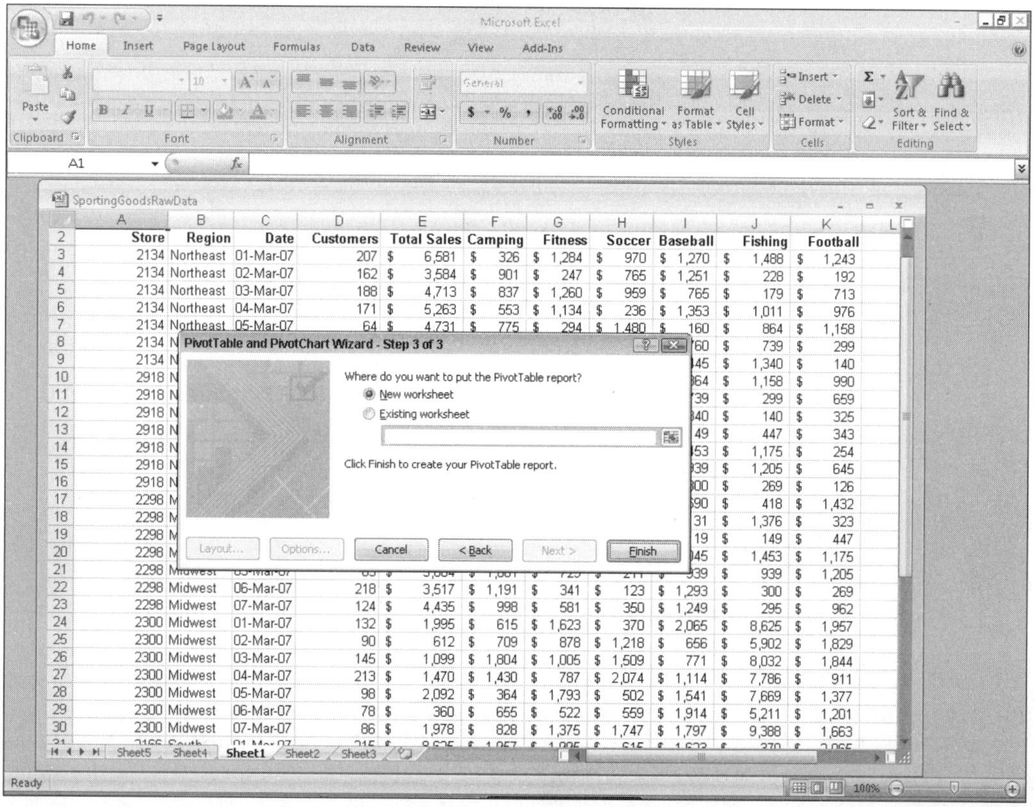

Figure 1-13: In the third and final step of the PivotTable and PivotChart Wizard you select the location for the new PivotTable.

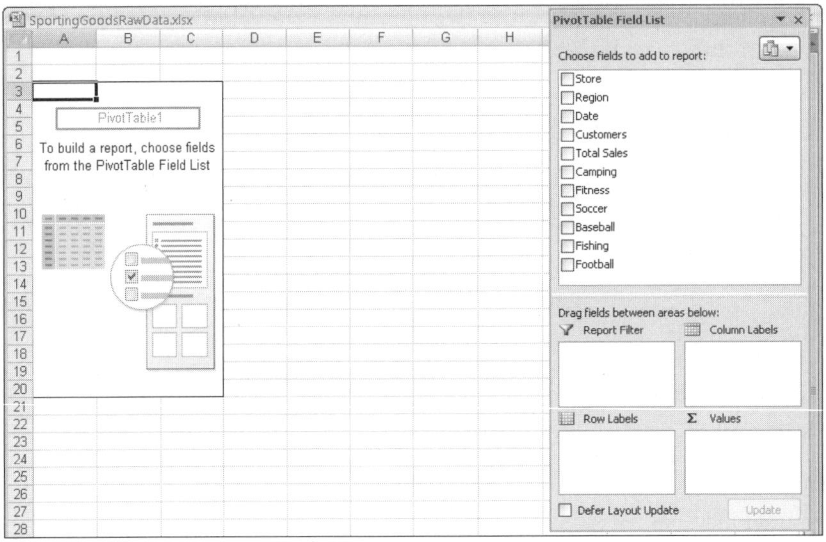

Figure 1-14: The newly created PivotTable report waiting to be customized.

Notice that the screen in Figure 1-14 looks identical to the one in Figure 1-3. That's right—if you use the PivotTable and PivotChart Wizard to create a PivotTable, the result is just the same as if you had used the newer tools in Excel 2007. You then follow the same steps to define the PivotTable columns and rows or to create a multi-column report, as described in the previous two sections.

Creating a PivotChart

A PivotChart is nothing more than a standard Excel chart created from the data in a PivotTable report. In fact there are a few features in PivotCharts that you will not find in charts based on other data—that is, data not in a PivotTable. For the most part, however, a PivotChart is like any other Excel chart and can be manipulated and formatted in the same way. The few differences will be covered as they come up.

Table and Chart in One Step?

If you know that you will want a PivotChart, you can create the PivotTable and PivotChart in one step. Instead of clicking the PivotTable button on the Insert ribbon, click the arrow underneath it and then select PivotChart from the menu. You'll then follow the usual procedures for creating a PivotTable, but when Excel creates the PivotTable it will automatically create a PivotChart as well.

Now you can go ahead and create a PivotChart based on the PivotTable report that you created earlier in this chapter, the one showed in Figure 1-9:

1. Make sure the PivotTable is active.

2. Click the PivotChart button on the Options ribbon. Excel displays the Insert Chart dialog box, shown in Figure 1-15.

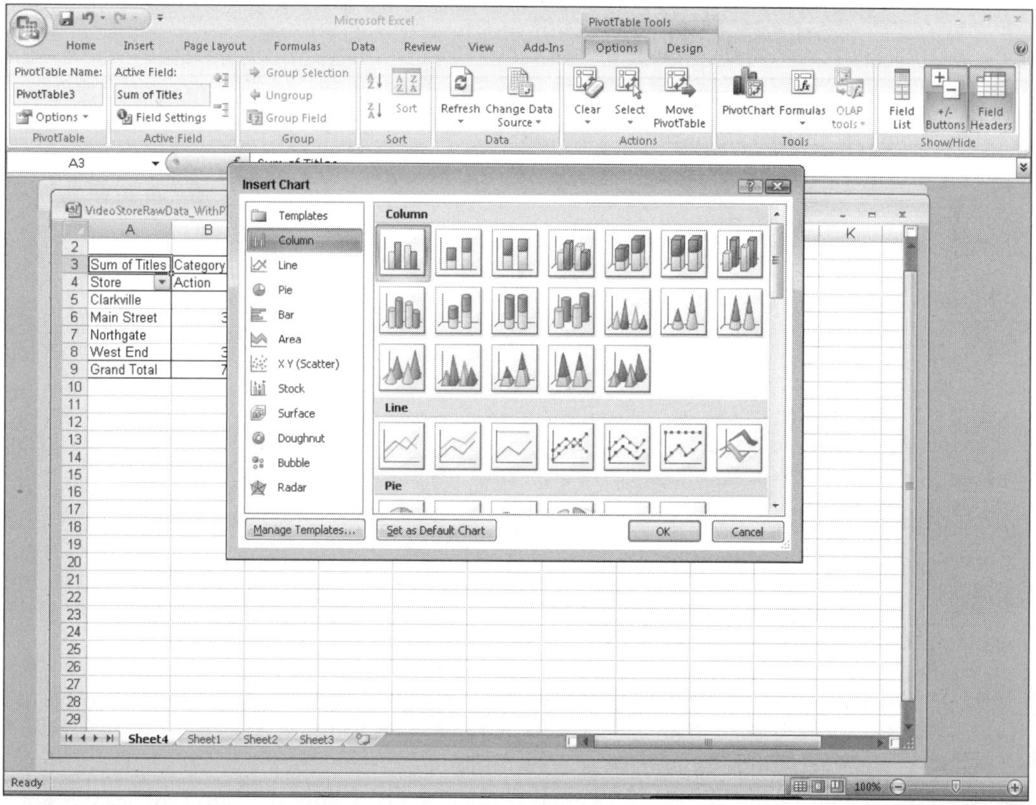

Figure 1-15: Selecting the type of chart for a PivotChart.

3. Select Column in the Templates list; then click the second chart template in the first row.

4. Click OK to create the chart.

The resulting chart is shown in Figure 1-16. Each store is represented by a bar in the chart, and within each bar the different categories are differentiated by color or shading.

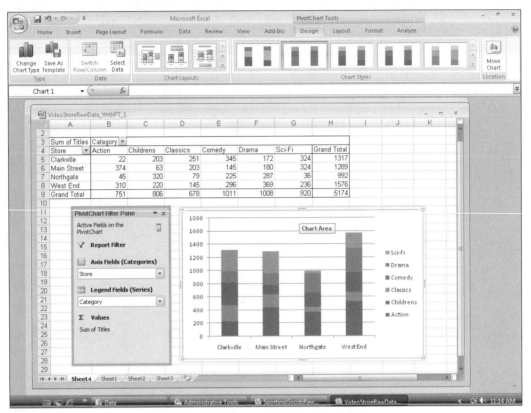

Figure 1-16: A PivotChart based on the video rental data PivotTable.

Although the chart or the underlying PivotTable is active, Excel displays the PivotChart Filter Pane, also shown in Figure 1-16. You can use the Axis Fields and Legend Fields elements in this pane to filter the data so that the PivotChart displays only a subset of the data. Any filtering that you select here is applied to the PivotTable itself, and the chart automatically reflects this change in the PivotTable. For example, Figure 1-17 shows the PivotTable and chart after filtering has been applied to show only the Clarkville and Main Street stores.

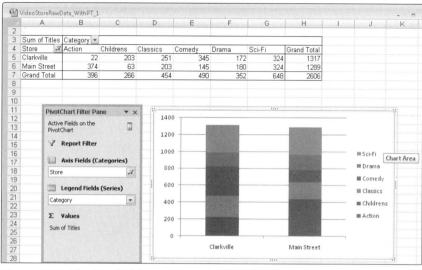

Figure 1-17: The PivotTable and PivotChart can be filtered to show a subset of the data.

Chapter 2

Understanding Data Sources for PivotTables

The first step in analyzing data with a PivotTable is, of course, specifying the data that the PivotTable will be based on. Excel provides you with a great deal of flexibility in this regard. You are not limited to analyzing data that have been entered into the workbook, although that is, in fact, a common scenario. The ability to use external data greatly enhances the power of PivotTable reports. This chapter explores the various data sources you can use with PivotTables.

In This Chapter

◆ Using data from an Excel workbook

◆ Using data from databases and other sources

◆ Creating a PivotTable report from an Access database

◆ Working with multiple consolidation ranges

◆ Basing a PivotTable on another PivotTable report

Using Excel Data from the Same Workbook

Perhaps the most common way to create a PivotTable is by basing it on data that already exist in an Excel workbook. The data can be in the same workbook as the PivotTable; this technique was used in Chapter 1. The data can also be in a separate workbook.

Things are at their simplest when you are creating a PivotTable in the workbook in which the data are located. The data should be organized as a standard Excel list, or table, as follows:

- The first row contains the field or column names.

- The second and subsequent rows contain the data.

- There are no blank rows, although individual blank cells may be present.

If the cell pointer is anywhere in the data table when you open the Create PivotTable dialog box, Excel automatically determines the address of the entire table and enters it in the Table/Range field of the dialog box. If you want to explicitly tell Excel where the input data range is located, you can do one of the following:

- Select the data before you display the dialog box. The address of the data will be entered automatically in the appropriate place in the dialog box.

- Type the address of the data into the Table/Range field of the dialog box (see Figure 2-1).

- Use the Select button in the dialog box to select the data range.

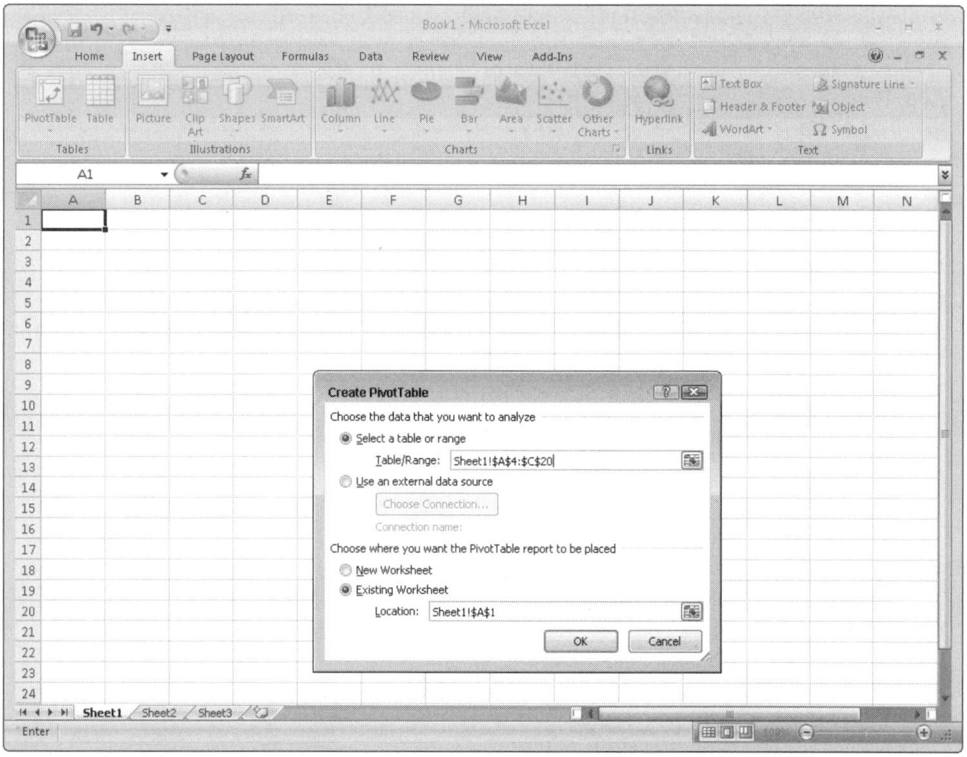

Figure 2-1: Specifying the data range in the Create PivotTable dialog box.

Actually, there is a fourth and preferred way to tell Excel where the data are—create a named range for the data. Using named ranges is more convenient than typing the address or selecting the data each time you want to refer to them. Named ranges also provide an advantage in that if you expand the range, perhaps to include additional data, the PivotTable report will automatically include the new data when it is refreshed. Here's how to create a named range:

1. Select the data range.

2. Click the Define Name button in the Defined Names section of the Formulas ribbon. The New Name dialog box is displayed (see Figure 2-2).

3. Type the name for the range in the Name field. You should use something descriptive such as SalesData or SurveyResults. It's best to avoid spaces, too; use an underscore if needed to separate words.

4. Click OK.

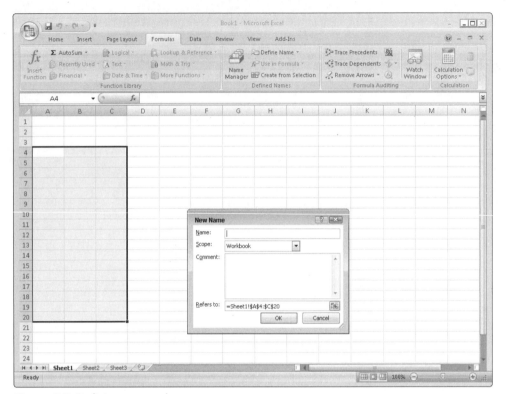

Figure 2-2: Defining a named range.

Then, when you are creating a PivotTable, simply enter the range name in the Table/Range field, as shown in Figure 2-3 for the range Name SalesData.

Of course, if you enter a name that does not exist, it will not work. Excel displays an error message when you click OK. You'll have to correct the range name you entered or use one of the other techniques to specify the source data range for your PivotTable.

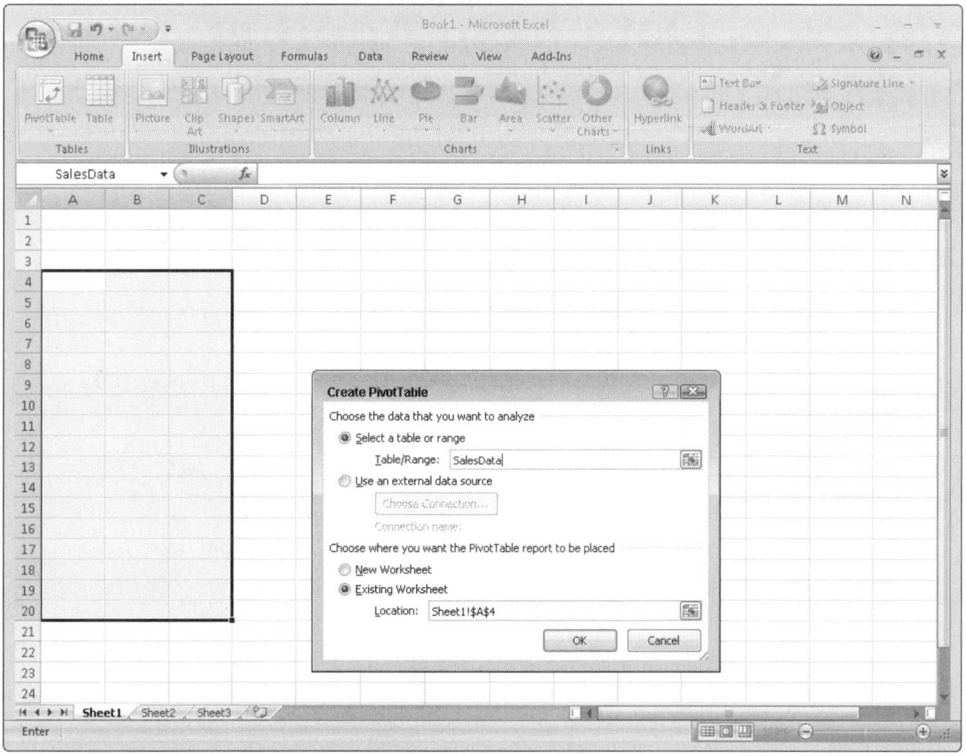

Figure 2-3: Specifying the data range by entering a range name in the Create PivotTable dialog box.

What About Filters and Subtotals?

If you have applied any autofilters or subtotals to your source data, they are ignored when you create a PivotTable from the data. If you want to create a PivotTable based on the filtered data, you must copy the data to a new list and use that as the basis for the PivotTable report.

Using Excel Data from Another Workbook

If the data you want to use in your PivotTable are in another workbook, the process is slightly different. You have to specify not only the range in which the data are located but also the name of the workbook they are in.

The easiest way to do this is to have both workbooks open; the one where you want to place the PivotTable should be the active one. Then follow these steps:

1. Click PivotTable on the Insert ribbon to display the Create PivotTable dialog box.

2. Make sure that the Select a Table or Range option is selected.

3. Click the Select button at the right end of the Table/Range field. The dialog box collapses to a single line.

4. Press Alt+Tab or click the Windows taskbar to activate the workbook that contains the data. The collapsed dialog box remains visible.

5. Select the data range for the PivotTable. Its address, including the workbook name, will be entered in the Create PivotTable dialog box.

6. Click the Select button in the dialog box to accept the selection and expand the dialog box.

7. Click OK to return to the original workbook with the PivotTable inserted.

When a PivotTable is linked to data in an external workbook, you can update it only if the linked data workbook is available. If this file has been moved, renamed, or deleted, you will not be able to update the PivotTable. Excel displays an error message when you attempt to do so. The original PivotTable data remains in place, however.

Why a Different Workbook?

You might be wondering why anyone would put a PivotTable in a different workbook from the data on which it is based. It is actually very useful to do so in some situations. Perhaps you have a huge amount of data and the workbook they are in is slow and cumbersome. By putting the PivotTable in a separate workbook you'll be able to view and manipulate the PivotTable summary without the extra overhead of all those data. Or perhaps you want to summarize data that are located in several different workbooks. You can create a summary workbook that contains several PivotTable reports, each linked to its own external data workbook.

PivotTables and Refreshing Data

It is important to be aware that PivotTables do not refresh automatically. This is true regardless of whether the data are in the same workbook as the PivotTable, in an external workbook, or in another external data source. Changes to the data will not be reflected in the PivotTable unless you refresh the data. You do this in one of two ways:

- Right-click the PivotTable and select Refresh Data from the pop-up menu.

- Click the Refresh button on the Options ribbon (available only when the PivotTable is active).

Recalculating the workbook does not refresh PivotTable data.

Using Data from Other Sources

Excel enables you to use data from a variety of other sources for your PivotTable reports. There are two general ways to do this:

- Link your PivotTable to the external data without importing them into Excel.

- Import the external data into Excel and then treat them as an Excel list.

This section covers the procedures for linking to external data. Importing data is discussed in "Using Other External Data Sources."

To create a PivotTable that is linked to external data:

1. Display the Create PivotTable dialog box.

2. Select the Use an External Data Source option.

3. Click the Choose Connection button. Excel displays the Existing Connections dialog box, shown in Figure 2-4.

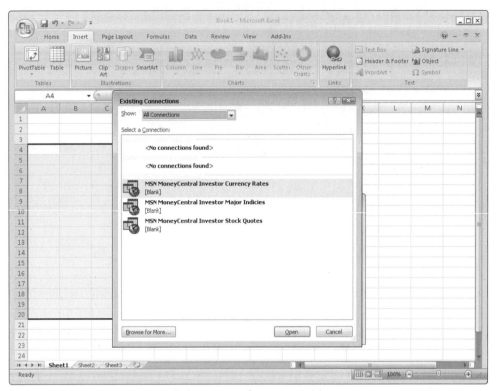

Figure 2-4: Selecting an external data source for a PivotTable.

The information shown in the Existing Connections dialog box depends on how your specific system has been set up—it is very unlikely that your Existing Connections dialog box contains the same elements as Figure 2-4. You can use the drop-down Show list at the top of the dialog box to control which data connections are displayed: those defined in the current workbook, those available on the network, and those available on your computer.

At this point you can do one of two things:

- Click the desired data connection; then click Open.
- Click Browse to locate a data connection that is not listed.

The next steps that you follow depend on the specific data connection you have selected. Some data connections are ready for immediate use in a PivotTable, whereas others require additional input from you before they can be used.

Note, however, that Excel offers another way to create a PivotTable that is based on external data. The end result is the same, but you may prefer using this method in some cases. On the Data ribbon there is a section labeled Get External Data. This command is usually used for importing data into a workbook but can also be used to create a PivotTable:

1. Click the Existing Connections button to see a list of existing connection, as shown earlier.

2. Click OK and continue the process until the Import Data dialog box is displayed, as shown in Figure 2-5.

3. Select either the PivotTable Report or the PivotChart and PivotTable Report option.

4. Specify whether the PivotTable should go in the current worksheet or a new worksheet.

5. Click OK.

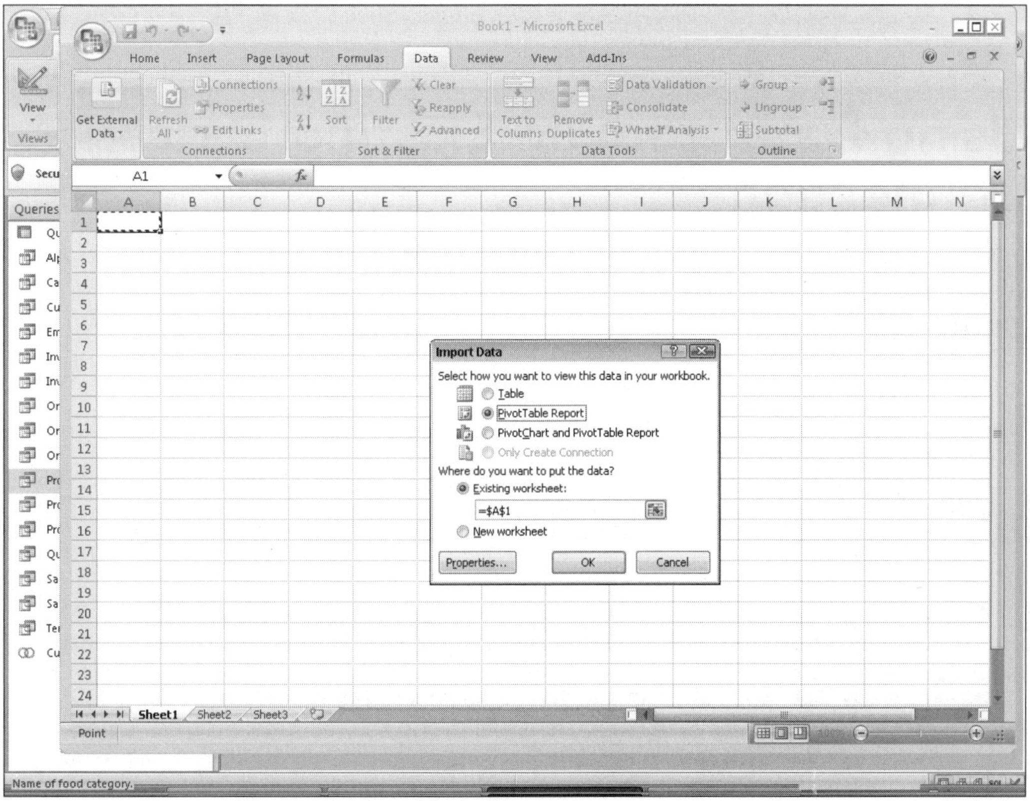

Figure 2-5: Importing data linked to a PivotTable.

Creating a New Data Connection

If the data connection that you need does not exist, you can define it yourself—but only if you are sure of what you are doing, because this can be a complex process with the potential to cause errors. Details on creating data sources are beyond the scope of this book, but if you want to give it a try, here's how to start: On the Data ribbon, click the From Other Sources button to display a list of the various types of connections you can create from within Excel. Then, follow the prompts to establish the connection. When you are finished, the connection will be available for you to use in Excel.

Connecting to external data is a potentially complex process, if only because you have so many options. That's one of the things that make PivotTable reports in Excel so powerful: you can base them on data from a wide variety of sources. Before trying to create a PivotTable based on external data, it is a good idea to have at least some idea of where the data are located and of the type of connection you will use. If you are not familiar with these topics, you may want to ask your network administrator or IT person to lend a hand.

Using Data from an Existing Data Connection

If you want to base your PivotTable report on an external data source that is already defined, follow these steps:

1. Click the PivotTable button on the Insert ribbon to display the Create PivotTable dialog box (shown earlier in Figure 2-1).

2. Select the Use an External Data Source option, and click the Choose Connection button to open the Existing Connections dialog box (shown earlier in Figure 2-4).

3. Click the data source that you want to use.

4. Click OK.

At this point one of two things will happen, depending on the nature of the data source. If the data source contains a single table of data, Excel will create the blank PivotTable and display the PivotTable field list, and you can proceed with the PivotTable design.

If, however, the data source contains more than one table, Excel will display the Select Table dialog box listing the available tables, as shown in Figure 2-6. You must click the table that you want to base your PivotTable on; then click OK to create the blank PivotTable and display the PivotTable Field List.

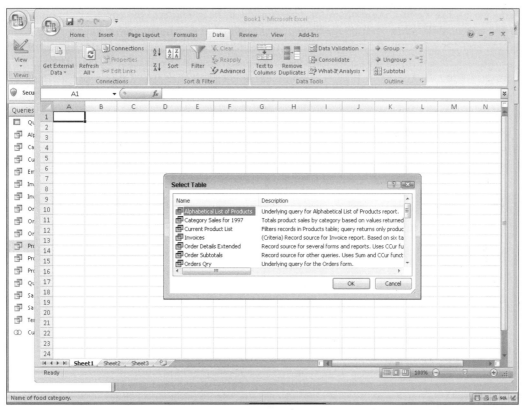

Figure 2-6: Selecting the table that you want the PivotTable to be based on.

Creating a PivotTable Report from Data in an Access Database

One of the beauties of the Excel PivotTable reports is that they are not limited to using data located in a workbook. In fact, it is fairly common to have your data in a database instead. Depending on the configuration of your system and the database drivers installed, you can access data in a wide variety of database formats. In this section I will show you how to create a PivotTable report based on data in a Microsoft Access database. Although some of the details will be different for other database formats, the general principles are the same.

For this section I will use the Northwind database. This is a sample database that is installed as part of most Microsoft Office installations. Its file name is Northwind.mdb and it is typically located in the Samples folder under the Microsoft Office installation in \Program Files. If you are not able to find it, you can use the Windows search feature to determine its location. (If you cannot find the file, it may not have been installed. You can get it from your Office installation CD and copy it to your hard disk.)

Before creating a PivotTable based on external data, be sure that you know which element in the external database you need. Typically the external database contains a variety of tables and queries and all of these will be available to you. For this demonstration I will use a query named Product Sales for 1997 that is defined in the Northwind database. This query is shown in Access in Figure 2-7; you can see that it contains data on product sales by category, product name, and quarter. Note that you do not have to have Access open to create the PivotTable.

Category Na ▾	Product Name ▾	ProductSale ▾	ShippedQua ▾
Beverages	Chai	$705.60	Qtr 1
Beverages	Chai	$878.40	Qtr 2
Beverages	Chai	$1,174.50	Qtr 3
Beverages	Chai	$2,128.50	Qtr 4
Beverages	Chang	$2,720.80	Qtr 1
Beverages	Chang	$228.00	Qtr 2
Beverages	Chang	$2,061.50	Qtr 3
Beverages	Chang	$2,028.25	Qtr 4
Beverages	Chartreuse verte	$590.40	Qtr 1
Beverages	Chartreuse verte	$360.00	Qtr 2
Beverages	Chartreuse verte	$1,100.70	Qtr 3
Beverages	Chartreuse verte	$2,424.60	Qtr 4
Beverages	Côte de Blaye	$25,127.36	Qtr 1
Beverages	Côte de Blaye	$12,806.10	Qtr 2
Beverages	Côte de Blaye	$7,312.12	Qtr 3
Beverages	Côte de Blaye	$1,317.50	Qtr 4
Beverages	Guaraná Fantástica	$529.20	Qtr 1
Beverages	Guaraná Fantástica	$467.55	Qtr 2
Beverages	Guaraná Fantástica	$219.37	Qtr 3
Beverages	Guaraná Fantástica	$337.50	Qtr 4
Beverages	Inoh Coffee	$1,398.40	Qtr 1

Record: ◄ ◄ 1 of 286 ► ►I ► No Filter Search

Figure 2-7: The PivotTable will be based on the Northwind database query named Product Sales for 1997.

After you have Excel open with a blank worksheet displayed, follow these steps:

1. Click the PivotTable button on the Insert ribbon to open the Create PivotTable dialog box.

2. Select the Use an External Data Source option.

3. Click the Choose Connection button to open the Existing Connections dialog box.

4. Click the Browse for More button to open the Select Data Source dialog box.

5. Navigate to and select the file Northwind.mdb as shown in Figure 2-8.

6. Click OK to display the Select Table dialog box. (See Figure 2-9.)

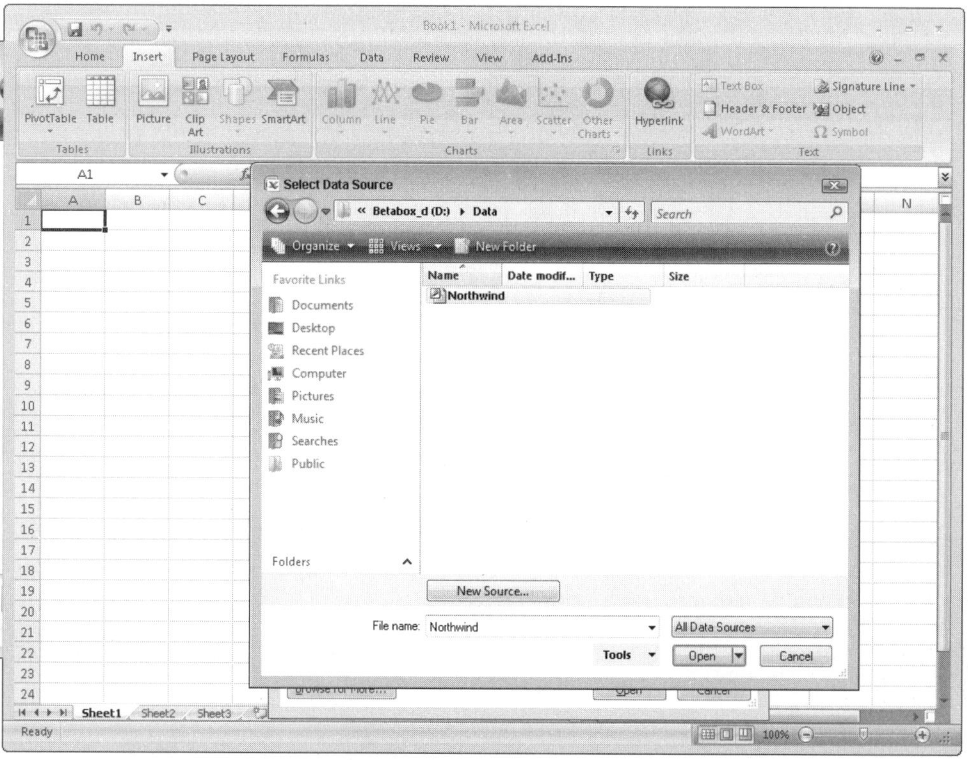

Figure 2-8: Navigate to and select Northwind.mdb.

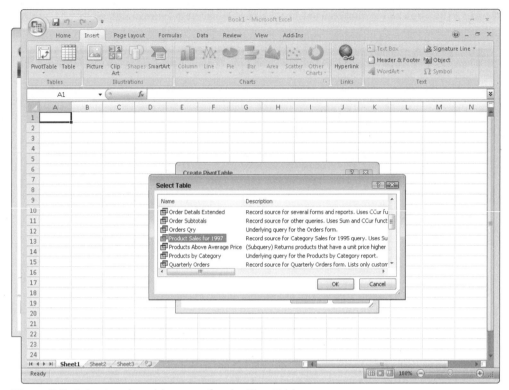

Figure 2-9: Selecting the table to use for the PivotTable.

7. In the list, select Product Sales for 1997.

8. Click OK to return to the Create PivotTable dialog box.

9. Click OK to close the Create PivotTable dialog box and create the blank PivotTable, which is shown in Figure 2-10.

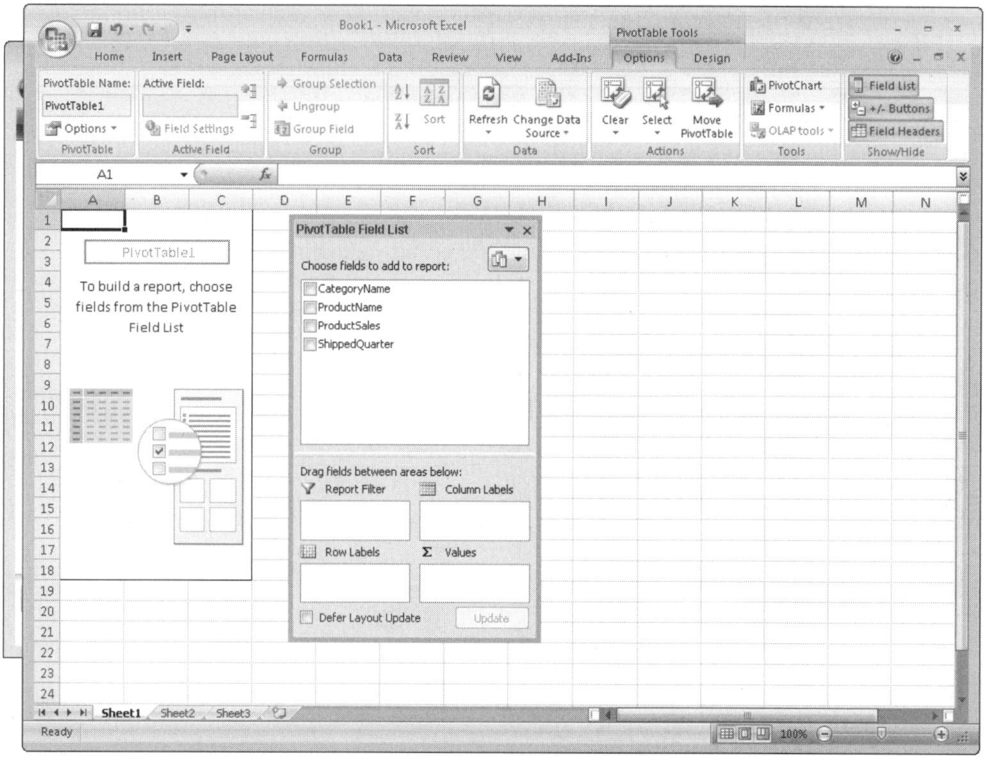

Figure 2-10: The blank PivotTable based on the Access query.

You can see that the four columns that were present in the Access query are listed in the Field List. Next you will add these fields to the blank PivotTable to achieve the data display you want. Because there are four fields, you have several ways to display these data. Follow these steps to create a PivotTable that displays total sales by category for each quarter:

1. Select the CategoryName field to add it to the Row Labels area.

2. Select the ShippedQuarter field to add it to the Row Labels area.

3. In the Row Labels area, click the arrow next to the ShippedQuarter field and select Move to Column Labels to move this field to the Column Labels area.

4. Select the ProductSales field to move it to the Values area.

5. In the Values area, click the down arrow next to the Sum of ProductSales field and select Value Field Settings from the popup menu to display the Value Field Settings dialog box.

Save Your Files!

When you complete this and other exercises be sure to save all your files. Some of them will be used in later exercises.

6. Click the Number Format button to open the Format Cells dialog box.
7. Select Currency format with no decimal places.
8. Click OK twice to close all dialog boxes.

The resulting PivotTable report is shown in Figure 2-11.

Sum of ProductSales	Column Labels				
Row Labels	Qtr 1	Qtr 2	Qtr 3	Qtr 4	Grand Total
Beverages	$35,858	$25,467	$20,845	$19,904	$102,074
Condiments	$11,922	$13,347	$14,002	$16,006	$55,278
Confections	$21,083	$22,066	$17,965	$19,781	$80,894
Dairy Products	$24,119	$27,254	$28,628	$34,749	$114,750
Grains/Cereals	$12,697	$14,629	$15,311	$13,312	$55,949
Meat/Poultry	$21,598	$13,695	$15,844	$30,202	$81,338
Produce	$8,981	$15,584	$8,303	$20,153	$53,020
Seafood	$7,445	$13,613	$23,424	$21,062	$65,544
Grand Total	**$143,703**	**$145,655**	**$144,320**	**$175,169**	**$608,847**

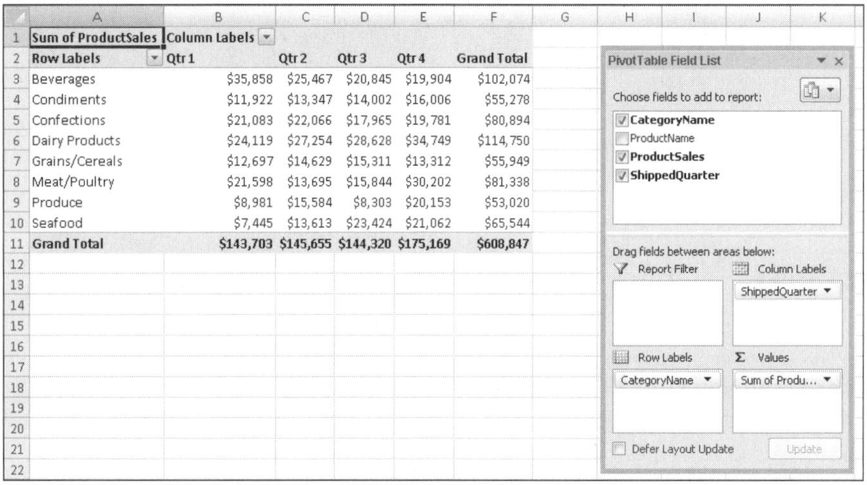

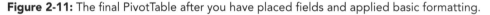

Figure 2-11: The final PivotTable after you have placed fields and applied basic formatting.

Accessing External Data

Many kinds of external data are protected against unauthorized access. You may need a user name and a password to access the data. If this is the case, you will be prompted for this information during the process.

Using Other External Data Sources

Excel provides you with tremendous power when it comes to accessing data. In some situations the data you want to use in your PivotTable report are located outside Excel but must be imported before you can use them. Even if you could connect directly to the external data, there may be scenarios where you prefer to import the data before creating your PivotTable report, for example, if the network connecting to the data source is not always available. A detailed explanation of all the ways Excel can import data is beyond the scope of this book. To import data, you always start by clicking the Get External Data on the Data ribbon to display the menu shown in Figure 2-12.

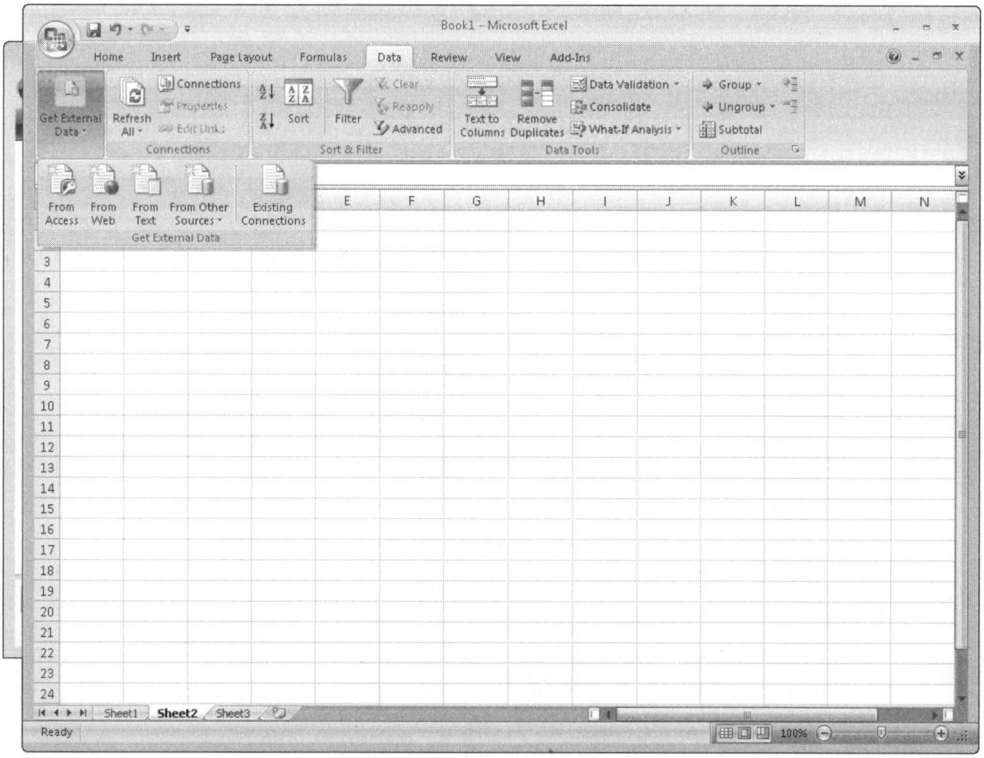

Figure 2-12: Choices available when importing external data.

Briefly, the choices on this menu are:

- **From Access**—Import data from an Access database (`*.mdb`, `*.mde`, `*.accdb`, `*.accde` files).

- **From Web**—Define a Web Query that imports data from a Web page.

- **From Text**—Import data from a text file (`*.txt`, `*.csv`, `*.prn`).

- **From Other Sources**—Import data from SQL Server, from Analysis Services, from XML files, and other sources.

Although the details of these various data-importing methods vary, the end result is the same: the data will be present in your workbook as a list. For the purposes of creating a PivotTable report, you can treat the data like any other Excel list, as was covered earlier. The fact that the data were imported is not relevant at this point.

Using Multiple Consolidation Ranges

The term *multiple consolidation ranges* sounds more complex than it actually is. All it means is creating a PivotTable based on two or more data tables or lists. The third option in Step 1 of the PivotTable Wizard for the location of the data is Multiple Consolidation Ranges. This is a fancy-sounding name for a simple idea—that your data are located in two or more separate lists in Excel. The lists can be in the same workbook or different workbooks. Oddly, the new Excel 2007 interface does not support creating PivotTables based on multiple consolidation ranges, but the old PivotTable and PivotChart Wizard, retained from earlier versions of Excel, still supports this.

To use multiple consolidation ranges, each list must have the same format, meaning that the column labels in the first row and the row labels in the first column must be the same in all lists. If the individual lists contain total rows or columns, these must not be included when you build the PivotTable report. Figure 2-13 shows an example of data in multiple ranges that can be consolidated into a PivotTable report.

	A	B	C	D	E	F	G	H	I
1									
2	**Cleveland Plant**			**Atlanta Plant**			**Newark Plant**		
3		Employees			Employees			Employees	
4	Accounting	4		Accounting	3		Accounting	11	
5	Human Resources	6		Human Resources	5		Human Resources	9	
6	Sales	12		Sales	9		Sales	16	
7	Development	7		Development	2		Development	22	
8	Manufacturing	45		Manufacturing	213		Manufacturing	135	
9	Support	8		Support	16		Support	10	
10									
11									

Figure 2-13: Data in multiple ranges suitable for consolidation.

To start the Wizard, press Alt+D followed by P. In Step 1, shown in Figure 2-14, select the Multiple Consolidation Ranges option.

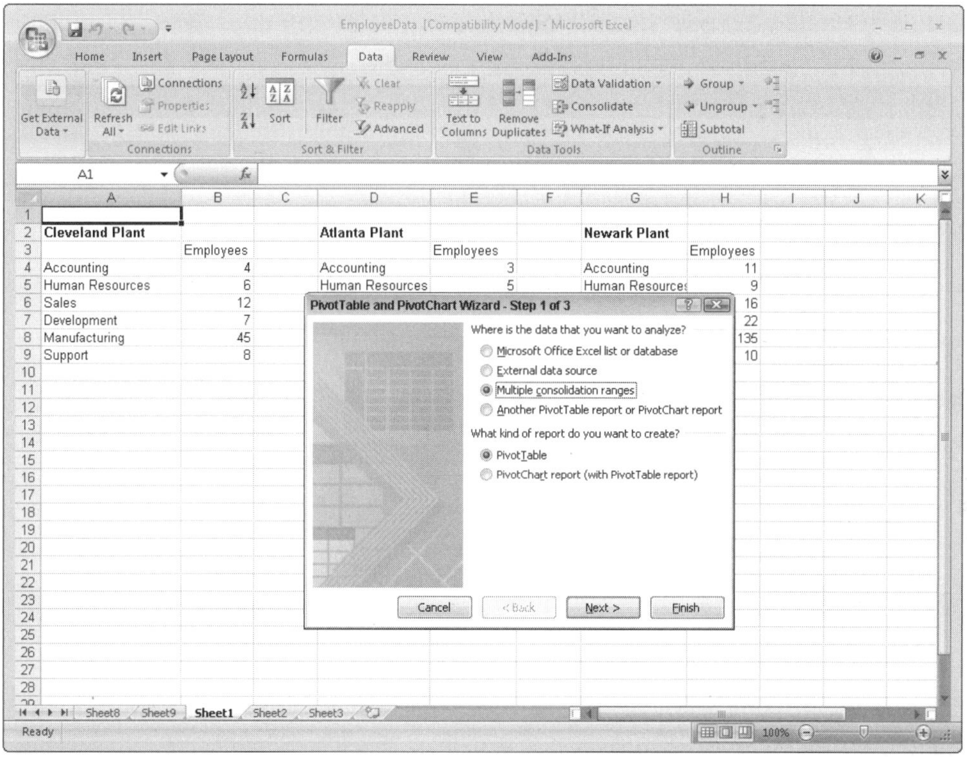

Figure 2-14: Step 1 of the PivotTable and PivotChart Wizard lets you use multiple consolidation ranges.

When you select Multiple Consolidation Ranges in Step 1 of the PivotTable Wizard and click Next, you go to Step 2a, where you are presented with two options, as shown in Figure 2-15.

You have the following options (recall that Page Field is the old term for a report filter):

- **Create a single page field for me**—Creates one page field with an item for each source range plus an item that consolidates all the ranges.

- **I will create the page fields**—Enables you to create your own page fields, up to a maximum of four, with each page consolidating different aspects of the data.

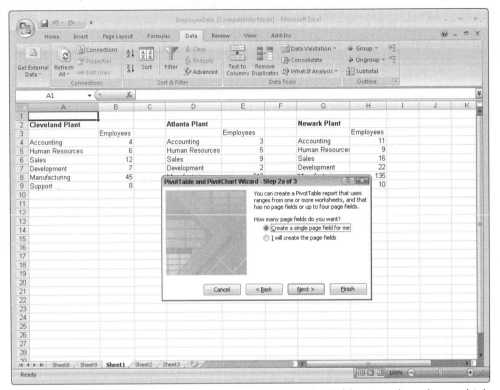

Figure 2-15: Setting page field options when creating a PivotTable report based on multiple consolidation ranges.

Basically, creating multiple page fields gives you greater data-filtering capabilities. (The differences between these two options will become apparent when you learn more.) In the following two sections I will explain the procedures for creating single- and multiple-page field PivotTable reports from multiple consolidation ranges. The details of using this kind of PivotTable will be covered in later parts.

Using Report Filters

Report filters, or page fields in the old terminology, are available in any PivotTable report, not just those based on multiple consolidation ranges. They serve the same purpose: permitting you to filter the entire report based on data values in the report filter fields. You must create report filter fields manually in other situations by adding them to the Report Filter area of the Field List.

Letting Excel Create a Single-Page (Report Filter) Field

When you opt to create a single-page field, the next step of the wizard—Step 2b—looks like Figure 2-16. You use this dialog box to select the multiple ranges that will be used for the PivotTable report.

To specify the ranges to use, follow these procedures:

- To specify each range, enter its address or assigned range name in the Range box, then click Add. You can also use the Select button to specify a range in any open workbook. The range should include only the data, not any identifying labels such as the plant locations in the example data.

- To specify a range in a workbook that is not open, click the Browse button to locate the workbook file and then follow the on-screen prompts.

- To remove a range, select it in the list and click Delete.

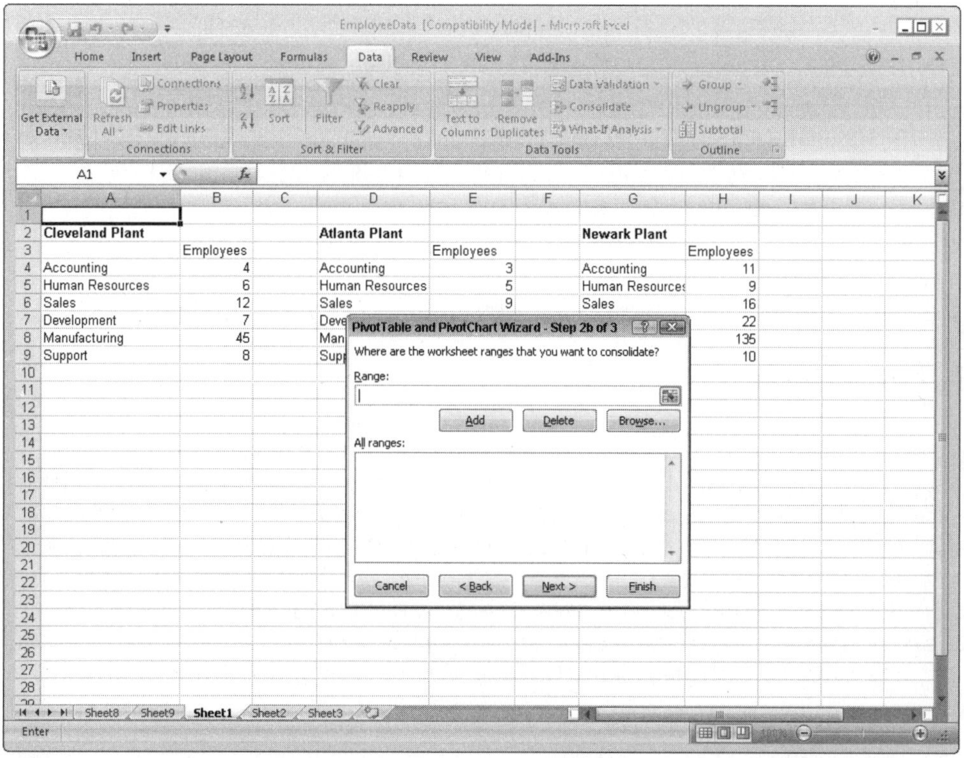

Figure 2-16: Specifying the ranges to be used in a single-page-field PivotTable report.

When you have specified all the ranges, click the Next button to go to the final wizard step (not shown here), in which you specify where to place the PivotTable report. When you finish the wizard, the report is created, as shown in Figure 2-17. (This PivotTable is based on the data shown earlier in Figure 2-13.)

	A	B	C
1	Page1	(All) ▼	
2			
3	Sum of Value	Column ▼	
4	Row ▼	Employees	Grand Total
5	Accounting	18	18
6	Development	31	31
7	Human Resources	20	20
8	Manufacturing	393	393
9	Sales	37	37
10	Support	34	34
11	Grand Total	533	533

Figure 2-17: A PivotTable report created from the multiple consolidation ranges shown in Figure 2-13.

You should notice a couple of differences between this PivotTable report and those created on the basis of a single data range. First of all, the report is created automatically; you do not have to add fields to the various areas to define the report. Second, there is a dropdown arrow next to the Page1 label that enables you to select which of the data ranges to include in the report. (You'll see how this works in a later section.)

You may also wonder about the Grand Total column in the report. Is it really necessary? In this example, it is not because the data have only one column, but Excel includes such totals in PivotTable reports by default. In Chapter 3, you will learn how to remove unneeded report elements such as this.

Creating Your Own Page (Report Filter) Fields

Creating a PivotTable report with multiple page fields is a source of confusion for some Excel users. To be honest, it is a bit confusing! This is partly because of what I consider a bad choice of terminology by Microsoft. When people hear the word *page* they naturally think that a PivotTable report with more than one page field will display multiple pages, but that's not how it works. A page field is a way to filter the PivotTable—in other words, to specify which of the consolidation ranges are summarized in the report. This may be why the old term *page fields* has been changed to *report filter* fields in Excel 2007. However, I will use page fields here because that what is used in the PivotTable and PivotChart Wizard.

In the process of defining a PivotTable that is based on multiple consolidation ranges and that has multiple page fields, you will specify the following:

- How many page fields there will be (zero to four)
- Which data range(s) are associated with each page field
- Descriptive names for the fields

If you select zero page fields, the resulting PivotTable report will lack any page-field filtering abilities. This type of report is actually simpler than the standard single-page field report that you learned how to create in the previous section. It's appropriate, however, when you do not need or want an extra level of filtering capability in the PivotTable.

If you select one page field, the resulting PivotTable will be almost identical to the standard single-page field report. You will have a few more customization options, such as the option to assign names to fields, but the filtering capabilities of the final PivotTable will be essentially the same.

It's when you create two or more page fields that things get interesting. This will become clearer as you gain experience and after you go through the section later in this chapter. The following steps are involved:

1. When you specify, in Step 2a of the wizard, that you will create the page fields, the next wizard step looks like Figure 2-18.

   The top part of this dialog box is used to select the data ranges, as you learned before. You can perform one of the following actions:

   - Type a range address or range name in the Range field.
   - Use the Select button to select a range with the mouse.
   - Click the Browse button to locate another workbook that contains a data range.
   - Click the Add button to add the defined range to the All Ranges list.

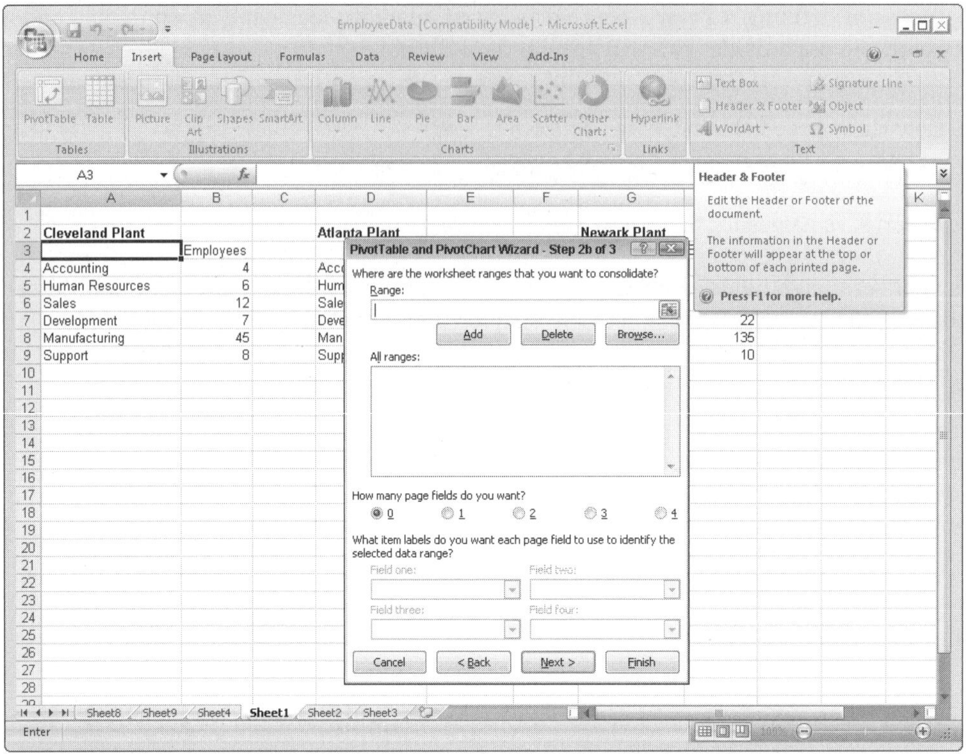

Figure 2-18: Creating a PivotTable based on multiple consolidation ranges and creating your own page fields.

2. So far this is pretty much the same process as defining the ranges when you are letting Excel create a single-page field, as described in the previous section. It's in the lower part of the dialog box that things get more interesting. First of all, you must select how many page fields you want. If you select 0, there is nothing more to do and you can click Next to proceed to the next step of the wizard.

3. If you select 1, 2, 3, or 4 page fields, the corresponding number of text boxes become active in the lower part of the dialog box. For example, if you click the 2 option, the text boxes Field one and Field two become active, as shown in Figure 2-19. This figure also shows the three data ranges from the example worksheet add to the All Ranges box.

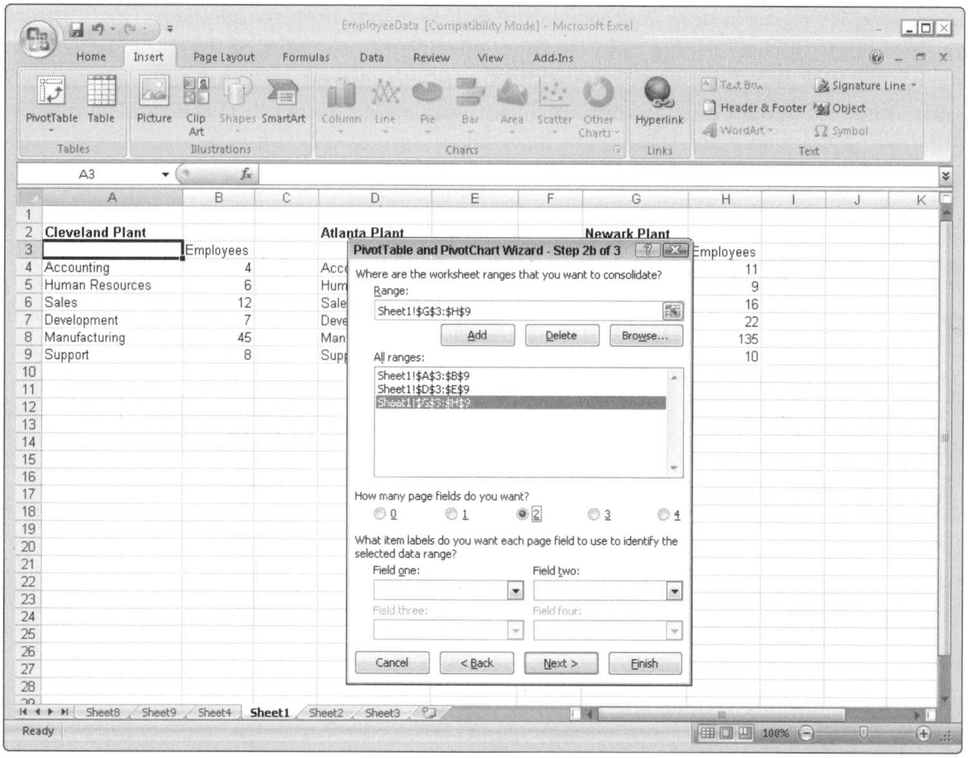

Figure 2-19: One Field box will become available for each page field you are creating; two in this figure.

4. Your next steps will depend on the kind of filtering you want to make available in the PivotTable. Your objective is to associate specific data ranges with specific fields and assign descriptive names to them. Here's how:

   a. In the All Ranges list, select a range (one of the consolidation ranges you added earlier) to be included in a filter.

   b. In the Field one box, type a descriptive name for this filter. If a name has already been assigned to a range and you want to assign it to this range as well, you can select it from the drop-down list.

   c. If you are using more than one field, enter a name for this filter in the Field two, Field three, and Field four boxes.

   d. Return to Step 1 to add another range.

   e. Repeat until all desired filters have been defined.

   f. Click Next to go to the final step of the wizard.

When the final PivotTable report is created, you will see that there is one page field item at the top of the report for each page field that you specified in the wizard. Each of these has a drop-down list that enables you to access the filters associated with that field. The judicious use of page fields can be a big help in filtering large data sets to make the PivotTable more understandable.

Creating a Single-Page Field PivotTable Report from Multiple Consolidation Ranges

To work through this project, you need to open the workbook `EmployeeData.xlsx`, which contains the raw data. (These data were shown in Figure 2-13.) You can see that there are three lists, each containing data from a specific plant. Each list contains the number of employees in each of several departments. To create a PivotTable based on these three data ranges, follow these steps:

1. Press Alt+D followed by P to open Step 1 of the PivotTable and PivotChart Wizard.
2. Select the Multiple Consolidation Ranges option.
3. Click Next to display Step 2a of the wizard.
4. Make sure the Create a Single-Page Field option is selected.
5. Click Next to display Step 2b of the wizard.
6. Click the Select button at the right end of the Range field.
7. Drag over cells A3:B9 in the worksheet.
8. Click the Select button again.
9. Click the Add button to add the range to the All Ranges list.
10. Repeat Steps 6 though 9 to select and add the ranges D3:D9 and G3:G9 to the All Ranges list. At this point the dialog box should look like Figure 2-20.
11. Click Next to go to the final wizard step.
12. Select the New Worksheet option.
13. Click Finish.

The completed PivotTable is shown in Figure 2-21.

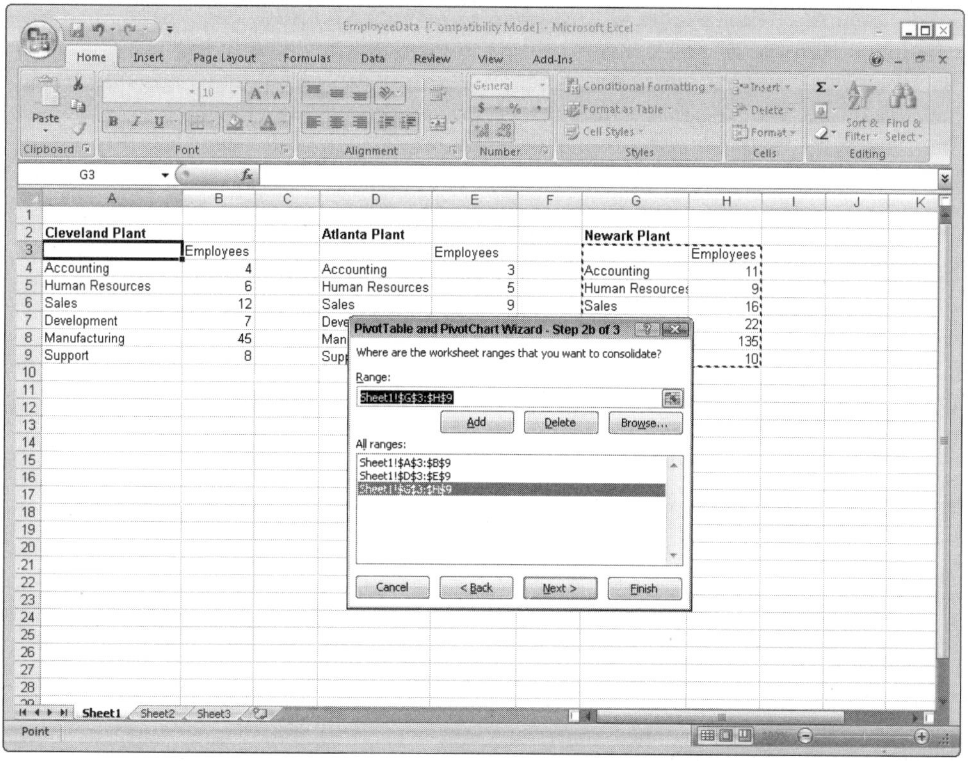

Figure 2-20: After selecting the three data ranges to be used in the PivotTable.

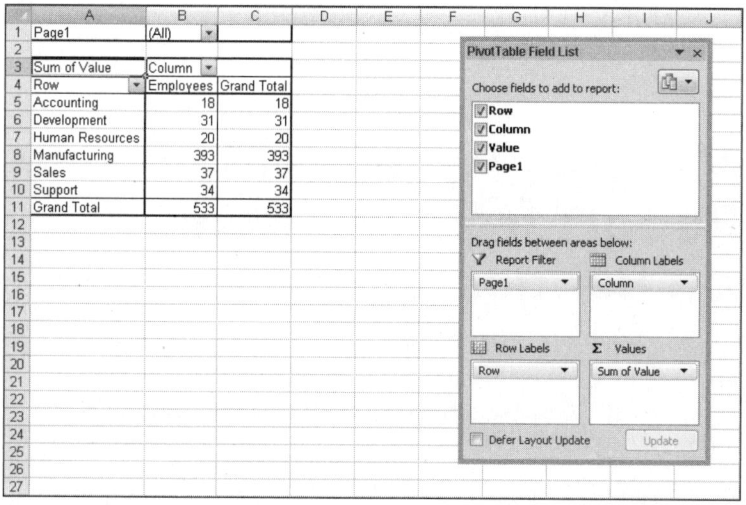

Figure 2-21: The completed PivotTable report is displayed on a new worksheet.

In the PivotTable, the Column label has an adjacent drop-down arrow that you can use to select which column(s) to display. Since the data used in this PivotTable have only one column, this feature isn't useful, but in reports that contain multiple columns, it would be. Note also that the Row label has a drop-down arrow that enables you to select which rows to include. These are features that you have seen in other PivotTable reports.

What's new is the drop-down arrow next to the Page1 label. This enables you to select which of the data ranges to include, as shown in Figure 2-22. The entries Item1, Item2, and Item3 refer to the three data ranges on which the PivotTable is based. You can select all the ranges or any single range to specify which data are summarized in the PivotTable report.

I suggest that you experiment with the filters in this PivotTable report to get a feel for how they work. Filters are an important aspect of PivotTables and you need to understand them to get the most out of PivotTables.

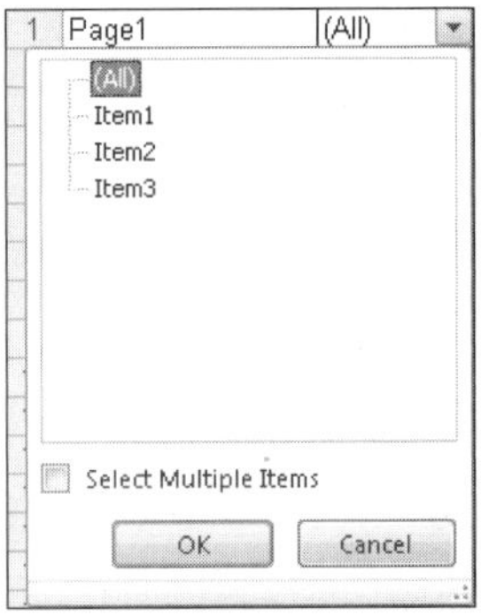

Figure 2-22: Selecting which data ranges to include in the PivotTable report.

Creating a Multiple Page-Field PivotTable Report from Multiple Consolidation Ranges

This section demonstrates the steps involved in creating a PivotTable from multiple consolidation ranges using multiple page fields. As I discussed earlier in this chapter, the concept of page fields is difficult for most Excel users to grasp. Seeing them in action is the best way to get a handle on them.

The data for this section are shown in Figure 2-23. There are four lists, each showing the number of students enrolled in a particular course for a specific year and semester. You'll find this data in CourseData.xlsx, which you will need to open to follow along.

⊿	A	B	C	D	E	F	G
1	Year 2005 Semester 1				Year 2006 Semester 1		
2		Students				Students	
3	Chemistry	21			Chemistry	32	
4	Biology	44			Biology	39	
5	Geology	94			Geology	83	
6	Physics	59			Physics	101	
7	Ecology	23			Ecology	82	
8	Marine Biology	70			Marine Biology	89	
9							
10	Year 2005 Semester 2				Year 2006 Semester 2		
11		Students				Students	
12	Chemistry	37			Chemistry	83	
13	Biology	101			Biology	74	
14	Geology	43			Geology	49	
15	Physics	96			Physics	86	
16	Ecology	28			Ecology	26	
17	Marine Biology	43			Marine Biology	25	
18							
19							

Figure 2-23: The source data are located in four lists.

Now follow these steps to begin creating the PivotTable:

1. Press Alt+D followed by P to start the PivotTable and PivotChart Wizard.

2. In Step 1 of the wizard, select the Multiple consolidation ranges option.

3. Click Next.

4. Select the I will create the page fields option.

5. Click Next.

6. In the Range box enter the range address A2:B8, or use the Select button to select the range.

7. Click the Add button to add the range to the All Ranges list.

8. Repeat Steps 6 and 7 three times to add the other three data ranges (E2:F8, A11:B17, and E11:F17) to the All Ranges list. At this point, the dialog box should look like the one in Figure 2-24.

9. Click the 2 option to specify two page fields. You'll see that the Field one and Field two boxes become available.

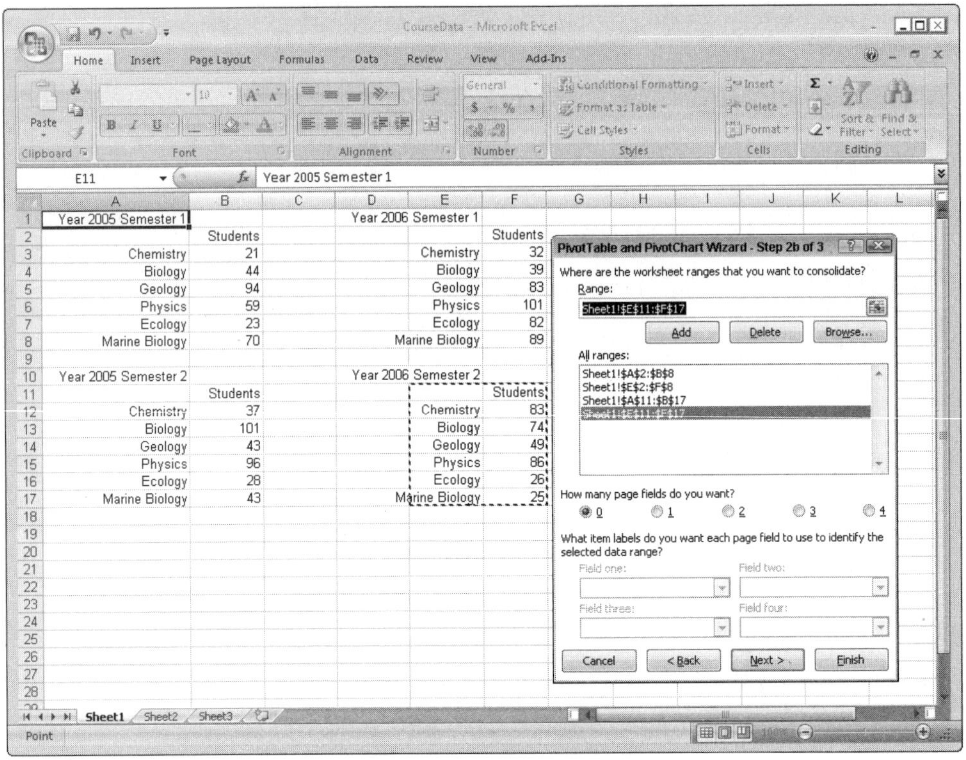

Figure 2-24: After selecting the four data ranges for the PivotTable.

At this point it will be wise to pause and do a little planning. How do you want the page fields to work? In other words, how do you want to be able to filter the data? Look at the data and you will see that two years are represented, 2005 and 2006, and two semesters, Semester 1 and Semester 2. It would be ideal to be able to filter on year to show data either from both years or from only one year, and also to filter on semester to show data either from both semesters or from a single one. That's the plan you will follow in the remaining steps.

1. In the All Ranges list select the first range, A2:B8. This range contains data from Year 2005, Semester 1.

2. Enter **Year 2005** in the Field one box.

3. Enter **Semester 1** in the Field two box.

4. Select E2:F8 in the All Ranges list. This range contains data from Year 2006, Semester 1.

5. Enter **Year 2006** in the Field one box.

6. Because you already used it, you can simply select Semester 1 from the drop-down list under Field two.

7. Select the range A11:B17 in the list. This contains data for Year 2005 and Semester 2.

8. Select Year 2005 from the drop-down list under Field one.

9. Enter **Semester 2** in the Field two box.

10. Select E11:F17 as the final range.

11. Select Year 2006 in the Field one box.

12. Select Semester 2 in the Field two box.

Now you can click Next and complete the wizard, placing the PivotTable on a new work-sheet. The result is shown in Figure 2-25.

When you examine this PivotTable report you will see that the design does just what you wanted. If you drop down Page1 you have three choices: All, Year 2005, and Year 2006. Likewise, if you drop down Page2 you have the choices All, Semester 1, and Semester 2. Make your selections to filter the PivotTable as needed.

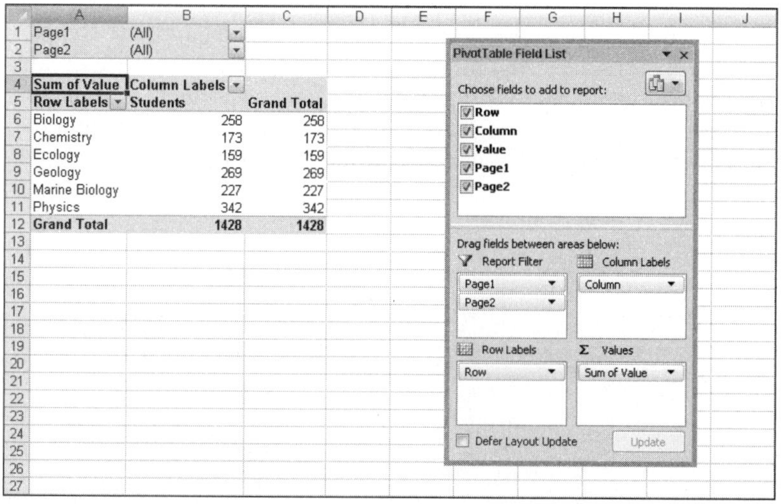

Figure 2-25: The completed PivotTable has two page fields with drop-down lists.

As a final task, get rid of the Grand Total column, which is really not needed. All you need to do is right-click the column heading and select Remove Grand Total from the pop-up menu. The column vanishes and your PivotTable report is complete.

Basing a PivotTable on Another PivotTable Report

A final option for creating a PivotTable report is to base it on an existing PivotTable or PivotChart. In other words, the summary data in the existing PivotTable report become the raw data for the second report.

There are two ways to create a PivotTable based on another PivotTable:

- If you are using the Excel 2007 interface, simply create the new PivotTable as usual, selecting the existing PivotTable as the input data range.

- If you are using the PivotTable and PivotChart Wizard, select the Another PivotTable or PivotChart Report option in Step 1 of the wizard. (This option will be available only if the workbook contains another PivotTable.) When you click Next, you'll see a list of all available PivotTables and PivotCharts. Simply select the desired source and proceed as usual.

Why base one PivotTable on another? In many cases the second PivotTable will, at least initially, look exactly like the source PivotTable. But by customizing the second PivotTable you can create two different views of the same data, which is useful in some situations. For example, the first PivotTable may summarize the original data but still be a rather complex table. By creating a second PivotTable that uses the first one for its data, you could create a more condensed summary that is easier to read. Also, basing a second PivotTable on an existing PivotTable uses less memory than basing the two PivotTables directly on the raw data. This may be a consideration when you are working with a large data set.

Chapter 3

Using PivotTable Tools and Formatting

Excel has some tools that are designed specifically for working with PivotTable reports. You find these tools on the Options and Design ribbons that Excel displays when a PivotTable report is active. You need to understand how to use these tools if you want to use PivotTables efficiently. This chapter also explains some of the options that you can set for PivotTables and the various techniques you can use to format PivotTable reports.

In This Chapter

◆ Working with the PivotTable Field List

◆ Using the classic PivotTable layout

◆ Getting the most out of the PivotTable ribbons

◆ Understanding PivotTable options

◆ Formatting PivotTables

Understanding the PivotTable Field List

Perhaps the most important tool at your disposal when working with a PivotTable is the Field List. You use the Field List to specify which data fields are included in the PivotTable report and how the data is arranged.

When you initially create a PivotTable report, the report itself is blank. The Field List displays all of the data fields that are available in the data source that the PivotTable is based on. An example is shown in Figure 3-1.

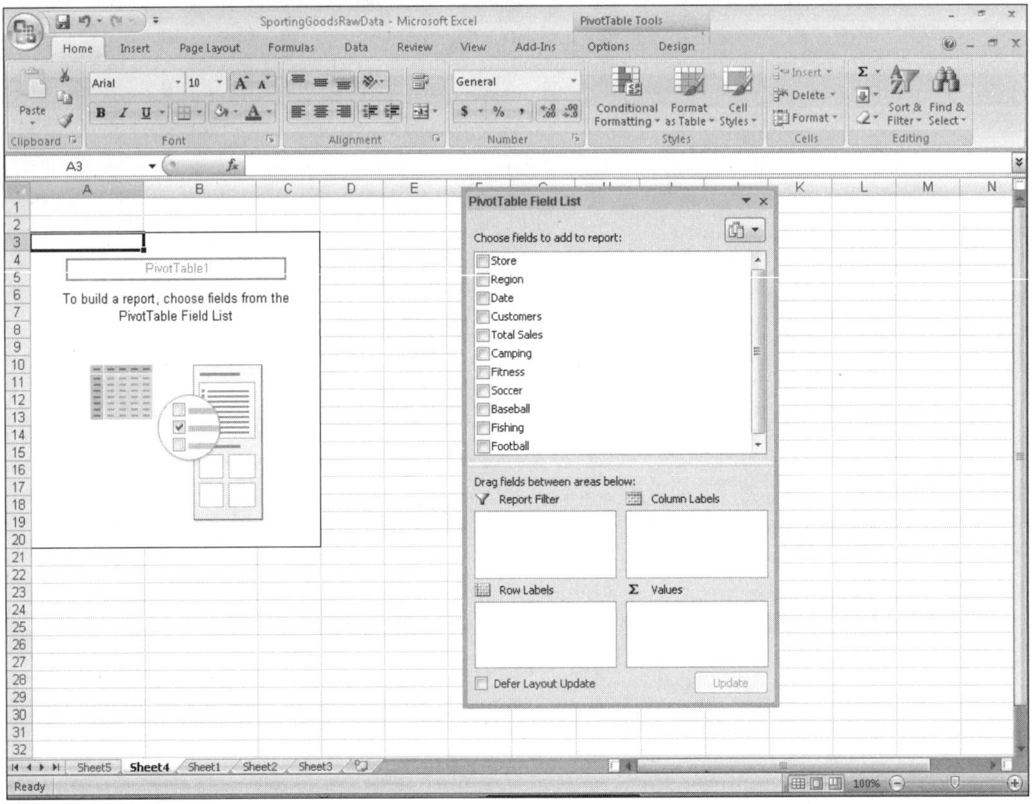

Figure 3-1: The Field List displays all of the data fields from the data source.

To add a field to the PivotTable, click the adjacent box. Excel will add the field to one of the four areas at the bottom of the Field List. These areas are:

- **Report Filter**—Data fields in this area can be used to filter the entire report—in other words, to display only selected data based on criteria that you specify.

- **Column Labels**—Data fields in this area are displayed as column headings in the report.

- **Row Labels**—Data fields in this area are displayed as row headings in the report.

- **Values**—Data fields in this area are summed by default and displayed in the main body of the report.

When you check a field, how does Excel know which area to place it in? It's simple, really—if the field contains numeric data it is placed in the Values area, and if it contains any other kind of data—text or a date, for example—it is placed in the Row Labels area. This is not really important seeing that you can move a field from one area to another as needed.

Let's look at an example, which will help make these concepts clear. Figure 3-2 shows a PivotTable and its associated Field List, with one field placed in each of the four areas. You'll see how to create this PivotTable in the next section. For now, look at the callouts which show how each field's placement in the Field List determines where that field appears in the PivotTable itself:

1. Region is placed in the Report Filter area and is placed in the Filter region of the report.

2. Date is placed in the Row Labels area and is displayed as row headings in the report.

3. Store is placed in the Column Labels area and is displayed as column headings in the report.

4. Camping—actually, Sum of Camping—is placed in the Values area and is displayed in the values section of the report.

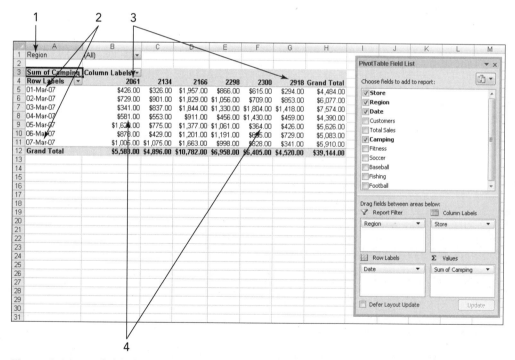

Figure 3-2: How field placement in the Field List affects the structure of the PivotTable.

The next section demonstrates how to use the Field List to get the PivotTable arrangement you want.

Using the Field List

The previous section shows you how the selection and placement of fields in the Field List determines the structure of the PivotTable report. This section shows you how to use the Field List to get the PivotTable structure you want.

To start, load the file SportingGoodsRawData. Then do the following:

1. Place the cell pointer on any cell in the data table.

2. Click the PivotTable button on the Insert ribbon to display the Create PivotTable dialog box.

3. Click OK. Excel creates a blank PivotTable as shown in Figure 3-3.

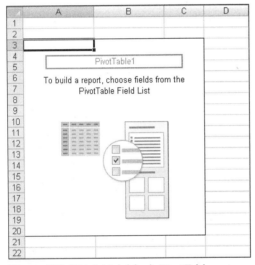

Figure 3-3: The initial, blank PivotTable.

4. In the PivotTable Field list, place checkmarks next to the Store, Region, Camping, and Date fields.

At this point, the worksheet looks like Figure 3-4.

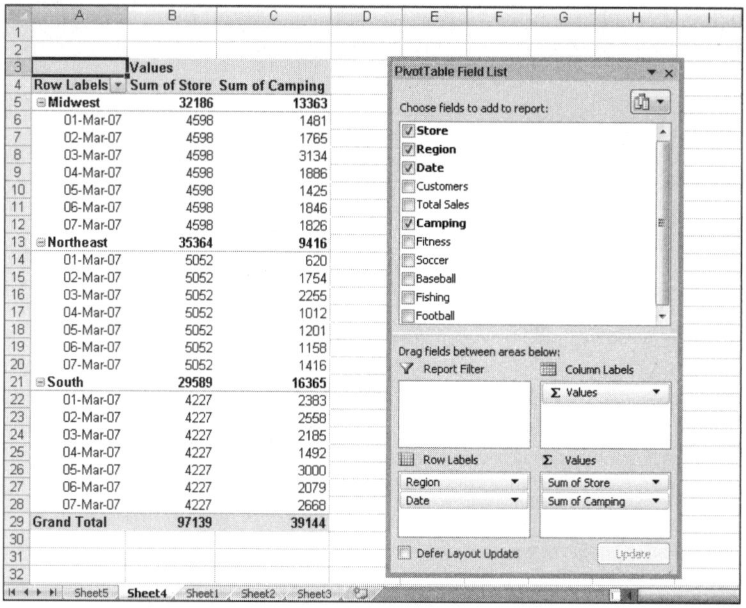

Figure 3-4: The default PivotTable arrangement.

Here's what has happened. The Camping and Store fields have been placed in the Values area because both of these fields contain numeric data. The Region and Date fields have been placed in the Row labels area because these fields contain text and date data, respectively. The PivotTable is not at all what you want—in fact, it is essentially useless. What's needed is to move some fields to different areas of the report.

You can move a field two ways:

- Drag the field and drop it in the desired area in the Field List.
- Click the down arrow adjacent to the field name and select Move to XXXX from the popup menu, where XXXX is the name of the destination area.

Then make the following changes:

- Move the Region field to the Report Filter area.
- Move the Store field—it is labeled Sum of Store—to the Column labels area.

The final step is to format the table values as currency:

1. Click the arrow next to the Sum of Camping field in the Values area.
2. Select Value Field Settings from the popup menu to open the Value Field Settings dialog box.

3. In the dialog box, click the Number Format button to open the Format Cells dialog box.

4. Select the Currency format.

5. Click OK twice to exit all dialog boxes.

Now the PivotTable report is what we want, as shown in Figure 3-5.

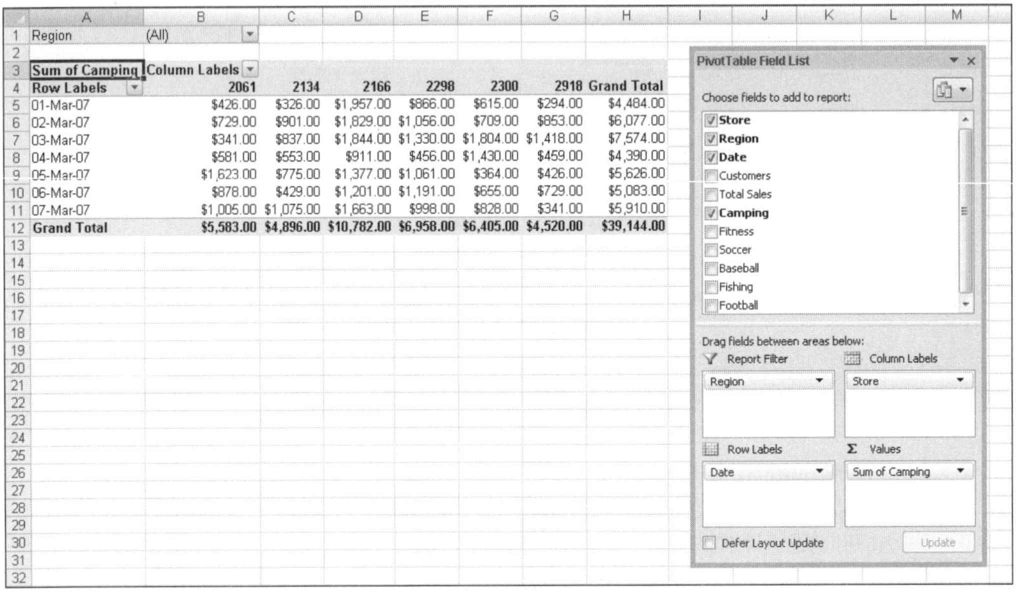

Figure 3-5: The final appearance of the PivotTable and Field List.

Setting Field List Options

The Field List dialog box provides some flexibility as to how it is displayed. It is displayed, by the way, whenever the associate PivotTable is active (that is, when the cell pointer is on a cell in the PivotTable). If for any reason you want to hide the Field List while the PivotTable is active, click the Field List button on the Options ribbon (and click this button again to re-display the Field List).

As with most windows, the Field List can be moved by pointing at its title bar and dragging. It can also be resized by pointing at its border or a corner and dragging.

Normally, the Field List dialog box displays the list of fields at the top with the four area boxes below. You can change this arrangement by clicking the button near the top-right of the dialog box and selecting one of five arrangements from the menu (see Figure 3-6). Note that the last two display options on this menu are useful when you have decided which fields will be part of the PivotTable and are working with their arrangement.

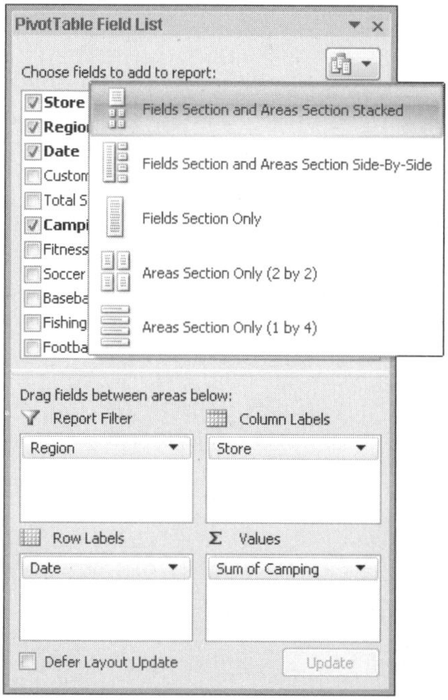

Figure 3-6: Selecting a display arrangement for the Field List.

The final Field List option, located at the bottom of the dialog box (see Figure 3-7), lets you defer updates to the PivotTable. If this option is turned off (the default), changes you make in the Field List are reflected immediately in the PivotTable. If you have a large, complex PivotTable, particularly if it is based on external data, such updates can take a significant amount of time. You can speed things up by selecting this option, making the required Field List changes, and then clicking the Update button to make all the required updates at one time.

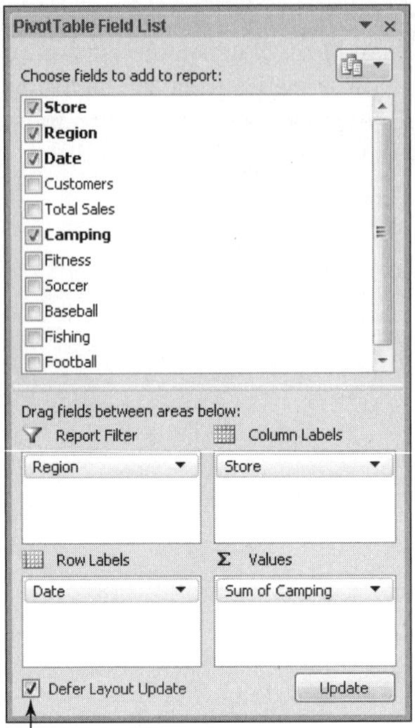

Select this option to defer PivotTable updates
when you are making changes in the Field List

Figure 3-7: Deferring layout updates can reduce delays when working with large, complex PivotTables.

Using Classic PivotTable Layout

As I have mentioned previously, Excel 2007 still supports some of the older techniques for working with PivotTables that were used in earlier versions of Excel. In addition to the PivotTable and PivotChart Wizard, which is covered in Chapter 1, Excel supports what is called *classic* PivotTable layout. This layout lets you rearrange fields in the PivotTable report by dragging them on the report itself rather than by making changes in the Field List. You may prefer using this layout, and this section shows you how.

To follow along, open the file SportingGoodsRawData and create a blank PivotTable by following these steps:

1. Place the cell pointer on any cell in the data table.

2. Click the PivotTable button on the Insert ribbon to display the Create PivotTable dialog box.

3. Click OK.

The next step is to switch to classic layout:

1. Click the Options button on the Options ribbon to open the PivotTable Options dialog box.

2. In the dialog box, click the Display tab (see Figure 3-8).

3. Select the Classic PivotTable Layout option.

4. Click OK.

Select this option to use classic PivotTable layout.

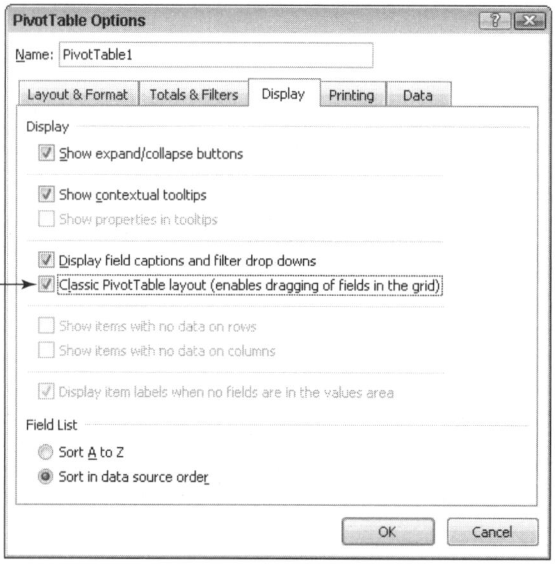

Figure 3-8: Selecting the Classic PivotTable Layout option.

Your empty PivotTable will change to resemble Figure 3-9. Compare this with the appearance of a default empty PivotTable as shown earlier in this chapter in Figure 3-3.

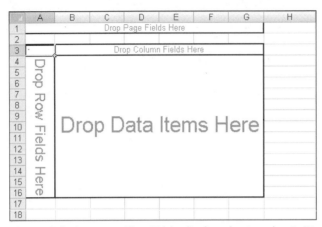

Figure 3-9: An empty PivotTable displayed using classic PivotTable layout.

You can see that the PivotTable has four areas labeled Drop XXXX Here where XXX is one of the following:

- **Page Fields**—A field that is used to filter the report, the same as the Report Filter area in the Field List.

- **Column Fields**—A field that is displayed as a column heading, the same as the Column Labels area in the Field List.

- **Row Fields**—A field that is displayed as a row heading, the same as the Row Labels area in the Field List.

- **Data Items**—A field that is displayed as a data item in the report, the same as the Values area in the Field List.

To design the report, drag fields from the Field List and drop them on the corresponding area of the report itself. Thus:

1. Drag the Region field and drop it on the Drop Page Fields Here section.

2. Drag the Date field and drop it on the Drop Row Fields Here section.

3. Drag the Store field and drop it on the Drop Column Fields Here section.

4. Drag the Region field and drop it on the Drop Data Items Here section.

After applying Currency formatting to the data, the resulting PivotTable looks like the one in Figure 3-10. If you compare this PivotTable with the same PivotTable created in normal view, shown earlier in Figure 3-5, you'll see that the two are essentially identical. You can switch back and forth between normal and classic layout as needed by following the steps presented earlier in this section.

	A	B	C	D	E	F	G	H	I	J	K	L	M
1	Region	(All)	▼										
2													
3	Sum of Camping	Store	▼										
4	Date ▼	2061	2134	2166	2298	2300	2918	Grand Total					
5	01-Mar-07	$426.00	$326.00	$1,957.00	$866.00	$615.00	$294.00	$4,484.00					
6	02-Mar-07	$729.00	$901.00	$1,829.00	$1,056.00	$709.00	$853.00	$6,077.00					
7	03-Mar-07	$341.00	$837.00	$1,844.00	$1,330.00	$1,804.00	$1,418.00	$7,574.00					
8	04-Mar-07	$581.00	$553.00	$911.00	$456.00	$1,430.00	$459.00	$4,390.00					
9	05-Mar-07	$1,623.00	$775.00	$1,377.00	$1,061.00	$364.00	$426.00	$5,626.00					
10	06-Mar-07	$878.00	$429.00	$1,201.00	$1,191.00	$655.00	$729.00	$5,083.00					
11	07-Mar-07	$1,005.00	$1,075.00	$1,663.00	$998.00	$828.00	$341.00	$5,910.00					
12	Grand Total	$5,583.00	$4,896.00	$10,782.00	$6,958.00	$6,405.00	$4,520.00	$39,144.00					

PivotTable Field List ▼ ×

Choose fields to add to report:

☑ Store
☑ Region
☑ Date
☐ Customers
☐ Total Sales
☑ Camping
☐ Fitness
☐ Soccer
☐ Baseball
☐ Fishing
☐ Football

Drag fields between areas below:

▽ Report Filter　　　　▦ Column Labels

Region ▼　　　　Store ▼

▦ Row Labels　　　　Σ Values

Date ▼　　　　Sum of Camping ▼

☐ Defer Layout Update　　　　Update

Figure 3-10: The finished PivotTable report using classic layout.

One additional capability of classic view is the ability to modify the PivotTable by dragging fields from one location in the table to another. You can try this by dragging the Region field from its location in the Page Fields area and dropping it in the Column Fields area, as shown in Figure 3-11. The result is that both Region and Store are now column fields, as shown in Figure 3-12.

Drag Region from here...

...and drop it here

	A	B	C	D	E	F	G	H
1	Region	(All)	▼					
2								
3	Sum of Camping	Store	▼					
4	Date ▼	2061	2134	2166	2298	2300	2918	Grand Total
5	01-Mar-07	$426.00	$326.00	$1,957.00	$866.00	$615.00	$294.00	$4,484.00
6	02-Mar-07	$729.00	$901.00	$1,829.00	$1,056.00	$709.00	$853.00	$6,077.00
7	03-Mar-07	$341.00	$837.00	$1,844.00	$1,330.00	$1,804.00	$1,418.00	$7,574.00
8	04-Mar-07	$581.00	$553.00	$911.00	$456.00	$1,430.00	$459.00	$4,390.00
9	05-Mar-07	$1,623.00	$775.00	$1,377.00	$1,061.00	$364.00	$426.00	$5,626.00
10	06-Mar-07	$878.00	$429.00	$1,201.00	$1,191.00	$655.00	$729.00	$5,083.00
11	07-Mar-07	$1,005.00	$1,075.00	$1,663.00	$998.00	$828.00	$341.00	$5,910.00
12	Grand Total	$5,583.00	$4,896.00	$10,782.00	$6,958.00	$6,405.00	$4,520.00	$39,144.00

Figure 3-11: Modifying the PivotTable report by dragging fields within the report.

	Midwest		Midwest Total	Northeast		Northeast Total	South		South Total	Grand Total
Sum of Camping Region ▾ Store ▾										
Date ▾	2298	2300		2134	2918		2061	2166		
01-Mar-07	$866.00	$615.00	$1,481.00	$326.00	$294.00	$620.00	$426.00	$1,957.00	$2,383.00	$4,484.00
02-Mar-07	$1,056.00	$709.00	$1,765.00	$901.00	$853.00	$1,754.00	$729.00	$1,829.00	$2,558.00	$6,077.00
03-Mar-07	$1,330.00	$1,804.00	$3,134.00	$837.00	$1,418.00	$2,255.00	$341.00	$1,844.00	$2,185.00	$7,574.00
04-Mar-07	$456.00	$1,430.00	$1,886.00	$553.00	$459.00	$1,012.00	$581.00	$911.00	$1,492.00	$4,390.00
05-Mar-07	$1,061.00	$364.00	$1,425.00	$775.00	$426.00	$1,201.00	$1,623.00	$1,377.00	$3,000.00	$5,626.00
06-Mar-07	$1,191.00	$655.00	$1,846.00	$429.00	$729.00	$1,158.00	$878.00	$1,201.00	$2,079.00	$5,083.00
07-Mar-07	$998.00	$828.00	$1,826.00	$1,075.00	$341.00	$1,416.00	$1,005.00	$1,663.00	$2,668.00	$5,910.00
Grand Total	$6,958.00	$6,405.00	$13,363.00	$4,896.00	$4,520.00	$9,416.00	$5,583.00	$10,782.00	$16,365.00	$39,144.00

Figure 3-12: After dragging the Region field from the Page Fields area to the Column Field area.

Note that using classic layout view does not preclude your using the Field List to arrange and change the PivotTable report—it just provides you with additional options.

Naming a PivotTable

Excel assigns default names to PivotTables in the form PivotTable1, PivotTable2, and so on. You can change the name to something more meaningful as follows:

1. Make the PivotTable active.

2. Click the Options button on the Options toolbar to open the PivotTable Options dialog box.

3. Type the new name in the Name field.

4. Click OK.

Using the PivotTable Ribbons

The new Office programs have greatly reduced the use of menus and toolbars in favor of *ribbons*, which are like toolbars in some ways but a lot more sophisticated and easier to use. Excel has several ribbons that are specifically related to PivotTables and PivotCharts.

Remember that all ribbons are dynamic and adjust to the size of the Excel window. If you have a large screen and the Excel window is wide, more ribbon elements will be shown. On a smaller screen with a narrower window, some ribbon elements will be hidden and you'll have to click an arrow on the ribbon to show them. Don't be surprised if your ribbon does not look exactly the same as the ones shown in the book's figures.

The PivotTable ribbons are available only when a PivotTable is active. Remember, click any cell in a PivotTable to make it active. There are two PivotTable-related ribbons that are collectively called PivotTable Tools and individually called Options and Design. Figure 3-13 shows the tabs for these ribbons.

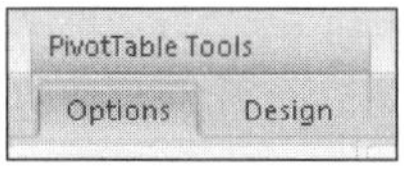

Figure 3-13: Excel has two ribbons, Options and Design, that are specifically related to PivotTables.

The Design ribbon is, as its name suggest, devoted to tools that let you change the appearance and layout of the PivotTable report. This ribbon is shown in Figure 3-14.

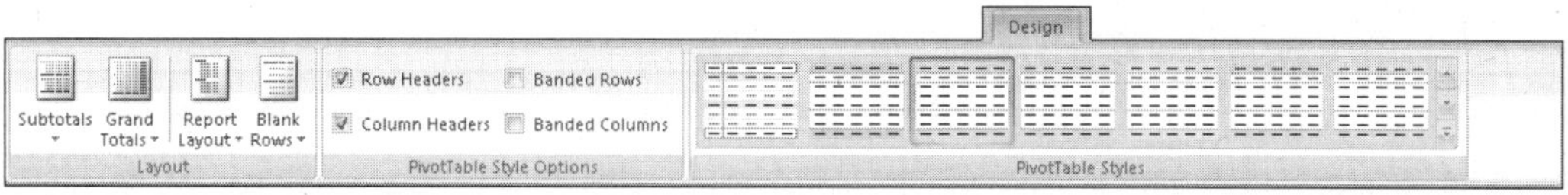

Figure 3-14: The Design ribbon lets you change the design and layout of a PivotTable report.

You can see on this ribbon, for example, that there are options for displaying row and column headers in the center, and on the right are some pre-defined styles that you can apply to a PivotTable.

The Options ribbon, shown in Figure 3-15, controls other aspects of a PivotTable such as the sorting and grouping of data.

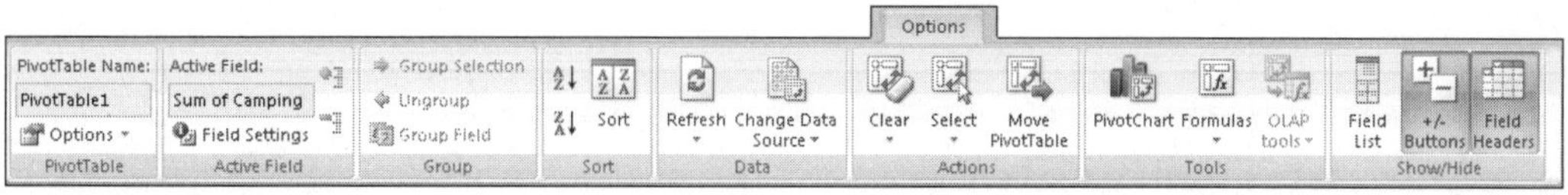

Figure 3-15: The Options ribbon controls aspects of PivotTable data display such as sorting and grouping.

You'll learn about the various tools on the PivotTable ribbons in upcoming tips that deal with that specific topic. For now, it's enough to remember that just about anything you want to do with a PivotTable report is done using commands on these two ribbons.

CROSS-REFERENCE

Excel also has several ribbons that are specifically related to PivotCharts. These will be covered in the section on PivotCharts in Chapter 4.

Setting PivotTable Options

Each PivotTable report has a set of options associated with it. You access these options for the active PivotTable report by clicking the Options button on the Options tab. The PivotTable Options dialog box contains five tabs, and the options on these tabs are explained in this section. Some of the explanations here are superficial, because a full explanation may not make sense before you know more about PivotTables. In these cases, you'll find a fuller explanation later in the book in the section that deals with the relevant aspects of PivotTables.

Figure 3-16 shows the Layout & Format tab of the PivotTable Options dialog box.

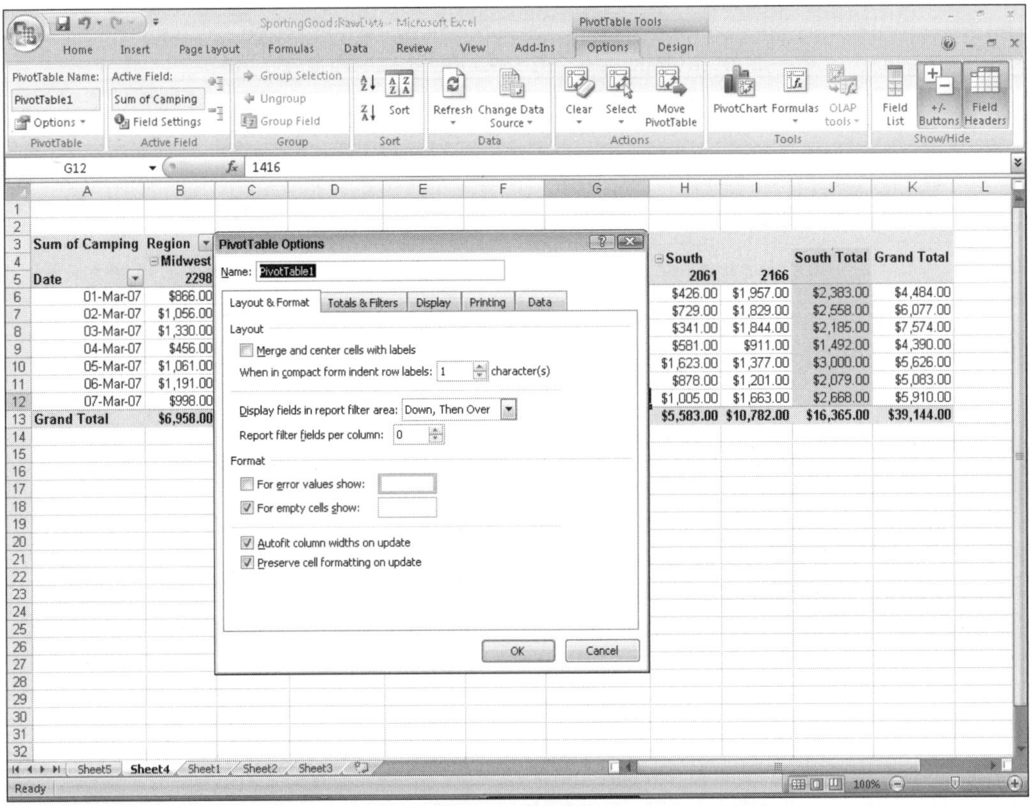

Figure 3-16: The Layout & Format tab of the PivotTable Options dialog box.

The following list discusses the options available on the Layout & Format tab of the PivotTable Options dialog box:

- **Merge and center cells with labels**—In some PivotTables, the same label, such as Quarter or Month, is repeated in the outer row or column cells. If you select this option, the repeated labels will be merged into a single label that spans the columns or months.

- **When in compact form indent row labels XXX characters**—Specifies by how much row labels would be indented when the PivotTable is in compact form.

- **Display fields in report filter area**—Determines how multiple fields are displayed in the report filter area. Select Down, Then Over to add new fields to an existing column before moving to a new column. Select Over, Then Down to add new fields to an existing row before moving to a new row.

- **Report filter fields per column**—Specifies how many fields are displayed in a row or column (depending on the setting of the Display fields in report filter area option) before starting a new row or column.

- **For error values show**—If you want PivotTable cells with an error to display text that you specify instead of the error message, select this option and enter the text in the adjacent box.

- **For empty cells show**—If you want blank PivotTable cells to display text that you specify, select this option and enter the text in the adjacent box.

- **Autofit column widths on update**—If this option is selected, Excel will, when the PivotTable is updated, automatically adjust the width of columns in the PivotTable to fit the widest text or number. Otherwise the original column widths will be retained.

- **Preserve cell formatting on update**—If this option is selected, the cell formatting and layout of the PivotTable will be preserved when certain operations, such as updating, are performed on the table.

The Totals & Filters tab of the PivotTable Options dialog box is shown in Figure 3-17.

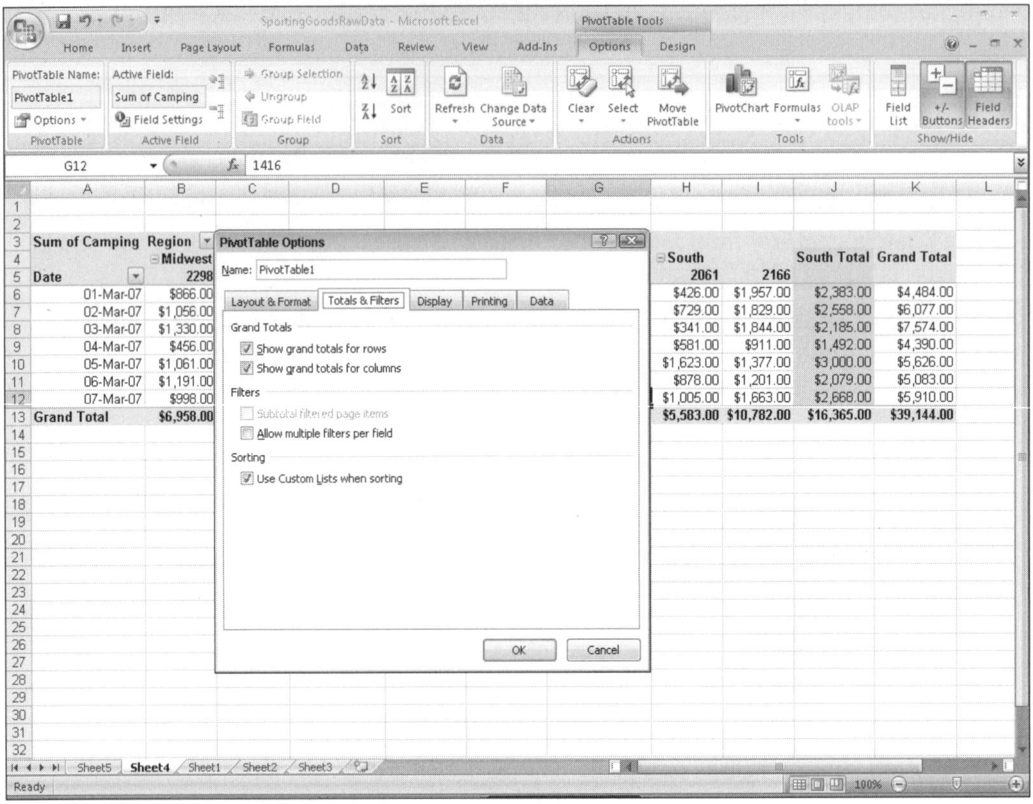

Figure 3-17: The Totals & Filters tab of the PivotTable Options dialog box.

The options on the Totals & Filters tab are as follows:

- **Show grand total for rows**—Select this option to display a grand total at the right end of each table row.

- **Show grand totals for columns**—Select this option to display a grand total at the bottom of each table column.

- **Subtotal filtered page items**—If this option is selected, subtotals include table values that are not displayed because of an applied filter. If this option is not selected, subtotals include only displayed table values.

- **Mark totals with**—If this option is selected, subtotals that include both displayed and non-displayed items (as per the Subtotal filtered page items option) are marked with an asterisk.

- **Allow multiple filters per field**—Select this option if you want subtotals and grand totals to include items that are hidden by filtering.

- **Use Custom Lists when sorting**—Select this option to enable the use of custom lists when sorting data. Please refer to Excel online help for information about using custom lists for sorting.

The Display tab of the PivotTable Options dialog box is shown in Figure 3-18.

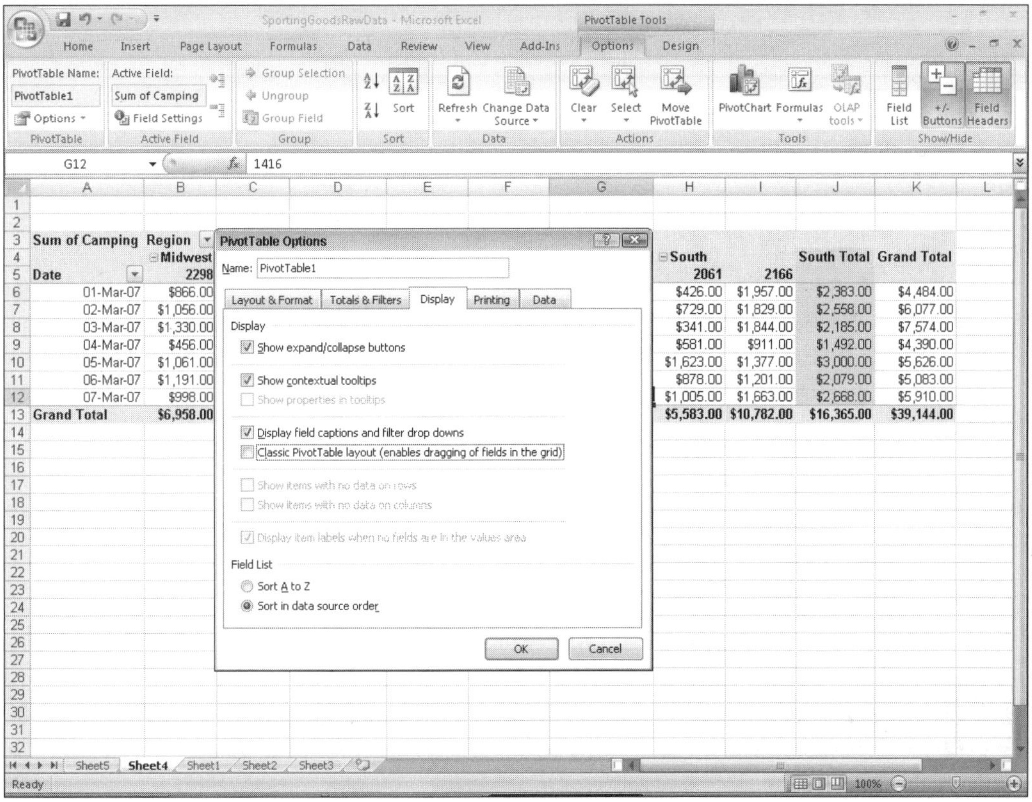

Figure 3-18: The Display tab of the PivotTable Options dialog box.

The options on the Display tab are as follows:

- **Show expand/collapse buttons**—When a PivotTable report has two or more levels of row or column labels, the higher level will, if this option is selected, display expand (+) or collapse (-) buttons that let you show or hide the lower levels of detail. This is illustrated in Figure 3-19, where stores 2061 and 2166 are expanded, showing the individual dates for each store, and store 2134 is collapsed, hiding the dates. Hiding these buttons may be desirable when you are printing or viewing (as opposed to manipulating) the PivotTable report.

- **Show contextual tooltips**—When this option is selected, Excel displays a contextual tooltip when you hover the mouse pointer over certain PivotTable elements. The tooltip shows information such as the name of the field, its value, and the row and column it is in (see Figure 3-20).

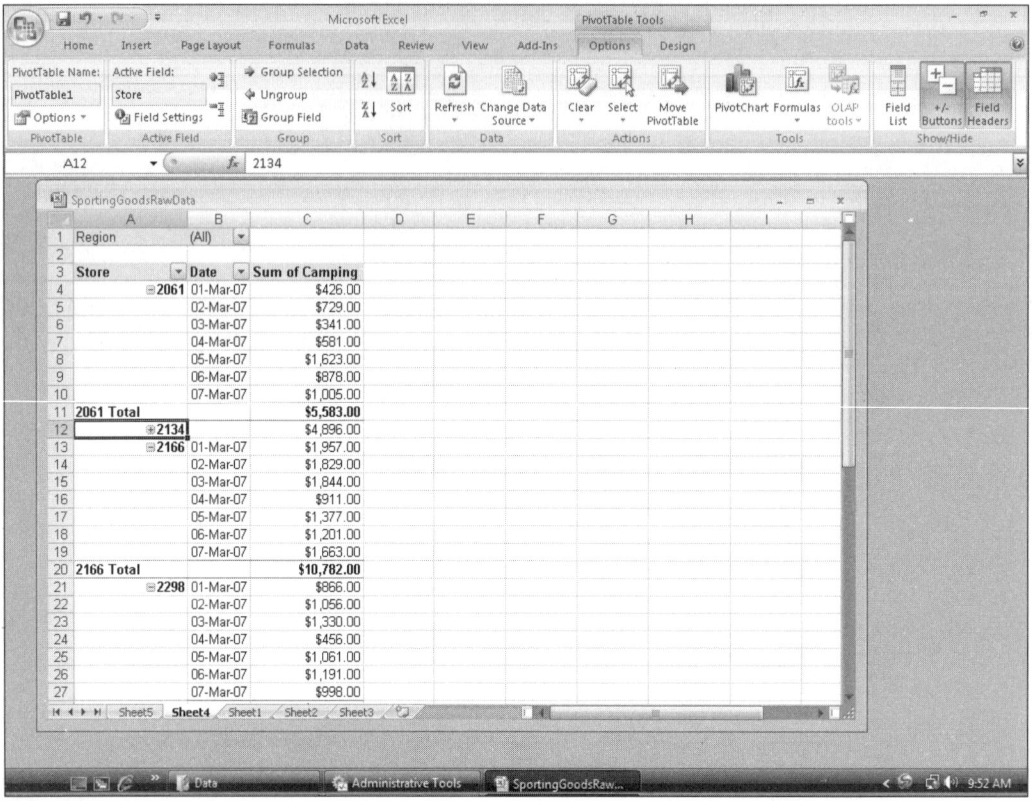

Figure 3-19: Expand/collapse buttons let you show or hide lower levels of column or row headings.

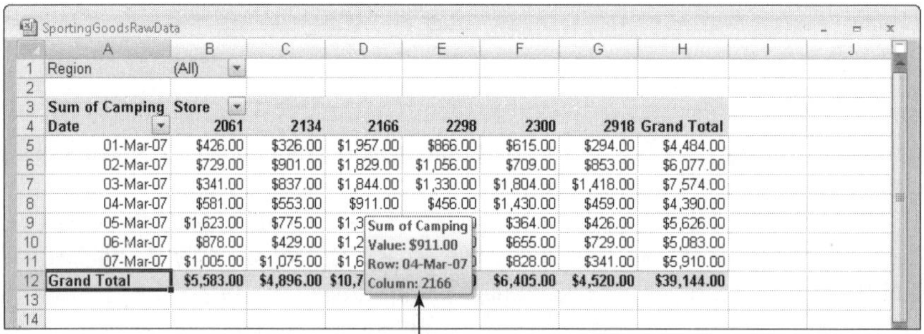

A contextual tooltip

Figure 3-20: A contextual tooltip displays information about a PivotTable element.

- **Show properties in tooltips**—Select this option if you want tooltips to include property information for an item. This option is available only if the data source supports properties.

- **Display field captions and filter drop-downs**—If this option is selected, the field captions and filter drop-downs are displayed on the report, as shown in Figure 3-21. You may want to hide these elements for viewing or printing the PivotTable.

1	Region	(All)	▼					
2								
3	**Sum of Camping**							
4		2061	2134	2166	2298	2300	2918	Grand Total
5	01-Mar-07	$426.00	$326.00	$1,957.00	$866.00	$615.00	$294.00	$4,484.00
6	02-Mar-07	$729.00	$901.00	$1,829.00	$1,056.00	$709.00	$853.00	$6,077.00
7	03-Mar-07	$341.00	$837.00	$1,844.00	$1,330.00	$1,804.00	$1,418.00	$7,574.00
8	04-Mar-07	$581.00	$553.00	$911.00	$456.00	$1,430.00	$459.00	$4,390.00
9	05-Mar-07	$1,623.00	$775.00	$1,377.00	$1,061.00	$364.00	$426.00	$5,626.00
10	06-Mar-07	$878.00	$429.00	$1,201.00	$1,191.00	$655.00	$729.00	$5,083.00
11	07-Mar-07	$1,005.00	$1,075.00	$1,663.00	$998.00	$828.00	$341.00	$5,910.00
12	**Grand Total**	$5,583.00	$4,896.00	$10,782.00	$6,958.00	$6,405.00	$4,520.00	$39,144.00
13								
14								

1	Region	(All)	▼					
2								
3	**Sum of Camping**	Store	▼					
4	**Date**	▼	2061	2134	2166	2298	2300	2918	Grand Total
5	01-Mar-07		$426.00	$326.00	$1,957.00	$866.00	$615.00	$294.00	$4,484.00
6	02-Mar-07		$729.00	$901.00	$1,829.00	$1,056.00	$709.00	$853.00	$6,077.00
7	03-Mar-07		$341.00	$837.00	$1,844.00	$1,330.00	$1,804.00	$1,418.00	$7,574.00
8	04-Mar-07		$581.00	$553.00	$911.00	$456.00	$1,430.00	$459.00	$4,390.00
9	05-Mar-07		$1,623.00	$775.00	$1,377.00	$1,061.00	$364.00	$426.00	$5,626.00
10	06-Mar-07		$878.00	$429.00	$1,201.00	$1,191.00	$655.00	$729.00	$5,083.00
11	07-Mar-07		$1,005.00	$1,075.00	$1,663.00	$998.00	$828.00	$341.00	$5,910.00
12	**Grand Total**		$5,583.00	$4,896.00	$10,782.00	$6,958.00	$6,405.00	$4,520.00	$39,144.00
13									
14									

Figure 3-21: A PivotTable with field captions and filter drop-downs displayed (top) and hidden (bottom).

- **Classic PivotTable layout**—Select this option to use classic PivotTable layout, as explained earlier in the part.

- **Show items with no data on rows**—Select this option if you want to display row items that have no values. This option will be available only if the PivotTable is based on an OLAP data source.

- **Show items with no data on columns**—Select this option if you want to display column items that have no values. This option will be available only if the PivotTable is based on an OLAP data source.

- **Display item labels when no fields are in the values area**—Select this option if you want to display item labels when there are no fields in the value area. This option applies only to PivotTables that were created in earlier versions of Excel.

- **Show calculated numbers from OLAP server**—Relevant only when the PivotTable is based on OLAP data. If selected, calculated items in a dimension are displayed.

- **Field list**—Select whether items in the files list are sorted in A-Z order or are displayed in the order specified by the data source (which may be, but is not necessarily, A-Z order).

The Printing tab of the PivotTable Options dialog box is shown in Figure 3-22.

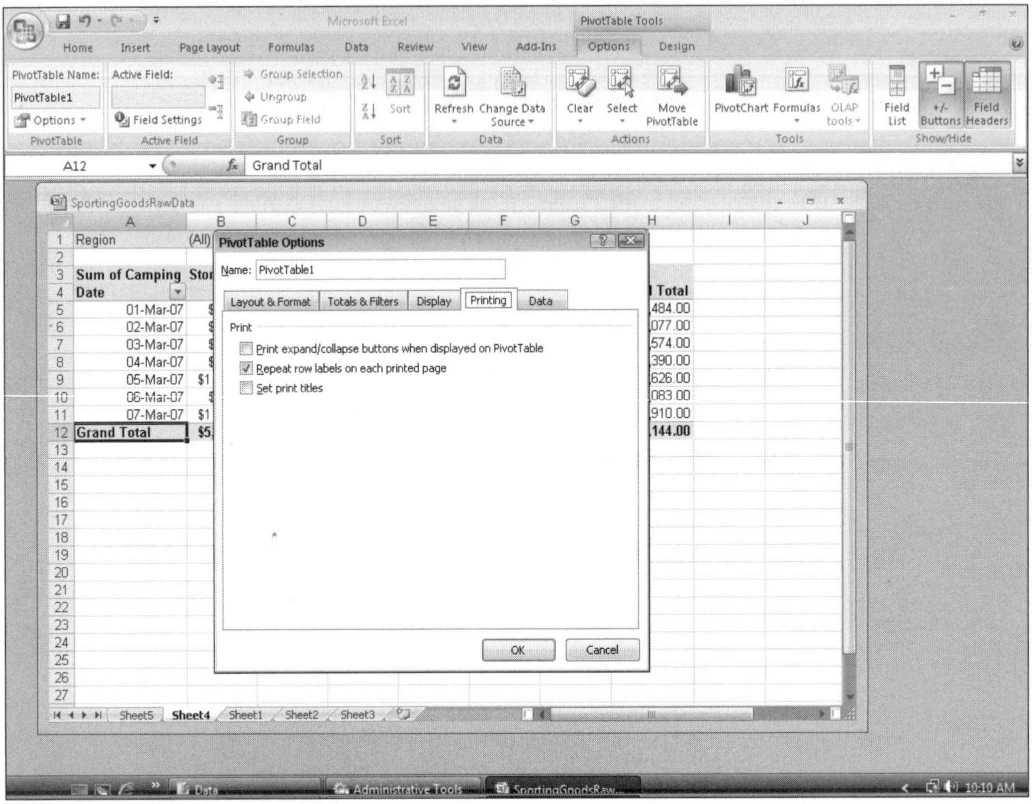

Figure 3-22: The Printing tab of the PivotTable Options dialog box.

The options on the Printing tab are as follows:

- **Print expand collapse buttons when displayed on the PivotTable**—If this option is selected, expand/collapse buttons are printed or not depending on whether they are displayed on the PivotTable, according to the setting of the Show expand/collapse buttons option on the Display tab. If this option is not selected, expand/collapse buttons are never printed.

- **Repeat row labels on each printed page**—If a PivotTable has more than one row field, selecting this option tells Excel to repeat the outer row labels on the second and subsequent pages when the report is printed. This is not the same as printing regular row and column labels on each page, which you can do with the Set print titles option.

- **Set print titles**—When this option is selected, row and column labels are repeated on each page of a multipage printed report.

The Data tab of the PivotTable Options dialog box is shown in Figure 3-23.

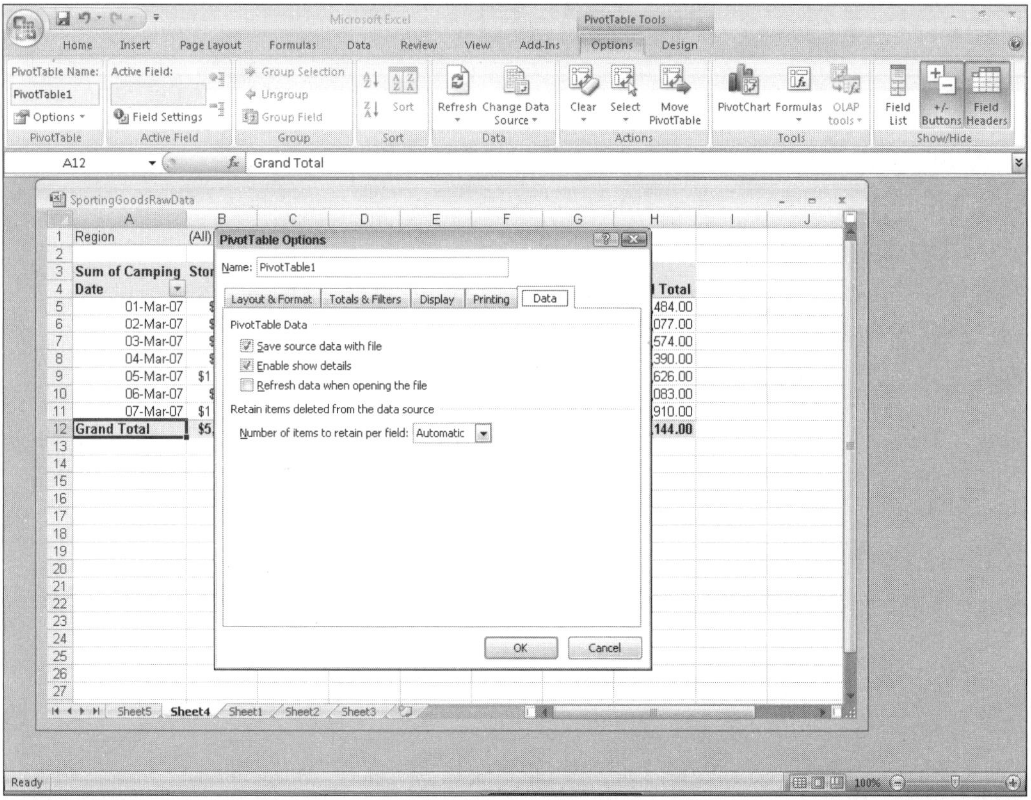

Figure 3-23: The Data tab of the PivotTable Options dialog box.

The options on the Data tab are as follows:

- **Save source data with file**—This option is relevant only for PivotTables that are based on external data. If selected, the data from the external source is saved as part of the workbook. This enables you to open the workbook and work on the PivotTable even when a connection to the data source is not available.

- **Enable show details**—Select this option to enable drilling to detail in the PivotTable report. This is covered in the section "Showing and Hiding Detail" in Chapter 5.

- **Refresh data when opening the file**—If this option is selected, the PivotTable is automatically refreshed from the data source each time the file is opened.

- **Number of items to retain per field**—This option is relevant only for PivotTables that are based on external data. It specifies the number of data items that are cached in the workbook for each field. Possible settings are:

  - *Automatic*—The default number of items for each field.

  - *None*—No unique items for each field.

  - *Max*—The maximum number of items for each field.

Formatting PivotTables

In some ways, a PivotTable is like any other data in Excel and you can use the same formatting techniques to get your report looking the way you want it. In other ways, PivotTable formatting is a different critter altogether.

Applying PivotTable Styles

Excel has a terrific assortment of styles that you can quickly apply to a PivotTable, and also lets you define your own styles. Styles can control the following aspects of a PivotTable's appearance:

- The font used for the table as a whole or for specific parts of the table, including type face, size, bold/italic, and color.

- The background color for the whole table, parts of the table, or alternating rows or columns.

- The borders, both vertical and horizontal, used within the table and on its outer edges.

To apply a style to the active PivotTable report, display the Design ribbon. Then, as shown in Figure 3-24, you can do the following:

- Select one of the displayed styles by clicking it. As you move the mouse pointer over the styles, the report previews that style.

- Scroll through the available styles using the scroll bar.

- Display the style menu by clicking where indicated in Figure 3-24.

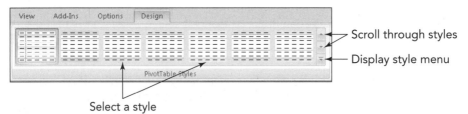

Figure 3-24: Working with PivotTable styles on the Design ribbon.

When you display the style menu, which is shown in Figure 3-25, you can view more of the defined styles. These are divided into three groups based on their general appearance: Light (shown in the figure), Medium, and Dark. Use the scroll bar on the right to view all available styles. As you view these styles, move the mouse pointer over the styles to preview the style on the report. On this menu you can also:

- Click Clear to remove a style from the active PivotTable report.

- Click New PivotTable Style to define a new custom style (more on this in the next section).

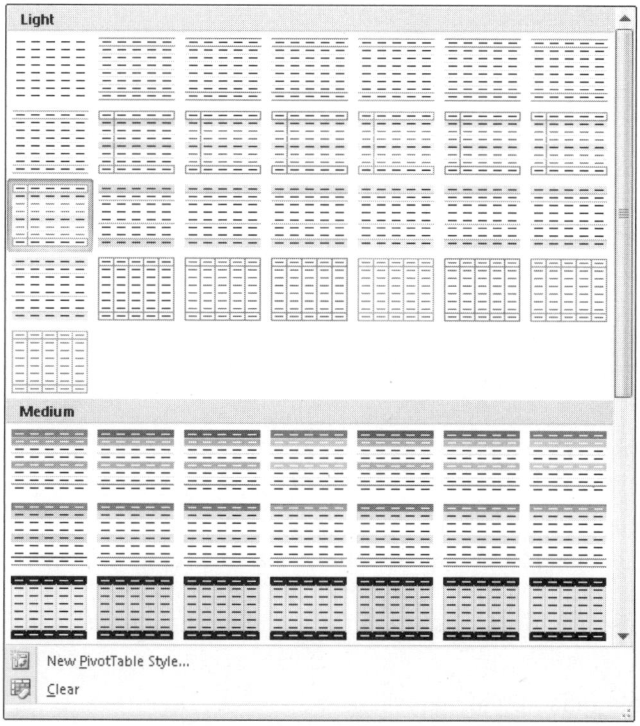

Figure 3-25: The styles menu gives you access to all defined styles.

Creating Custom PivotTable Styles

You can define your own style by clicking New PivotTable Style on the style menu. Excel opens the dialog box shown in Figure 3-26. You use the elements in this dialog box to define your new custom style.

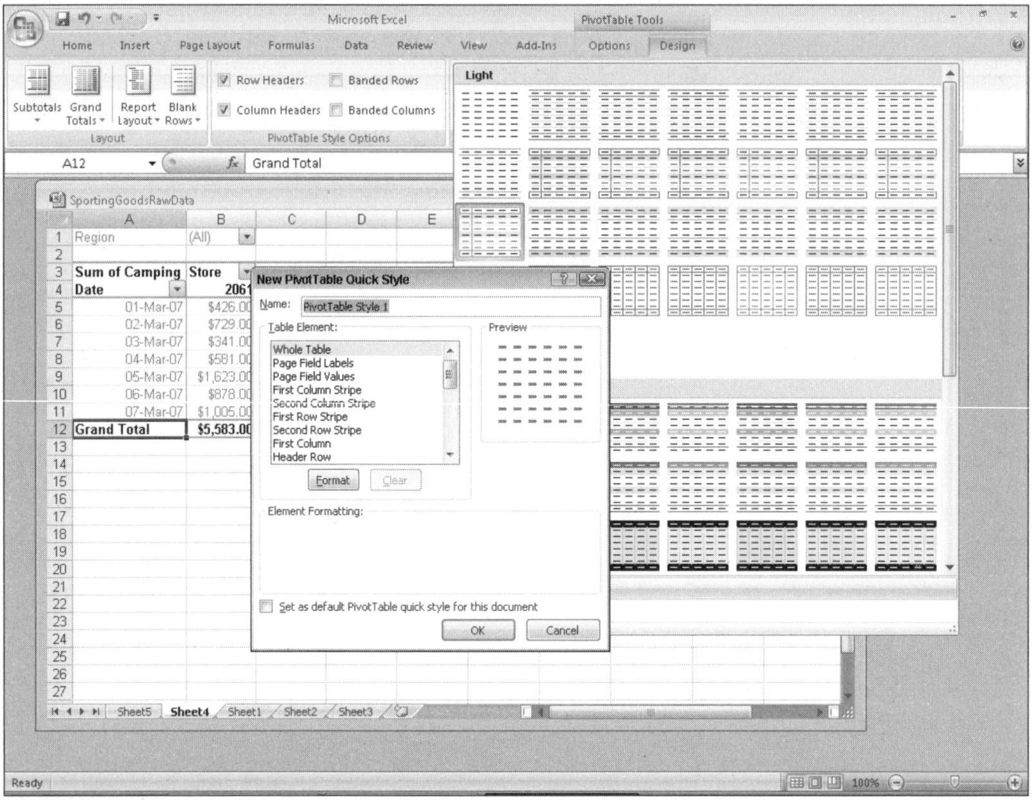

Figure 3-26: Defining a custom PivotTable style.

Each entry in the Table Element list corresponds to a part of the PivotTable report ranging from the entire report to single subheading rows. To define the formatting for an element, select it in the list and then click the Format button. Excel displays the Format Cells dialog box, shown in Figure 3-27. You use the three tabs at the top to define the font, border, and fill attributes for the element.

Other elements in the New PivotTable Quick Style dialog box are:

- **Name**—Enter the display name for the style.

- **Preview**—Shows a preview of the style as you define it.

- **Clear**—Click this button to remove all special formatting from the selected PivotTable element.

- **Set as default**—Select this option if you want the style you are defining to be the default style for all new PivotTables in the workbook.

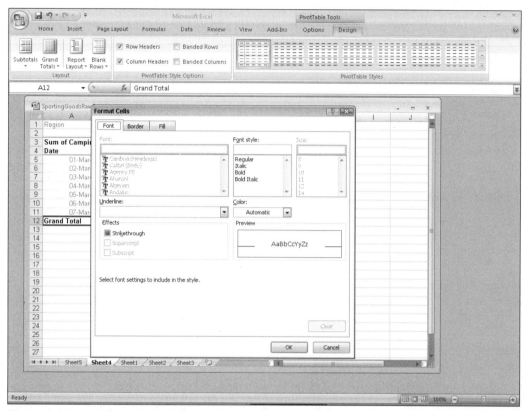

Figure 3-27: Specifying the style format for a specific PivotTable element.

When you have defined one or more custom PivotTable styles they are displayed at the top of the style menu in the Custom section.

Formatting Value Cells

Value cells in a PivotTable report can be assigned a number format. However, you do not assign the format directly to the cells, as you would with non-PivotTable data in a workbook, but rather to the data field that the cells display. To do so:

1. Click the down arrow to the right of the field name in the Values area of the Field List (see Figure 3-28).

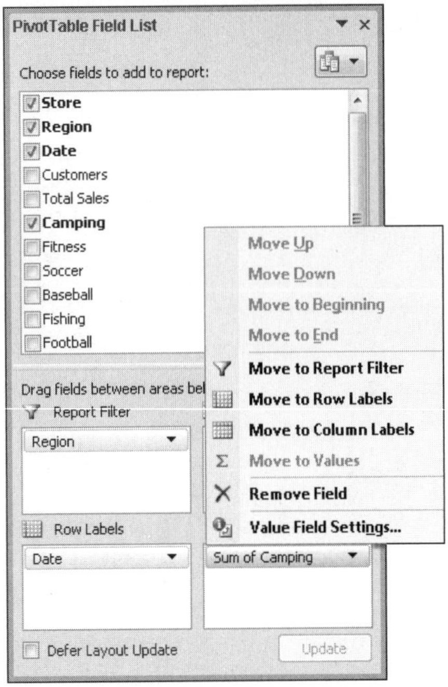

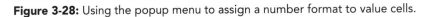

Figure 3-28: Using the popup menu to assign a number format to value cells.

2. Select Value Field Settings from the popup menu to display the Value Field Settings dialog box.

3. Click the Number Format button to open the Format Cells dialog box (see Figure 3-29).

4. Select a number format from the list on the left.

5. If necessary, specify format details on the right. Note that the Sample field displays what the selected format will look like.

6. Click OK twice to return to the worksheet.

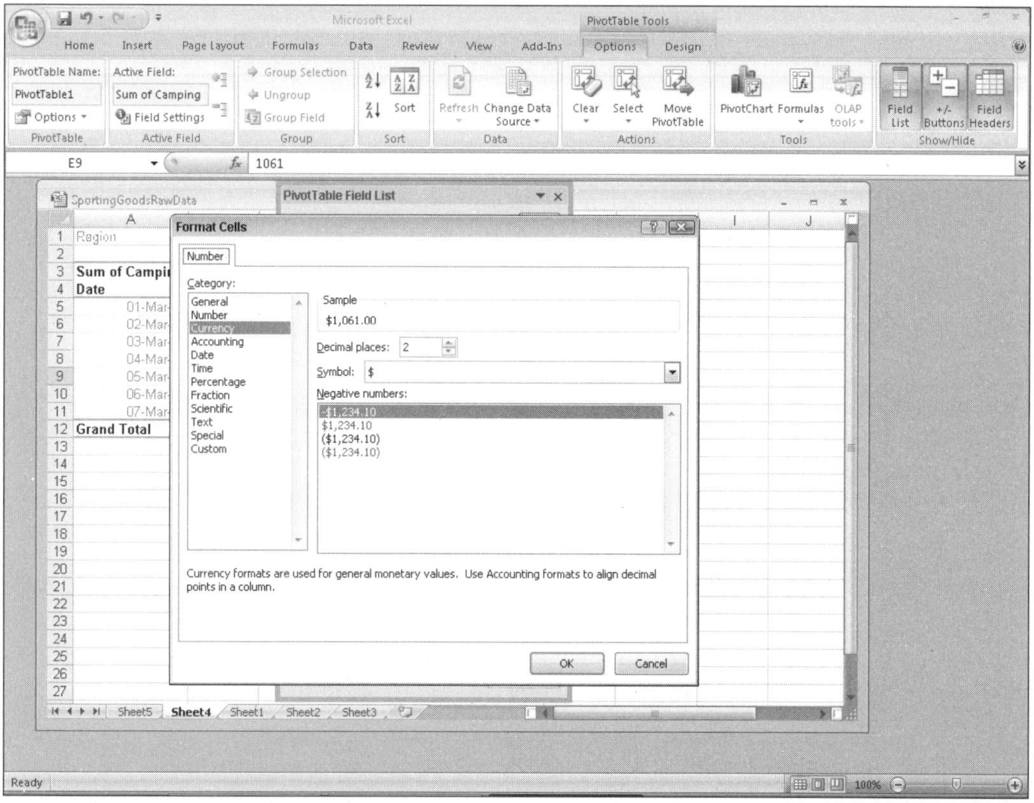

Figure 3-29: The Format Cells dialog box.

Setting Report Layout

Excel offers three report layouts that control the overall layout of the report. You select a layout using the Report Layout button on the Design ribbon. The layouts are:

- **Compact Form**—This layout, shown in Figure 3-30, arranges the PivotTable report to take up as little space as possible. It is useful when you are trying to fit a wide PivotTable report onto a single sheet of paper when printing or to make the entire table visible on-screen at one time.

- **Outline Form**—This layout, shown in Figure 3-31, displays the table like an outline. Subsidiary row fields—Category in the example—are displayed indented under the parent field. Rows are not separated by borders.

- **Tabular Form**—This layout, shown in Figure 3-32 displays the table in tabular form. Subsidiary row fields get their own column to the right of the parent field, and top-level row fields are separated by a horizontal border.

	A	B	C
1	Drop Page Fields Here		
2			
3	Sum of Titles		
4	Row Labels ▾	Total	
5	⊟Clarkville	1317	
6	Action	22	
7	Childrens	203	
8	Classics	251	
9	Comedy	345	
10	Drama	172	
11	Sci-Fi	324	
12	⊟Main Street	1289	
13	Action	374	
14	Childrens	63	
15	Classics	203	
16	Comedy	145	
17	Drama	180	
18	Sci-Fi	324	
19	⊟Northgate	992	
20	Action	45	
21	Childrens	320	
22	Classics	79	
23	Comedy	225	
24	Drama	287	
25	Sci-Fi	36	
26	⊟West End	1576	
27	Action	310	
28	Childrens	220	

Figure 3-30: A PivotTable report in compact form layout.

	A	B	C	D
1	Drop Page Fields Here			
2				
3	Sum of Titles			
4	Store ▾	Category ▾	Total	
5	⊟Clarkville		1317	
6		Action	22	
7		Childrens	203	
8		Classics	251	
9		Comedy	345	
10		Drama	172	
11		Sci-Fi	324	
12	⊟Main Street		1289	
13		Action	374	
14		Childrens	63	
15		Classics	203	
16		Comedy	145	
17		Drama	180	
18		Sci-Fi	324	
19	⊟Northgate		992	
20		Action	45	
21		Childrens	320	
22		Classics	79	
23		Comedy	225	
24		Drama	287	
25		Sci-Fi	36	
26	⊟West End		1576	
27		Action	310	
28		Childrens	220	

Figure 3-31: A PivotTable report in outline form layout.

	A	B	C	D
1	Drop Page Fields Here			
2				
3	Sum of Titles			
4	Store ▼	Category ▼	Total	
5	⊟Clarkville	Action	22	
6		Childrens	203	
7		Classics	251	
8		Comedy	345	
9		Drama	172	
10		Sci-Fi	324	
11	Clarkville Total		1317	
12	⊟Main Street	Action	374	
13		Childrens	63	
14		Classics	203	
15		Comedy	145	
16		Drama	180	
17		Sci-Fi	324	
18	Main Street Total		1289	
19	⊟Northgate	Action	45	
20		Childrens	320	
21		Classics	79	
22		Comedy	225	
23		Drama	287	
24		Sci-Fi	36	
25	Northgate Total		992	
26	⊟West End	Action	310	
27		Childrens	220	
28		Classics	145	

Figure 3-32: A PivotTable report in tabular form layout.

Changing Other Formatting

Because a PivotTable report is part of a worksheet, like any other Excel data, you can use regular Excel formatting tools to apply formats such as font, background color, and cell borders to a PivotTable—in essence, anything you can change for other parts of a worksheet can also be changed for a PivotTable report. There are a few things you need to keep in mind when formatting a PivotTable.

First of all, you want to make sure that the formatting you apply is preserved when the PivotTable is refreshed or its layout changes. This requires selecting the Preserve Cell Formatting on Update option on the Layout & Format tab of the PivotTable Options dialog box as mentioned earlier in this chapter. To display this dialog box, click the Options button on the Options ribbon.

A second concern is ensuring that the formatting is applied to parts of the PivotTable that are not visible. For example, you may have used a page field to filter the PivotTable to display a subset of the data. Before applying the formatting changes, select (All) in the page-field drop-down list to display all the data.

Finally, you need to use the correct technique to select the part of the PivotTable that you want to format. As I have mentioned before, cells in the PivotTable that are linked to the same field are connected, and you can select linked cells simultaneously by clicking the field heading. To do this, ensure that the mouse cursor changes to a right- or down-pointing arrow before clicking the heading to select a table element. After you have selected the desired element(s), use the usual formatting commands on the Formatting toolbar or the Format menu to apply the desired formatting.

For example, look at Figure 3-33. The mouse pointer is on the field heading Main Street and has changed to a right-pointing arrow. Click here to select all value cells that are associated with this heading. You can now apply formatting, such as italics or a background color, to all these cells at once.

Mouse cursor changes to an arrow

Figure 3-33: Clicking a field heading to select all associated cells.

Applying Formatting to a PivotTable Report

This section takes you through the process of formatting a PivotTable report with a style and with cell formats. I will use the PivotTable that you created in Chapter 2 from data in an Access database. This PivotTable is shown in Figure 3-34 with the default formatting. You need to open the workbook containing this PivotTable before proceeding.

Figure 3-34: The PivotTable report with its default formatting.

The first step is to ensure that the PivotTable options are set so that the formatting you will apply is preserved. Although these options are on by default, it is always a good idea to double-check:

1. Click any cell in the PivotTable to make it active.

2. Click the Options tab to display the Options ribbon.

3. Click the Options button to display the PivotTable Options dialog box.

4. On the Layout & Format tab, make sure that the Preserve Cell Formatting on Update option is checked.

5. Click OK.

The next step is to apply a style to the PivotTable:

1. With the PivotTable still active, click the Design tab to display the Design ribbon.

2. Use the PivotTable Styles section of the ribbon to select the desired style. I used the first style listed in the Medium section of the full Styles menu.

3. Click anywhere outside the PivotTable to deselect it.

Your PivotTable now resembles the one in Figure 3-35.

	A	B	C	D	E	F	G
1		ShippedQuarter ▾					
2	CategoryName ▾	Qtr 1	Qtr 2	Qtr 3	Qtr 4	Grand Total	
3	Beverages	$ 35,858.20	$ 25,466.95	$ 20,845.09	$ 19,904.05	$102,074.29	
4	Condiments	$ 11,922.16	$ 13,347.27	$ 14,001.95	$ 16,006.18	$ 55,277.56	
5	Confections	$ 21,082.75	$ 22,065.51	$ 17,964.86	$ 19,780.99	$ 80,894.11	
6	Dairy Products	$ 24,118.72	$ 27,254.12	$ 28,627.54	$ 34,749.37	$114,749.75	
7	Grains/Cereals	$ 12,697.10	$ 14,629.30	$ 15,310.72	$ 13,311.70	$ 55,948.82	
8	Meat/Poultry	$ 21,598.15	$ 13,694.55	$ 15,843.51	$ 30,201.85	$ 81,338.06	
9	Produce	$ 8,980.74	$ 15,583.66	$ 8,302.97	$ 20,152.61	$ 53,019.98	
10	Seafood	$ 7,445.41	$ 13,613.41	$ 23,423.57	$ 21,061.80	$ 65,544.19	
11	Grand Total	$ 143,703.23	$ 145,654.77	$ 144,320.21	$ 175,168.55	$608,846.76	
12							
13							

Figure 3-35: The PivotTable after you have applied the style.

So far so good, but suppose you want to emphasize certain parts of the report. For example, you might want to emphasize the Dairy Products row, because it has shown a lot of improvement, and you might also want to emphasize the Qtr 4 column, because the total sales figure was so good. Here's how:

1. Point the mouse at the left end of the Dairy Products row, right about where the D in Dairy is. The mouse cursor changes to a right-pointing arrow (see Figure 3-36).

	A	B
1		ShippedQuarter ▼
2	CategoryName ▼	Qtr 1	Qtr 2
3	Beverages	$ 35,858.20	$
4	Condiments	$ 11,922.16	$
5	Confections	$ 21,082.75	$
6	Dairy Products	$ 24,118.72	$
7	Grains/Cereals	$ 12,697.10	$
8	Meat/Poultry	$ 21,598.15	$
9	Produce	$ 8,980.74	$
10	Seafood	$ 7,445.41	$
11	Grand Total	$ 143,703.23	$
12		
13		

Selecting a field

Figure 3-36: When enabling you to select an entire PivotTable element, the mouse cursor changes to an arrow.

2. Click once. The entire row will be selected.

3. Click the Bold button on the Home ribbon. The entire selected row becomes boldfaced.

4. Point the mouse at the top of the Qtr 4 column, just above the label. The cursor changes to a downward-pointing arrow.

5. Click to select the entire column.

6. Click the Italics button on the Home ribbon. The entire selected column will become italicized.

7. Click anywhere outside the PivotTable to deselect it.

At this point your PivotTable resembles the one in Figure 3-37. The combination of applying a style and the custom cell formatting results in an attractive, easy-to-read table with the important information emphasized.

	A	B	C	D	E	F	G
1		ShippedQuarter ▼					
2	CategoryName ▼	Qtr 1	Qtr 2	Qtr 3	Qtr 4	Grand Total	
3	Beverages	$ 35,858.20	$ 25,466.95	$ 20,845.09	$ 19,904.05	$102,074.29	
4	Condiments	$ 11,922.16	$ 13,347.27	$ 14,001.95	$ 16,006.18	$ 55,277.56	
5	Confections	$ 21,082.75	$ 22,065.51	$ 17,964.86	$ 19,780.99	$ 80,894.11	
6	**Dairy Products**	$ 24,118.72	$ 27,254.12	$ 28,627.54	$ 34,749.37	$114,749.75	
7	Grains/Cereals	$ 12,697.10	$ 14,629.30	$ 15,310.72	$ 13,311.70	$ 55,948.82	
8	Meat/Poultry	$ 21,598.15	$ 13,694.55	$ 15,843.51	$ 30,201.85	$ 81,338.06	
9	Produce	$ 8,980.74	$ 15,583.66	$ 8,302.97	$ 20,152.61	$ 53,019.98	
10	Seafood	$ 7,445.41	$ 13,613.41	$ 23,423.57	$ 21,061.80	$ 65,544.19	
11	**Grand Total**	$ 143,703.23	$ 145,654.77	$ 144,320.21	$ 175,168.55	$600,846.76	
12							
13							

Figure 3-37: The final PivotTable after all formatting has been applied.

Part II

PivotTables and Charts: Going Beyond the Basics

Chapter 4

Working with PivotTable Components

PivotTables have a lot of power hidden within them. The PivotTable components discussed in this chapter may not be visible on the surface in all cases, but they are waiting for you to use them to organize and display your PivotTable data in the precise way you need. This is the first of two chapters that delve into the use of these tools. With these techniques under your belt, you will be able to go beyond the simple creation of a PivotTable and learn how to customize it to suit your data and your needs.

In This Chapter

- ◆ Working with row and column fields
- ◆ Filtering and sorting a PivotTable
- ◆ Using multiple value fields
- ◆ Understanding report filter fields
- ◆ Working with summary functions
- ◆ Setting options for PivotTable fields

Using Report Areas

Every PivotTable report starts out as a group of empty areas, and you create the report by adding fields to these areas in the Field List. Perhaps the most important part of designing the PivotTable to display the data you want in the way you want is how you use these areas. Previous chapters introduce only relatively simple uses of the report areas with usually only one field per area. This is perfectly legitimate for some needs, but PivotTables have much more power when you place two or more fields in one area. To do this correctly, you need an understanding of how the Field List and the various drops work. Chapter 3 introduces this topic, but there is a lot more to learn.

The Field List

The Field List contains the names of all the fields in your source data. Figure 4-1 shows an example (you'll see the raw data on which it is based in the next section). If a field has already been added to the PivotTable, its name is checked and displayed in one of the areas at the bottom of the Field List. In Figure 4-1, no fields have yet been added to the PivotTable.

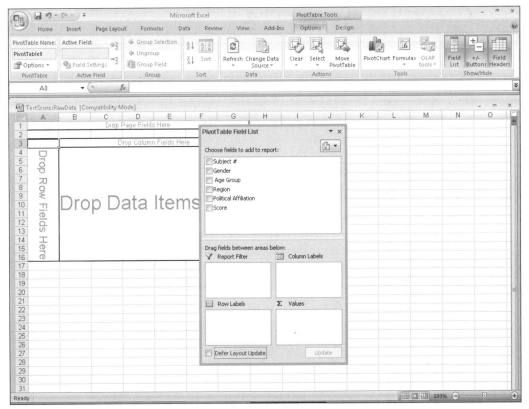

Figure 4-1: The Field List displays the names of all the data fields.

NOTE
The Field List will be visible only when the PivotTable is active. To make a PivotTable active click any cell in it. If the Field List is still not visible, click the Field List button on the Options tab (visible only when a PivotTable is active).

To add a field to a PivotTable, select it in the Field List. Excel automatically adds the field to an area depending on the field's data:

- If the field contains numeric data it is added to the Values area and becomes data displayed in the main body of the report.

- If the field contains non-numeric data, such as text or dates, it is added to the Row Labels area and becomes a row heading in the PivotTable.

NOTE
If the PivotTable is in Classic PivotTable Layout (as explained in the Chapter 3), you can also drag a field from the Field List and drop it directly on the target area of the report.

Moving a Field to a Different Area

After you have selected a field to add it to the PivotTable report, you may want to move it to a different area. To do so, click the down arrow that is displayed next to the field name in the area where it is currently located (see Figure 4-2). Then, from the popup menu, select the area that you want to move the field to. You can also drag a field from one area of the Field List to another area without using this menu.

If the PivotTable is in Classic PivotTable Layout, you can move a field to a different area by dragging on the report itself.

Removing a Field

If you make a mistake when adding a field to a PivotTable, you can correct it by removing the check mark from the field in the Field List. If the PivotTable is in Classic PivotTable Layout you can also drag the field off the PivotTable and drop it outside the PivotTable.

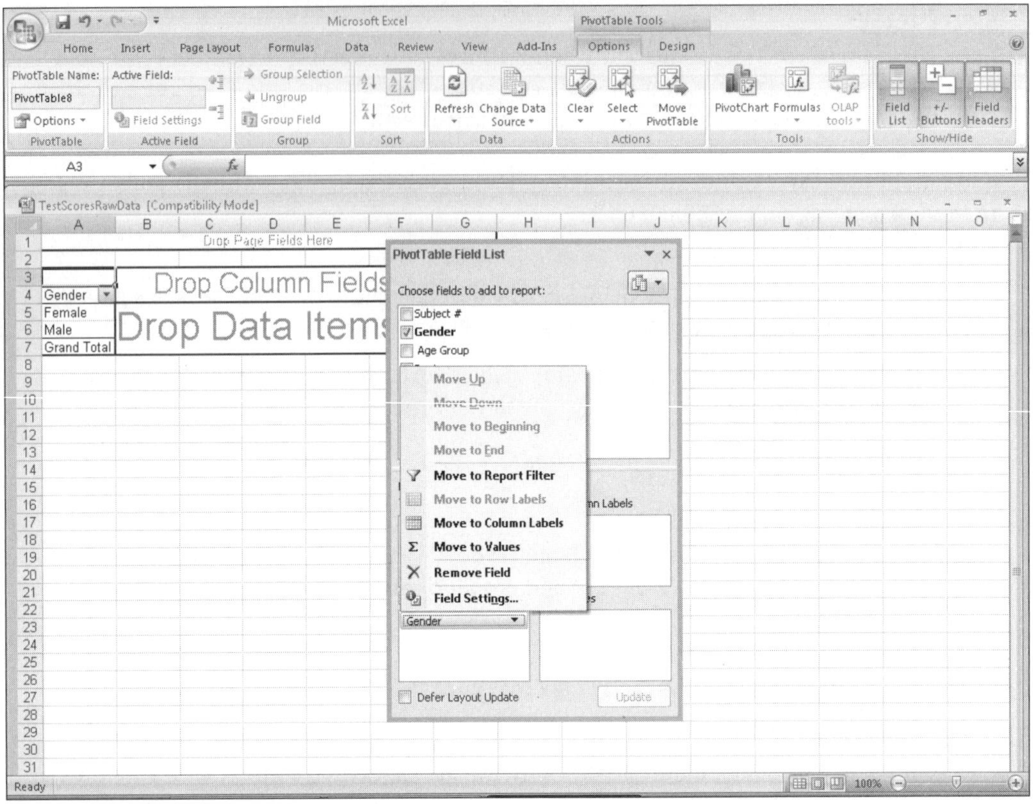

Figure 4-2: Moving a field to a different area.

Using the Row Labels Area

You add a field to the Row Labels area when you want the PivotTable to display data organized by rows based on the values in that field. To see how this works, look at the test score data in Figure 4-3. This figure shows only the first few rows of the data.

Suppose you created a PivotTable based on these data and added the Gender field to the Row Labels area (before adding any other fields). Your still-incomplete PivotTable would look like Figure 4-4.

	A	B	C	D	E	F	G
2	Subject #	Gender	Age Group	Region	Political Affiliation	Score	
3	1	Male	20-29	NorthEast	Dem	92	
4	2	Female	40-49	Midwest	Ind	94	
5	3	Male	30-39	South	Dem	84	
6	4	Male	20-29	NorthEast	Ind	94	
7	5	Female	50-59	NorthEast	Rep	95	
8	6	Female	30-39	SouthWest	Rep	88	
9	7	Male	40-49	Midwest	Rep	80	
10	8	Female	50-59	Midwest	Ind	83	
11	9	Male	30-39	South	Dem	87	
12	10	Male	20-29	NorthWest	Rep	81	
13	11	Male	40-49	NorthEast	Dem	97	
14	12	Female	50-59	NorthWest	Dem	88	
15	13	Male	30-39	Midwest	Rep	88	
16	14	Female	60-69	South	Rep	96	
17	15	Female	50-59	SouthWest	Dem	80	
18	16	Female	50-59	NorthEast	Rep	83	
19	17	Male	40-49	NorthWest	Rep	100	
20	18	Male	40-49	NorthWest	Ind	83	
21	19	Female	50-59	Midwest	Ind	86	
22	20	Female	20-29	SouthWest	Rep	93	
23	21	Male	30-39	Midwest	Dem	87	
24	22	Male	20-29	NorthWest	Dem	90	
25	23	Female	40-49	SouthWest	Rep	96	
26	24	Female	30-39	South	Ind	98	
27	25	Male	30-39	NorthWest	Dem	91	
28	26	Female	50-59	NorthWest	Dem	82	
29	27	Female	20-29	South	Dem	98	

Sheet4 **Sheet1** Sheet2 Sheet3

Figure 4-3: The sample test score data.

	A	B
1		
2		
3	Gender ▾	
4	Female	
5	Male	
6	Grand Total	
7		
8		

Figure 4-4: After you add the Gender field to the Row Labels area, the table has two rows.

The PivotTable now has two rows (not counting the default Grand Total row): Male and Female. This is because the Gender field contains either the value Male or the value Female for every subject. There are two possible values for Gender; hence, there are two rows in the PivotTable. A label at the top, Gender in this example, displays the name of the field. The drop-down button next to the field name is used to filter the PivotTable, but that's a topic for another section.

Part II

Suppose that instead of adding the Gender field to the Row Labels area you added the Age Group field—what do you think would happen? Looking at the raw data you can see that the Age Group column contains the following five possible values:

- 20–29
- 30–39
- 40–49
- 50–59
- 60–69

You would therefore expect the resulting PivotTable to have five rows, one for each of these data values, and that's exactly what you get, as shown in Figure 4-5.

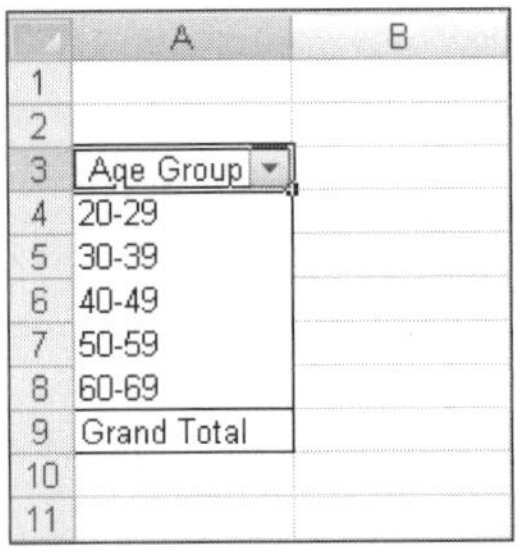

Figure 4-5: If you add the Age Group field to the Row Labels area, the table will have five rows.

Using Multiple Row Fields

So far you have looked at PivotTables in which only one field has been added to the Row Labels area. PivotTables can accommodate more complex scenarios in which you have multiple row fields. If you add two fields to the Row Labels area, one will become the inner row field and the other will become the outer row field. Data are organized first according to the values in the outer row field; then within each group of outer row fields, they are organized by the values in the inner row field.

To create inner and outer row fields, add both of the fields to the Row Labels area. The one that you add first becomes the outer row field, and the one that you add second becomes the inner row field (although this arrangement can be changed at any time).

Suppose you are creating a PivotTable from the score data shown in Figure 4-3. If you first add the Age Group field to the Row Labels area and then add the Gender field, the resulting PivotTable will look like Figure 4-6.

	A	B	C
1			
2			
3	Age Group	Gender	
4	⊟20-29	Female	
5		Male	
6	20-29 Total		
7	⊟30-39	Female	
8		Male	
9	30-39 Total		
10	⊟40-49	Female	
11		Male	
12	40-49 Total		
13	⊟50-59	Female	
14		Male	
15	50-59 Total		
16	⊟60-69	Female	
17		Male	
18	60-69 Total		
19	Grand Total		
20			
21			

Figure 4-6: In this PivotTable, Age Group is the outer row field and Gender is the inner row field.

If you reverse the order of adding the fields to the Row labels area, however, you will get Gender as the outer row field and Age Group as the inner row field, as shown in Figure 4-7.

	A	B	C
1			
2			
3	Gender	Age Group	
4	⊟Female	20-29	
5		30-39	
6		40-49	
7		50-59	
8		60-69	
9	Female Total		
10	⊟Male	20-29	
11		30-39	
12		40-49	
13		50-59	
14		60-69	
15	Male Total		
16	Grand Total		
17			
18			

Figure 4-7: Age Group as the inner row field and Gender as the outer row field.

Why would you select one field for the inner and another for the outer row field? The answer lies in the subtotals. Excel automatically creates subtotals for each outer row field. For example, in Figure 4-7 there is a row labeled Male Total and another labeled Female Total. Likewise, Figure 4-6 shows a total row for each age group. Therefore, you choose your inner and outer row fields based on which you need subtotals for.

Moving Fields Within an Area

When you have two or more fields within an area, their initial position—that is, inner or outer—is determined by the order in which they were added. They are listed in the Field List in this order. For example, Figure 4-8 shows the Row Labels area of the Field List with Gender as the outer row field and Age Group as the inner row field.

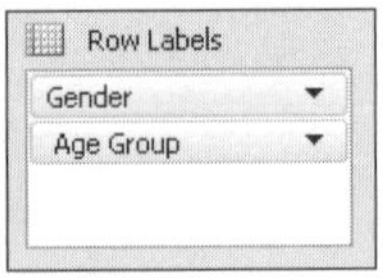

Figure 4-8: Fields are listed in order in their area.

You can change the order of the fields in an area and thus their inner/outer relationships by clicking the arrow next to the field name and selecting one of the following from the popup menu:

- **Move up**—Moves the field up one position in the list.
- **Move down**—Moves the field down one position in the list.
- **Move to beginning**—Moves the field to the start of the list.
- **Move to end**—Moves the field to the end of the list.

Using More Than Two Fields in the Row Area

You can use as many fields in the Row Labels area as you want. When you go beyond three or perhaps four fields, PivotTables tend to be a bit confusing, but your data analysis may require this number of fields. For example, Figure 4-9 shows a PivotTable with four fields in the Row labels area. Here, Gender is the outer field, Age Group is the inner field, and Region and Political Affiliation fall in between. Note how the four fields are listed in the Row labels section of the Field List.

If you look at Figure 4-9, you may wonder why, in the top rows of the PivotTable, only the age groups 20–29 and 50–59 are listed (cells D4 and D5). This part of the report is for data from subjects where Gender=Female, Region=Midwest, and Political Affiliation=Dem. There were no subjects in the other age groups that met these criteria, so those age groups are not listed.

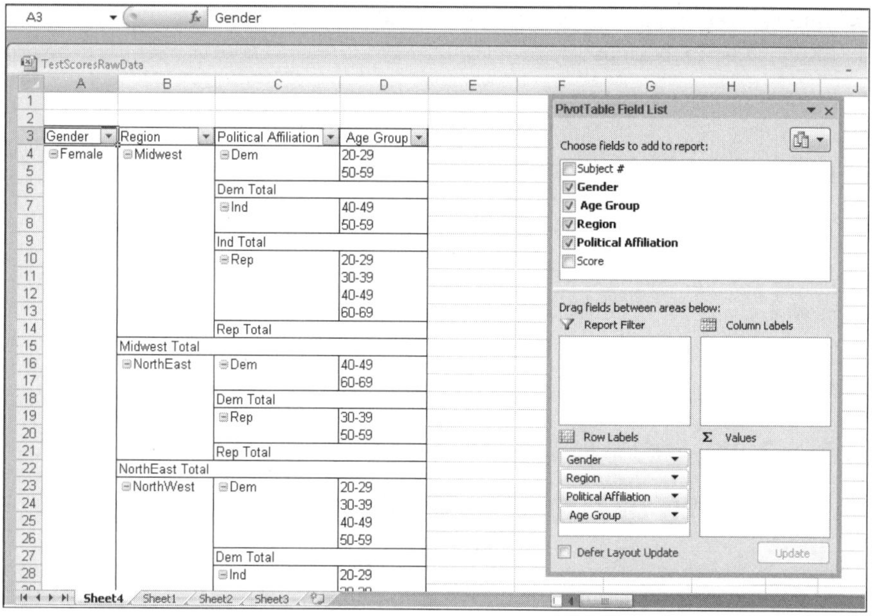

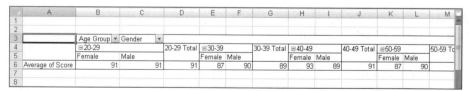

Figure 4-9: A PivotTable that has four fields in the Row Labels area.

Using the Column Labels Area

The Column Labels area works the same way as the Row Labels area except that you get a separate column, rather than a row, for each data value.

A PivotTable can use multiple column fields as well. They work much like multiple row fields. Even though you might think that column fields would be called `upper` and `lower` they are still referred to as `inner` and `outer`, just like multiple row fields, including the creation of subtotal columns for outer fields.

Figure 4-10 shows a portion of a PivotTable in which the Gender and Age Group fields have been placed in the Column Labels area with Age Group as the outer field.

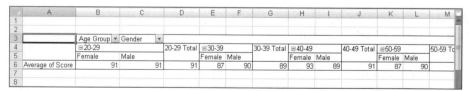

Figure 4-10: You can define inner and outer column fields as well.

You can have multiple column fields and multiple row fields in the same PivotTable. The resulting table is likely to be rather complex, but this may be necessary for certain kinds of data presentation.

NOTE

There's nothing preventing you from creating a PivotTable with more than two fields in the Column or Row area. The only problem is that the resulting PivotTable is usually too complex to understand easily. It is usually better to use filtering or multiple PivotTables in situations where you might consider three or more row/column fields.

Creating a PivotTable with Two Column Fields and Two Row Fields

By actually creating a PivotTable with multiple column and row fields, you will gain a better understanding of how this works. For this walkthrough you need the data in the workbook TestScoresRawData.xls. (You saw these data earlier in Figure 4-3.) After opening the workbook the first steps are to create a blank PivotTable:

1. Place the cell pointer on any cell in the data range A2:F122.

2. Click the PivotTable button on the Insert ribbon to display the Create PivotTable dialog box.

3. Click OK to accept the default options and create the blank PivotTable.

The resulting blank PivotTable is shown in Figure 4-11.

Before continuing, it is a good idea to do some planning. You want your PivotTable to be set up as follows:

- Gender is the outer row field because you want subtotals for this variable.

- Age Group is the inner row field.

- Political Affiliation is the outer column field. You do not actually want subtotals for this variable. Although Excel automatically creates them, you can get rid of them after the PivotTable is created.

- Region is the inner column field.

- Score is the value field.

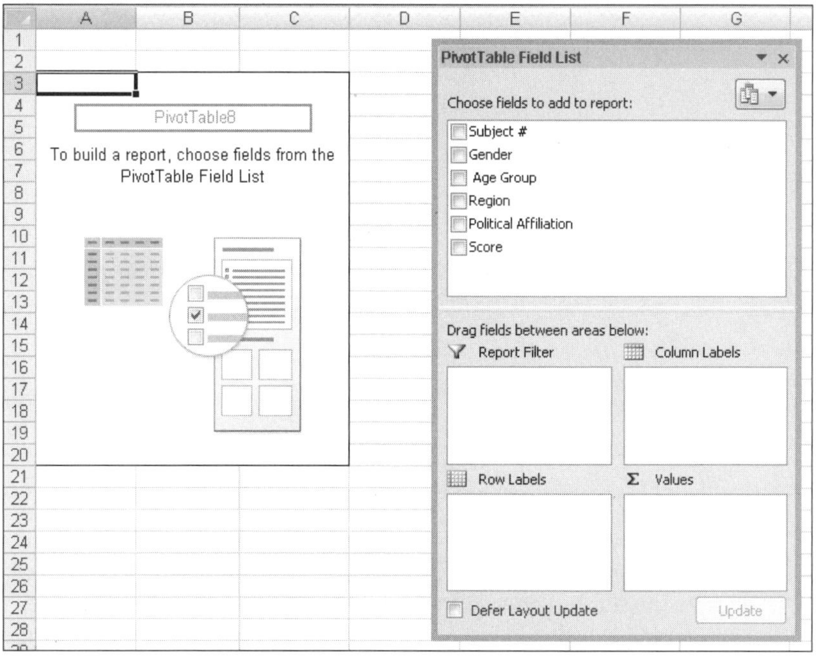

Figure 4-11: The blank PivotTable before any fields are added to it.

With your plan in place, you can create the PivotTable:

1. In the Field List, select all fields except Subject #.

2. To make the Field List easier to work with, change the Field List display to Areas Section Only (2 by 2). Remember to click the button at the top right of the Field List to display a menu of display options.

3. The Field List now appears as shown in Figure 4-12. You can see that Score has been added to the Values area and all other fields have been added to the Row Labels area.

4. Click the arrow next to the Region field and select Move to Column Labels from the popup menu.

5. Click the arrow next to the Political Affiliation field and select Move to Column Labels from the popup menu.

6. If necessary, change the order of fields so that Political Affiliation is listed first under Column Labels and Gender is listed first under Row Labels. Remember, to change field order, click the adjacent arrow and select Move Up or Move Down from the popup menu.

Figure 4-12: The Areas boxes in the Field List after creating the initial PivotTable report.

At this point, your PivotTable will resemble the one in Figure 4-13 (which shows only part of the PivotTable). Note that I adjusted the column widths to show more columns. If you want column widths to be preserved through refreshes and layout changes, you must turn on the Preserve Cell Formatting on Update option in the PivotTable Options dialog box. As you discussed in Chapter 3, you access this dialog box by clicking the Options button on the Options ribbon.

Gender	Age Group	Midwest	NorthEast	NorthWest	South	SouthWest	Dem Total	Midwest	NorthEast	NorthWest	South
								⊟Ind			
⊟Female	20-29	88		100	83	189	460			82	
	30-39			434		252	686			94	
	40-49		81	98		99	278	94		278	
	50-59	94		333		80	507	169			
	60-69		99			195	294			279	
Female Total		182	180	965	83	815	2225	263		733	
⊟Male	20-29		92	177		179	448		94		
	30-39	177	94	363	171	86	891				
	40-49	95	180	89	91	91	546	87	94	83	
	50-59	96		96			192	94			
	60-69			95			95				
Male Total		368	366	820	262	356	2172	181	188	83	
Grand Total		550	546	1785	345	1171	4397	444	188	816	1

Figure 4-13: The partially completed PivotTable.

There are two more steps required to complete this PivotTable. The first has to do with the value data that is displayed. By default, a PivotTable report sums numerical data, but that's not appropriate for the test score data in this example. You want to have the average score displayed. Here's how:

1. In the Field List, click the arrow next to the Sum of Score field and select Value Field Settings from the popup menu. Excel displays the Value Field Settings dialog box (Figure 4-14).

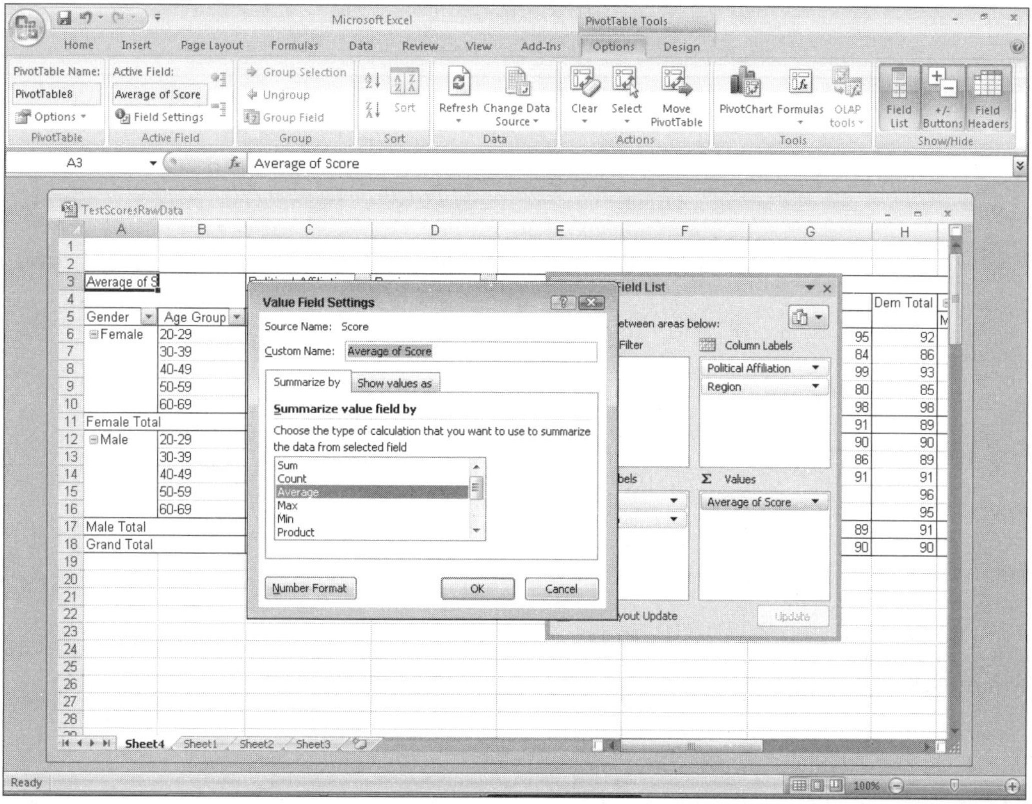

Figure 4-14: The Value Field Settings dialog box lets you change how a value field is summarized.

2. On the Summarize tab, click Average in the Summarize value field by list.

3. Click the Number Format button to open the Format Cells dialog box (see Figure 4-15).

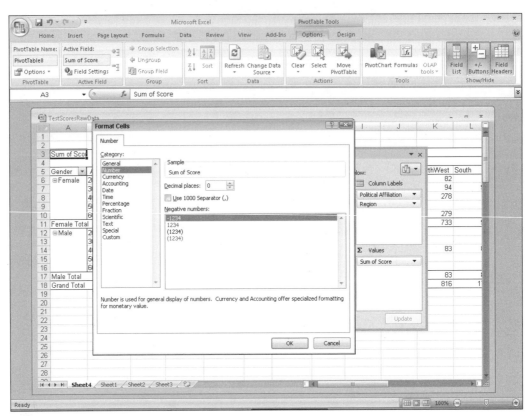

Figure 4-15: Specifying the number format for the value cells.

4. In the Category list, click Number.

5. On the right, specify no decimal places.

6. Click OK twice.

Figure 4-16 shows what the PivotTable looks like at this point. You can see that the PivotTable now displays average scores and that the value field is now called Average of Score.

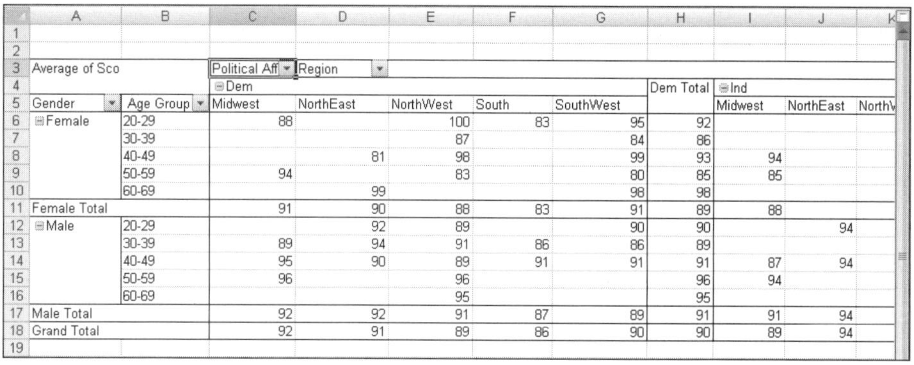

	A	B	C	D	E	F	G	H	I	J	K
1											
2											
3	Average of Sco		Political Aff ▼	Region	▼						
4			⊟Dem					Dem Total	⊟Ind		
5	Gender ▼	Age Group ▼	Midwest	NorthEast	NorthWest	South	SouthWest		Midwest	NorthEast	NorthV
6	⊟Female	20-29	88		100	83	95	92			
7		30-39			87		84	86			
8		40-49		81	98		99	93	94		
9		50-59	94		83		80	85	85		
10		60-69		99			98	98			
11	Female Total		91	90	88	83	91	89	88		
12	⊟Male	20-29		92	89		90	90		94	
13		30-39	89	94	91	86	86	89			
14		40-49	95	90	89	91	91	91	87	94	
15		50-59	96		96			96	94		
16		60-69			95			95			
17	Male Total		92	92	91	87	89	91	91	94	
18	Grand Total		92	91	89	86	90	90	89	94	
19											

Figure 4-16: After setting the PivotTable to display average scores rather than sums.

The final step in this walkthrough is to remove the column subtotals. Although subtotals are useful for some kinds of data, they are not in this situation. The simplest way to get rid of these columns is to hide them:

1. Right-click the Political Affiliation label at the top of the PivotTable (in column C) to display the popup menu shown in Figure 4-17.

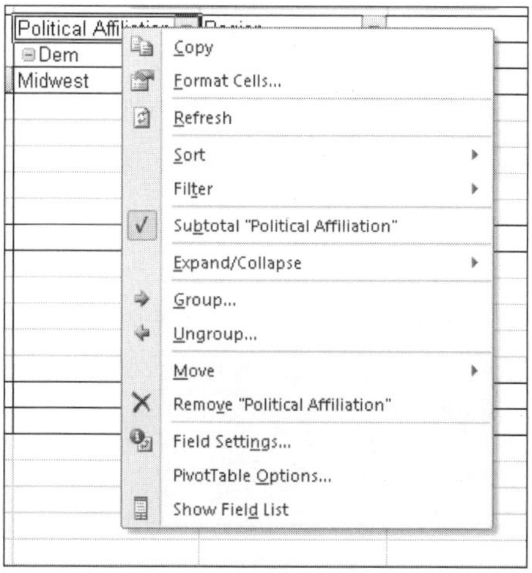

Figure 4-17: Turning subtotals off for a column field.

2. Click Subtotal Political Affiliation to remove the adjacent check mark.

The PivotTable now is complete and should appear as shown in Figure 4-18.

| C3 | ▼ | f_x | Political Affiliation |

TestScoresRawData

	A	B	C	D	E	F	G	H	I	J
1										
2										
3	Average of Score		Political Aff ▼	Region ▼						
4			⊟Dem					⊟Ind		
5	Gender ▼	Age Group ▼	Midwest	NorthEast	NorthWest	South	SouthWest	Midwest	NorthEast	NorthWest Sc
6	⊟Female	20-29	88		100	83	95			82
7		30-39			87		84			94
8		40-49		81	98		99	94		93
9		50-59	94		83		80	85		
10		60-69		99			98			93
11	Female Total		91	90	88	83	91	88		92
12	⊟Male	20-29		92	89		90		94	
13		30-39	89	94	91	86	86			
14		40-49	95	90	89	91	91	87	94	83
15		50-59	96		96			94		
16		60-69			95					
17	Male Total		92	92	91	87	89	91	94	83
18	Grand Total		92	91	89	86	90	89	94	91
19										
20										

Figure 4-18: The completed PivotTable report.

Before you leave this PivotTable, note that some of the cells in the Data area are blank. This is not an error but the result of the data. For example, cell D6 is blank because there were no test scores from females in the 20–29 age group who were in the NorthEast region and reported a Dem political affiliation.

Filtering and Sorting a PivotTable on Row and Column Fields

One of the powerful features of PivotTable reports is the ability to filter the data that are displayed. You specify the criteria, and the PivotTable changes to display on the data that match. You can also specify how row and column fields are sorted.

Look again at the test scores PivotTable that you created in the previous section. As shown in Figure 4-19, each row and column field label has an adjacent button that you can click to sort or filter that field.

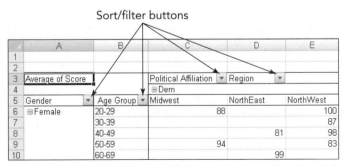

Figure 4-19: In a PivotTable, each row and column field label displays a sort/filter button.

When you click one of these buttons, Excel displays a menu like the one shown in Figure 4-20 (which is for the Region field in the example PivotTable).

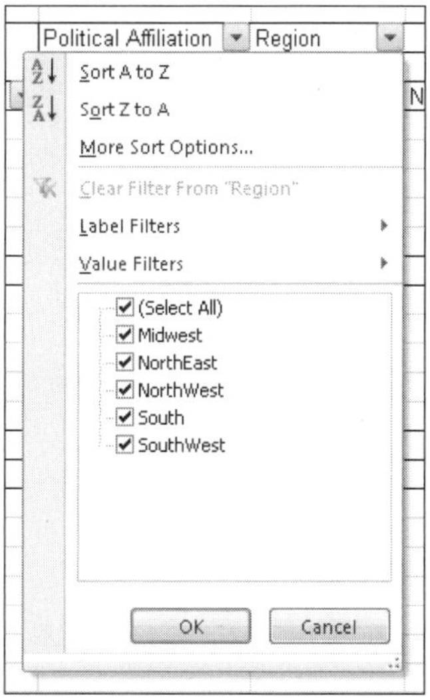

Figure 4-20: The sort and filter options for the Region field.

To specify the sort order for the field, select either Sort A-Z or Sort Z-A. The more advanced sorting options available with the More Sort Options command will be covered in a later section.

To filter the display based on this field, select or clear the field values at the bottom of the menu. For example, selecting only Midwest results in the PivotTable report shown in Figure 4-21.

The other filter commands on this menu are covered in later sections.

	A	B	C	D	E	F
1						
2						
3	Average of Score		Political Affiliation ▼	Region ▼		
4			⊟Dem	⊟Ind	⊟Rep	Grand Total
5	Gender ▼	Age Group ▼	Midwest	Midwest	Midwest	
6	⊟Female	20-29	88		97	93
7		30-39			84	84
8		40-49		94	100	97
9		50-59	94	85		88
10		60-69			100	100
11	Female Total		91	88	95	92
12	⊟Male	20-29			98	98
13		30-39	89		88	88
14		40-49	95	87	86	88
15		50-59	96	94	84	91
16		60-69			84	84
17	Male Total		92	91	88	90
18	Grand Total		92	89	91	90
19						
20						

Figure 4-21: Filtering the PivotTable report to show only the Midwest region.

Using the Value Area

The Value area is where you place the field or fields that contain the data to be summarized by the PivotTable. Each cell in the report's data area summarizes a subset of the data based on the row and column the cell is in. For an example, look at the data and PivotTable in Figure 4-22. In this PivotTable the data or value field is Sold.

	A	B	C	D	E
1					
2					
3	Sum of Sold	Size			
4	Flavor	Large	Small	Grand Total	
5	Chocolate	109	44	153	
6	Vanilla	67	107	174	
7	Grand Total	176	151	327	
8					
9					

Figure 4-22: A simple PivotTable report.

Look at the value 109 in cell B5. Where did this number come from? You can see that this cell is in the Large column and the Chocolate row. This tells you that the value 109 is the sum of the Sold field values for all data records where Flavor=Chocolate and Size=Large. In other words, it is the sum of the Sold values. The other cells in the PivotTable work the same way.

What if you do not want to sum the data but rather display some other calculation such as the average or count? You can do this using the field settings, which are covered later in this chapter in the section, "Working with Field Settings."

Using Multiple Value Fields

There's no reason that the data area of the PivotTable has to be limited to a single value field, although this is often all you need. Sometimes you want to summarize two or more data items in the table. Look, for example, at the data in Figure 4-23, which shows the total sales for both 2005 and 2006 for several salespeople over four quarters. Can you include both the 2005 and 2006 sales amounts in your PivotTable? You bet.

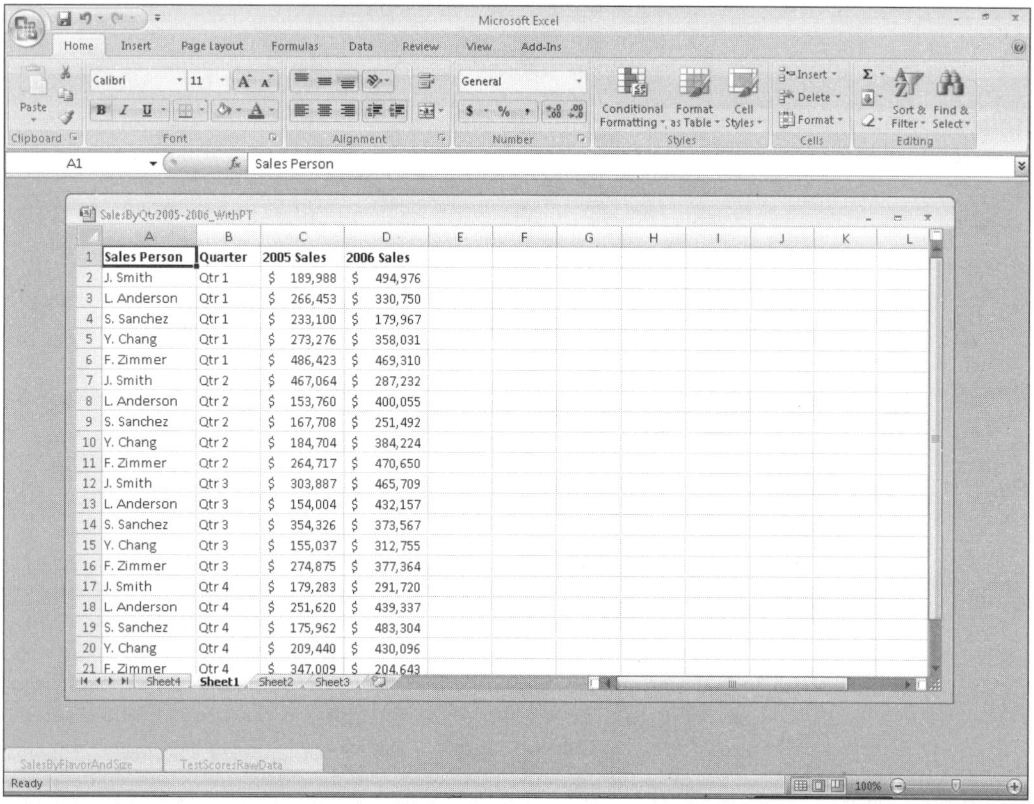

Figure 4-23: These raw data contains two data items, 2005 Sales and 2006 Sales, both of which can be included in the same PivotTable report.

To create a PivotTable with more than one value field, you add each data field to the Values area. The resulting PivotTable created from the data in Figure 4-23 (after the application of numeric formatting) is shown in Figure 4-24. You can see that for each salesperson there is a sum for each of the data fields, 2005 Sales and 2006 Sales.

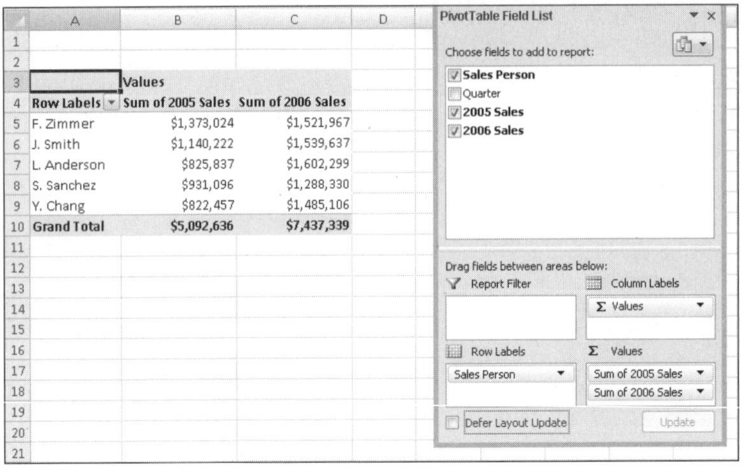

Figure 4-24: A PivotTable created with two value fields.

NOTE

You may be thinking that the labels in column B of this PivotTable report aren't right; after all, the values in the cells are not actually sums but single values brought over from the raw data. Can you change this? Yes, it's another action you can take with field settings, covered later in this chapter in the section, "Working with Field Settings." You can drop the same field twice or more on the Data area. What's the point of this? Initially both instances of the data field display the sum of the data, which is not at all useful. You can, however, change the way one of the fields summarizes the data. For example, you can set it to display the average or count of the data rather than the sum. For an Amount field you can display the sum, the average, and the maximum—three different summaries based on the same raw data. You'll learn how to do this later in this chapter.

Using the Report Filter Area

Although some PivotTable reports do not use them, report filter fields—called page fields in earlier versions of Excel—are powerful tools and are essential for many advanced tasks. A report filter enables you to filter the entire report based on the data in the field.

This is similar in concept to the kind of filtering you can do with row and column fields, but the results are somewhat different. A given field cannot be both a page field and a row or column field at the same time. If you add to the report filter a field that is already a row or column field, it is removed from its original location.

For each report filter field that you add, the PivotTable displays a filter button with the name of the field. To the right of this button a cell displays the current filter setting. By default this is (All), indicating that data from all report field values are included in the PivotTable. For example, look at the data in Figure 4-25, which presents sales for a group of five sales reps for the years 2005 and 2006, broken out by quarter.

	A	B	C	D
1	Sales Person	Quarter	2005 Sales	2006 Sales
2	J. Smith	Qtr 1	$ 189,988	$ 494,976
3	L. Anderson	Qtr 1	$ 266,453	$ 330,750
4	S. Sanchez	Qtr 1	$ 233,100	$ 179,967
5	Y. Chang	Qtr 1	$ 273,276	$ 358,031
6	F. Zimmer	Qtr 1	$ 486,423	$ 469,310
7	J. Smith	Qtr 2	$ 467,064	$ 287,232
8	L. Anderson	Qtr 2	$ 153,760	$ 400,055
9	S. Sanchez	Qtr 2	$ 167,708	$ 251,492
10	Y. Chang	Qtr 2	$ 184,704	$ 384,224
11	F. Zimmer	Qtr 2	$ 264,717	$ 470,650
12	J. Smith	Qtr 3	$ 303,887	$ 465,709
13	L. Anderson	Qtr 3	$ 154,004	$ 432,157
14	S. Sanchez	Qtr 3	$ 354,326	$ 373,567
15	Y. Chang	Qtr 3	$ 155,037	$ 312,755
16	F. Zimmer	Qtr 3	$ 274,875	$ 377,364
17	J. Smith	Qtr 4	$ 179,283	$ 291,720
18	L. Anderson	Qtr 4	$ 251,620	$ 439,337
19	S. Sanchez	Qtr 4	$ 175,962	$ 483,304
20	Y. Chang	Qtr 4	$ 209,440	$ 430,096
21	F. Zimmer	Qtr 4	$ 347,009	$ 204,643
22				

Figure 4-25: The sales rep data.

Next, Figure 4-26 shows a PivotTable report created from this data. You can look at the Field List to see that the Quarter field has been placed in the Report Filter area. As a result, the Quarter field is not displayed as part of the PivotTable's main area but rather separately in the Report Filter area in cells A1:B1. Cell A1 shows the name of the filter field and cell B1 shows the current filter set, which is by default All. This means that the report itself displays all of the data for all quarters.

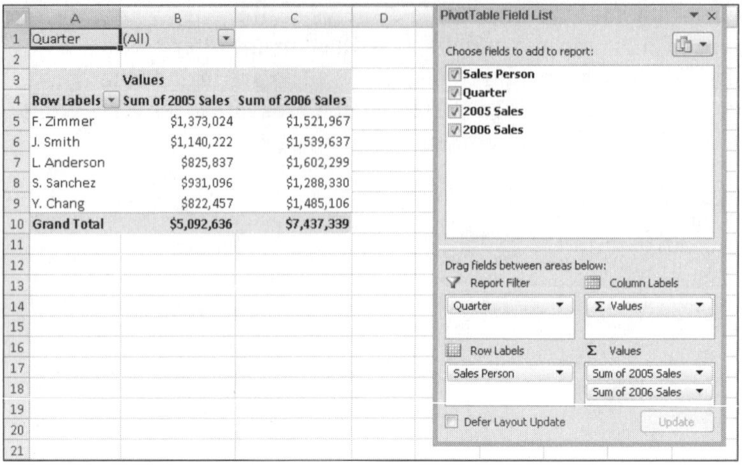

Figure 4-26: The PivotTable report created from the sales rep data, with the Quarter field placed in the Report Filter area.

To change the filter, click the arrow adjacent to the filter setting in cell B2. Excel displays a menu with the possible filter settings on it. This is shown in Figure 4-27. You can select any one of the possible values for this field, in this case Qtr1, Qtr2, Qtr3, or Qtr4. For example, Figure 4-28 shows the PivotTable report filtered on Qtr4.

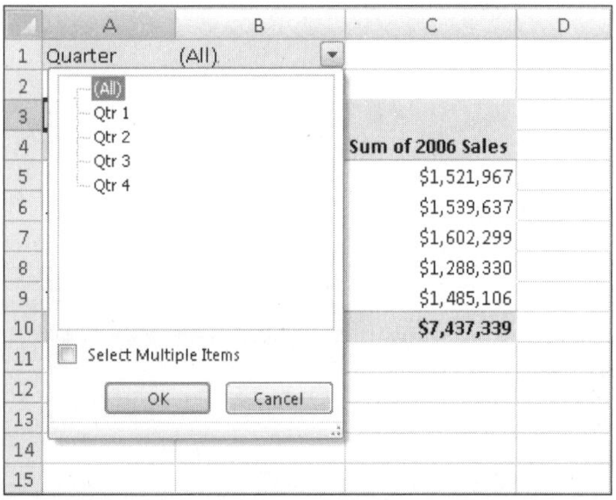

Figure 4-27: Selecting a filter setting for a filter field.

	A	B	C	D
1	Quarter	Qtr 4		
2				
3		Values		
4	Row Labels	Sum of 2005 Sales	Sum of 2006 Sales	
5	F. Zimmer	$347,009	$204,643	
6	J. Smith	$179,283	$291,720	
7	L. Anderson	$251,620	$439,337	
8	S. Sanchez	$175,962	$483,304	
9	Y. Chang	$209,440	$430,096	
10	Grand Total	$1,163,314	$1,849,100	
11				
12				

Figure 4-28: The PivotTable report filtered to show only data where the Quarter field is equal to Qtr4.

Suppose you want to filter on two or more field values, such as showing data for only Qtr1 and Qtr2? Then, as shown in Figure 4-29, select the Select Multiple Items option in the filter menu and select the values to include in the filter.

	A	B	C	D
1	Quarter	(All)		
2	☑ (All)			
3	☑ Qtr 1			
4	☑ Qtr 2		Sum of 2006 Sales	
5	☑ Qtr 3		$1,521,967	
6	☑ Qtr 4		$1,539,637	
7			$1,602,299	
8			$1,288,330	
9			$1,485,106	
10			$7,437,339	
11	☑ Select Multiple Items			
12	OK Cancel			
13				
14				
15				

Figure 4-29: Filtering a PivotTable report on more than one filter field value.

Creating a PivotTable with Three Report Filter Fields

This section takes you through the steps involved in creating a PivotTable with three report filter fields. The data, part of which is shown in Figure 4-30, are sales of items with five variables: Store, Month, Item, Color, and Size. The goal is to create a PivotTable that shows total sales for each store for each month, and that gives you the ability to filter on the Item, Color, and Size variables.

	A	B	C	D	E	F	G
1							
2	Store	Month	Item	Color	Size	Amount	
3	Downtown	Jan	4	Red	Large	19.64	
4	Northside	Feb	1	Blue	Small	4.37	
5	East End	Feb	2	Red	Medium	4.58	
6	Downtown	Mar	5	Green	Small	15.3	
7	South Plaza	Jan	5	White	Large	13.43	
8	East End	Feb	2	Blue	Medium	5.53	
9	Downtown	Mar	4	Green	Small	13.96	
10	Downtown	Mar	3	White	Large	19.37	
11	Northside	Mar	2	Red	Large	12.81	
12	South Plaza	Jan	5	Red	Medium	11.98	
13	Downtown	Feb	4	Blue	Large	11.78	
14	Northside	Feb	5	Red	Medium	10.71	
15	East End	Jan	3	Green	Small	16.56	
16	South Plaza	Jan	3	White	Medium	1.66	
17	Downtown	Jan	4	Blue	Medium	10.16	
18	East End	Mar	4	White	Medium	11.08	
19	Downtown	Mar	1	White	Small	16.58	
20	Downtown	Jan	1	Red	Large	12.71	
21	Northside	Mar	5	Red	Small	3.38	
22	South Plaza	Jan	4	Blue	Medium	14.73	
23	Downtown	Mar	2	Red	Large	4.72	
24	Northside	Feb	3	Green	Small	15.14	
25	East End	Feb	5	White	Medium	17.75	
26	Downtown	Mar	1	Blue	Small	2.83	
27	South Plaza	Mar	1	Green	Large	14.79	
28	East End	Jan	2	White	Large	10.54	

Figure 4-30: The sample sales data.

To start, open the workbook `ThreePageFields.xls`. Then do the following:

1. Place the cell pointer on any cell in the data range (A2:F162).

2. Click the PivotTable button on the Insert ribbon to display the Create PivotTable dialog box.

3. Click OK to create a blank PivotTable report. The blank PivotTable looks like the one in Figure 4-31.

4. In the Field List, select all of the fields.

5. Move the Sum of Item field from the Values area to the Report Filter area.

6. Move the Color and Size fields from the Row Labels area to the Report Filter area.

7. Move the Month field from the Row Labels area to the Column Labels area.

8. Click the Sum of Amount field name in the Values area and select Value Field Settings from the popup menu to display the Value Field Settings dialog box.

9. Click the Number Format button to open the Format Cells dialog box.

10. In the Category list, click Currency.

11. Click OK twice.

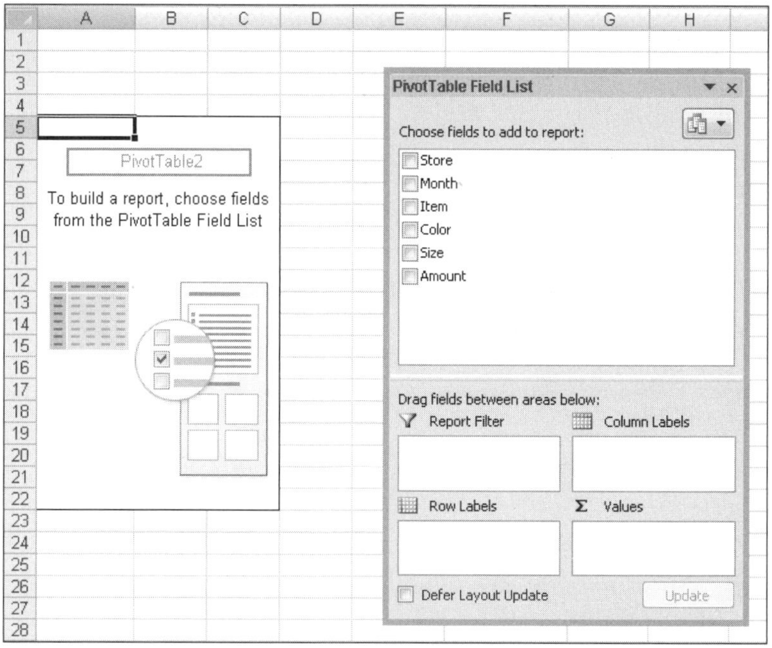

Figure 4-31: The blank PivotTable before any fields have been added.

At this point, your PivotTable should look like Figure 4-32. You can see that there is a button for each of the three report filter fields. The drop-down arrow next to each button enables you to select how the data in the table is filtered. By default, the setting is (All) for each page field, meaning that all data for the field are displayed.

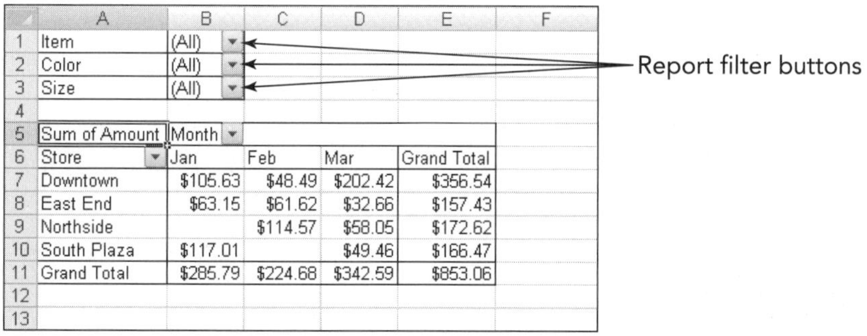

	A	B	C	D	E	F
1	Item	(All)				
2	Color	(All)				
3	Size	(All)				
4						
5	Sum of Amount	Month				
6	Store	Jan	Feb	Mar	Grand Total	
7	Downtown	$105.63	$48.49	$202.42	$356.54	
8	East End	$63.15	$61.62	$32.66	$157.43	
9	Northside		$114.57	$58.05	$172.62	
10	South Plaza	$117.01		$49.46	$166.47	
11	Grand Total	$285.79	$224.68	$342.59	$853.06	
12						
13						

Report filter buttons

Figure 4-32: The completed PivotTable report displays three report filter field buttons.

Try some filtering. Click the arrow next to the Size field to see the list shown in Figure 4-33. You can select any one of the three Size values—Large, Medium, and Small—. and the PivotTable report will change to include only data that pass the filter. You can also select (All) to remove any filtering based on this field.

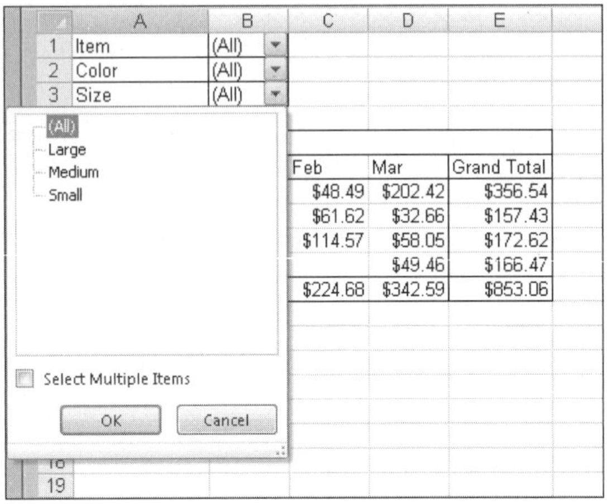

Figure 4-33: The Size filter options.

Follow these steps to experiment with filtering:

1. Pull down the Color filter list and select Red; then click OK.

2. Pull down the Item filter list and select 4; then click OK.

3. Pull down the Size filter list and select Large; then click OK.

After you have applied these filters, your PivotTable will look like the one in Figure 4-34.

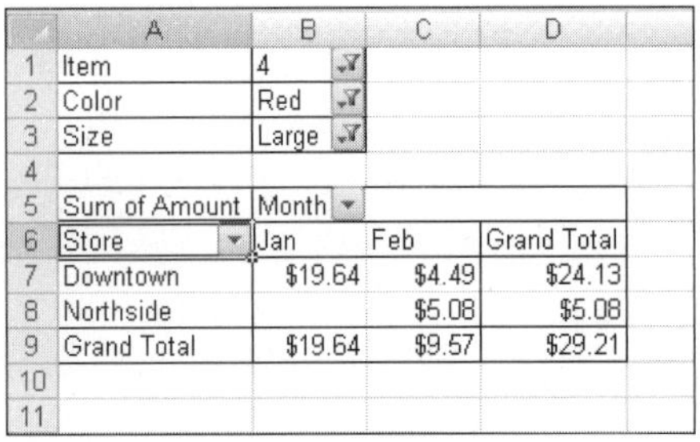

Figure 4-34: The PivotTable report after the application of three filters.

Note the following:

- Each page field button displays the current filter setting: Red for Color, 4 for Item, and Large for Size.

- The PivotTable no longer has a column for Mar because the filtered data did not include any results where Month=Mar. This is also why only two stores are listed; the other stores did not have any matching data.

- The cell for the Northside store in Jan is blank. This means no data passed the filter and matched these criteria.

This walkthrough is an example of how page fields can be used to add flexibility to a PivotTable. As you gain experience with PivotTables, you will develop a feeling for whether it is better to drop a field on the Page area or on the Row or Column area. There is no right way to do things; it all depends on your data and what you want to get out of them.

Working with Field Settings

A PivotTable report is made up of fields, and each field has a group of settings associated with it. These settings control how (and whether) the field displays its number format, the summary calculation used, and a few other things. It's essential that you understand these settings.

To change field settings, you must display the PivotTable Field dialog box using one of these methods:

- In one of the areas of the Field List, click the arrow next to the field name and select Field Settings (or Value Field Settings in the case of a value field) from the popup menu.

- In the PivotTable report itself, right-click a cell associated with the field and select Field Settings (or Value Field Settings in the case of a value field) from the popup menu.

Field settings are different depending on the type of field you are working with: a value field, a row/column field, or a report filter field. These are covered in the following tips.

Understanding Settings for Value Fields

Figure 4-35 shows the PivotTable Field Settings dialog box for a Value field.

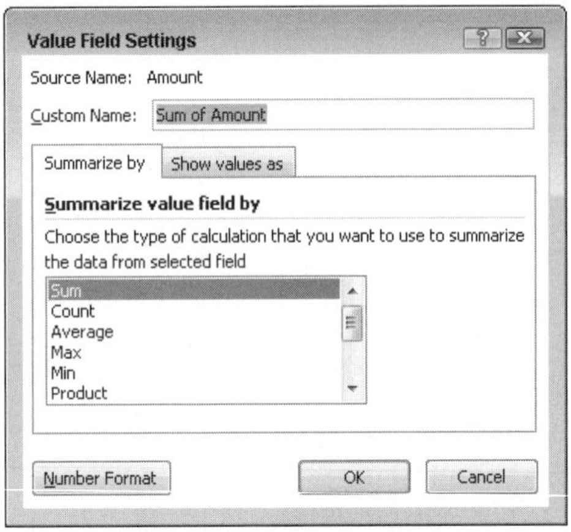

Figure 4-35: The Field Settings dialog box for a value field.

This dialog box contains the following elements:

- **Source Name**—Lists the name of the data source field on which this PivotTable field is based. You cannot change this.

- **Custom Name**—Shows the display name of the field. Edit this name to change the way it is displayed in the PivotTable report.

- **Number Format**—Click this button to display the Format Cells dialog box where you can select the number format for this field.

- **Summarize by**—Enables you to select how the field summarizes the data (Sum, Count, Average, and so on).

- **Show values as**—Use this tab to set advanced data field options. These options are covered later in this chapter in the section, "Setting Advanced Value Field Options."

The Summarize by setting gives you great flexibility in the way the PivotTable presents the data. By default, a value field is set to Sum if the field contains number data. This means that the numbers displayed in the PivotTable will be the sums of the corresponding data items. If a value field contains text data, the default is Count. The other summary options available are:

- **Count**—The number of data items.

- **Average**—The average of the data values.

- **Max**—The largest data value.

- **Min**—The smallest data value.

- **Product**—The result of multiplying all the data values together.

- **Count nums**—The number of data items that are numeric.

- **StdDev**—The sample standard deviation of the data values.

- **StdDevp**—The population standard deviation of the data values.

- **Var**—The sample variance of the data values.

- **Varp**—The population variance of the data values.

Obviously, most of these summary functions are applicable only to numeric data.

Using Different Summary Functions

This section shows you how to use field settings to summarize data in different ways, as introduced in the previous section. It uses the test score data shown in Figure 4-36. These data are located in `TestScores2.xls`. After you open that file, you can proceed.

	A	B	C	D
	TestScores2			
	A	B	C	D
2	**Student #**	**Gender**	**Score**	
3	1	Male	81	
4	2	Male	79	
5	3	Female	86	
6	4	Male	92	
7	5	Female	87	
8	6	Female	99	
9	7	Male	70	
10	8	Male	98	
11	9	Female	85	
12	10	Male	87	
13	11	Female	91	
14	12	Female	97	
15	13	Male	98	
16	14	Male	78	
17	15	Female	88	
18	16	Male	77	
19	17	Female	97	
20	18	Female	87	
21	19	Male	74	
22	20	Male	93	
23	21	Female	78	
24	22	Male	70	
25	23	Female	83	
26	24	Female	81	
27	25	Male	70	
28	26	Male	85	
29	27	Female	71	
30	28	Male	82	

Figure 4-36: The sample test score data.

The first steps are to create the basic PivotTable report:

1. Place the cell pointer on any cell in the data range (A2:C45).

2. Click the PivotTable button on the Insert ribbon to open the Create PivotTable dialog box.

3. Click OK to create the blank PivotTable.

4. Add the Gender field to the Row Labels area.

5. Add the Score field to the Values area.

6. Point at the Score field in the list and drag it to the Values area, as shown in Figure 4-37. This adds a second Score field, called Sum of Score2, to the Values area.

7. Repeat step 6 to add a third Sum of Scores field to the Values area.

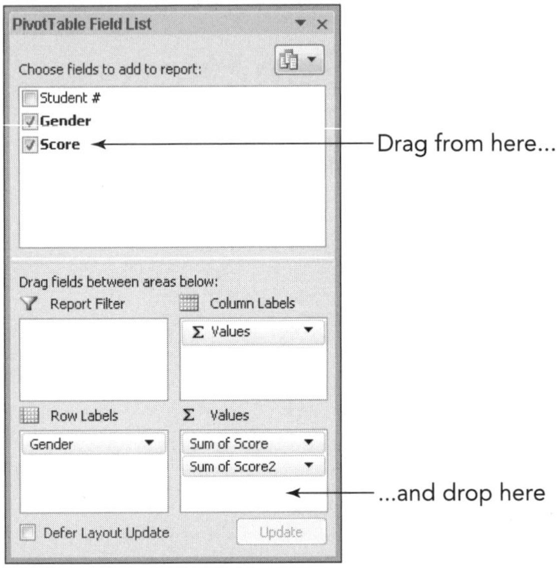

Figure 4-37: Dragging a field to add multiple copies to an area of the PivotTable.

At this point the PivotTable will look like the one shown in Figure 4-38. It has three Score fields in the Values area, Sum of Score, Sum of Score2, and Sum of Score3. Each displays the same result, but this is not what you want. In fact, you don't want a sum at all; rather, you want the average, the maximum, and the minimum for each group.

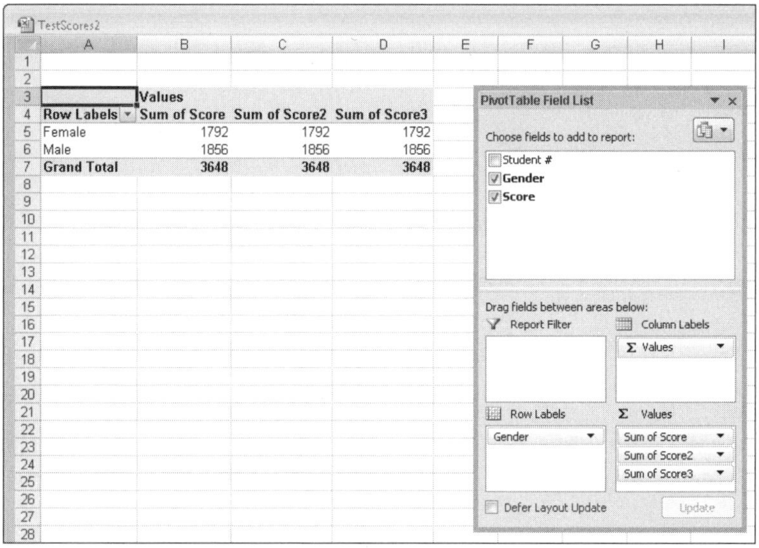

Figure 4-38: The PivotTable report with three copies of the Sum of Score field.

To continue, follow these steps:

1. Right-click one of the Sum of Score field cells—one of the cells that contain the field name Sum of Score or one of the adjacent cells that contain the sum itself.

2. Select Value Field Settings from the popup menu to display the Value Field Settings dialog box (shown in Figure 4-39).

3. Select Average in the Summarize by list. The Custom Name box changes to Average of Score. Edit the name to say simply Average.

4. Click OK.

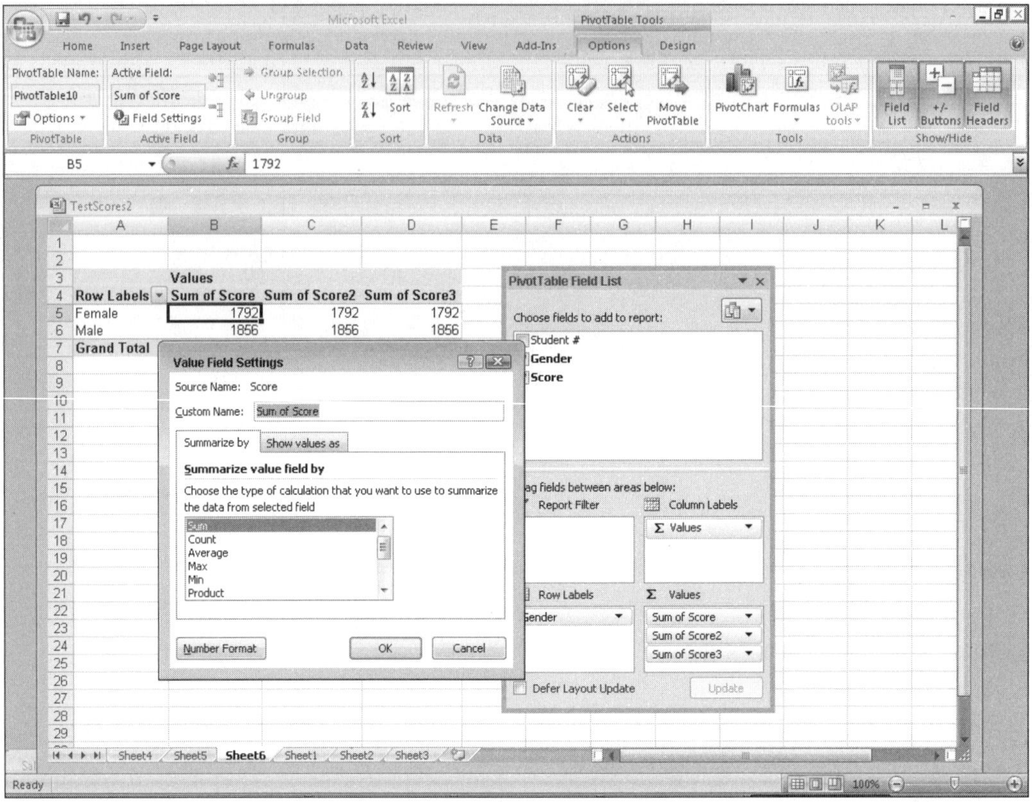

Figure 4-39: Changing the field settings for the Sum of Score field.

At this point the PivotTable should look like the one in Figure 4-40. You successfully changed one value field to display the average, but you really do not need so many decimal places.

Row Labels	Values Average	Sum of Score2	Sum of Score3
Female	85.33333333	1792	1792
Male	84.36363636	1856	1856
Grand Total	84.8372093	3648	3648

Figure 4-40: The PivotTable after one of the Sum of Score fields has been changed to summarize by average.

Changing the number of decimal places displayed requires another visit to the Field Settings dialog box:

1. Display the Value Field Settings dialog box again for this field, which is now named Average.

2. Click the Number Format button to display the Format Cells dialog box.

3. Select Number in the Category list and enter 1 in the Decimal places box.

4. Click OK twice.

The remaining steps in this section change the summary for the other two fields:

1. Right-click one of the Sum of Score2 field cells.

2. Select Value Field Settings from the popup menu to display the Value Field Settings dialog box.

3. Select Max in the Summarize by list.

4. Edit the Custom Name box to read Maximum.

5. Click OK.

6. Right-click one of the Sum of Score3 field cells.

7. Select Value Field Settings from the popup menu to display the Value Field Settings dialog box.

8. Select Min in the Summarize by list.

9. Edit the Custom Name box to read Minimum.

10. Click OK.

There's one more thing to do. The total row at the bottom of the table is not needed. Here's how to get rid of it:

1. Display the Design ribbon.

2. Click the Grand Totals button.

3. Select Off for rows and columns.

Now the PivotTable report looks like Figure 4-41. It's just what you wanted, providing three different summaries for the Score value.

	Values		
Gender ▼	Average	Maximum	Minimum
Female	85.3	99	70
Male	84.4	98	70

Figure 4-41: The PivotTable after the three data fields have been changed to summarize by average, maximum, and minimum.

Working with Settings for Row and Column Fields

Field settings for row and column fields are essentially identical to each other, with the only real difference being where on the report the field is placed. They are, however, somewhat different from the settings for value fields. Figure 4-42 shows the Field Settings dialog box for a row or column field.

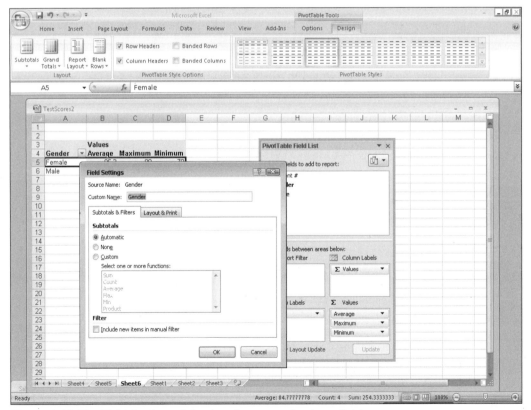

Figure 4-42: The Field Settings dialog box for row and column fields.

This dialog box offers the following options:

- **Source Name**—Lists the name of the data source field on which this PivotTable field is based. You cannot change this.

- **Custom Name**—The display name of the field. Edit this name to change the way it is displayed in the PivotTable report.

- **Subtotals & Filters tab**—Lets you set options for field subtotals (explained in the next section).

- **Layout & Print tab**—Lets you set options for field layout and printing

- **Include new items in manual filter**—Determines whether new items that are added to the data source are automatically included or excluded by a filter that has been applied to the PivotTable report.

Subtotal and Filter Options

By default, rows and columns are subtotaled automatically as a sum of data items. This is what you get if the Automatic option is selected under Subtotals. You can also select None to have no subtotals or Custom to use the subtotal calculation selected in the list. (Of course, most of these subtotal options don't really provide totals, but that's the term Excel uses for all of them.) You can click more than one custom subtotal and the PivotTable displays a separate row/column for each one. Click again to deselect. The following custom subtotal options are available:

- **Sum**—The sum of the data items.

- **Count**—The number of data items.

- **Average**—The average of the data items.

- **Max**—The largest data item.

- **Min**—The smallest data item.

- **Product**—The result of multiplying the data items together.

- **Count Nums**—The number of data items with a numeric value.

- **StdDev**—The sample standard deviation.

- **StdDevp**—The population standard deviation.

- **Var**—The sample variance.

- **Varp**—The population variance.

Layout and Print Options

Figure 4-43 shows the Layout & Print tab of the Field Settings dialog box.

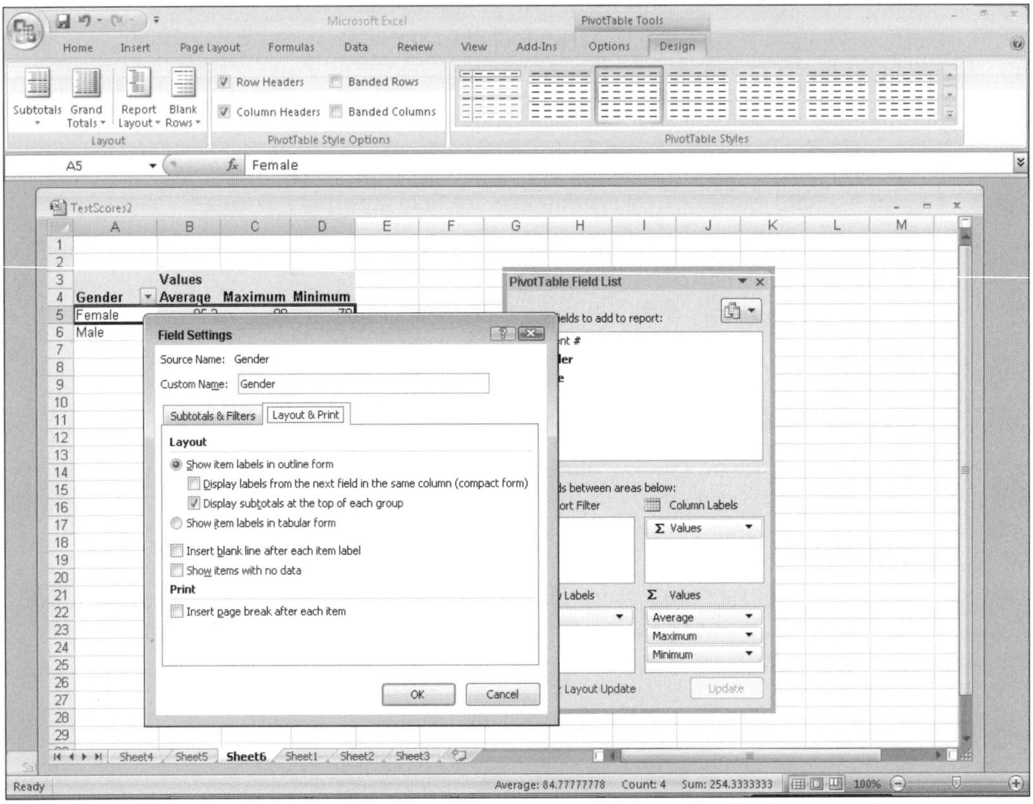

Figure 4-43: The Layout & Print tab of the Field Settings dialog box.

The first two options let you choose between Outline form and Tabular form for the field. If you select Outline Form, you then can select to display labels from the next field in the same column (compact form). These options are similar to the Outline Form, Tabular Form, and Compact Form options that are available from the Report Layout button on the Design tab (as explained in Chapter 3), but apply to a single field rather than to the whole report.

These options affect only the report appearance, not the data it contains. The effects of these options on a PivotTable report are shown in Figures 4-44, 4-45, and 4-46. For these examples, the settings were applied to the Gender field. Each figure shows the Layout & Print options along with the resulting PivotTable appearance:

- Figure 4-44 shows the effects of selecting the Show item labels in outline form option but not selecting any of the sub-options.

- Figure 4-45 shows the effects of selecting the Show item labels in outline form option and also selecting the Display labels in the next field in the same column (compact form) sub-option.

- Figure 4-46 shows the effects of selecting the Show item labels in tabular form option.

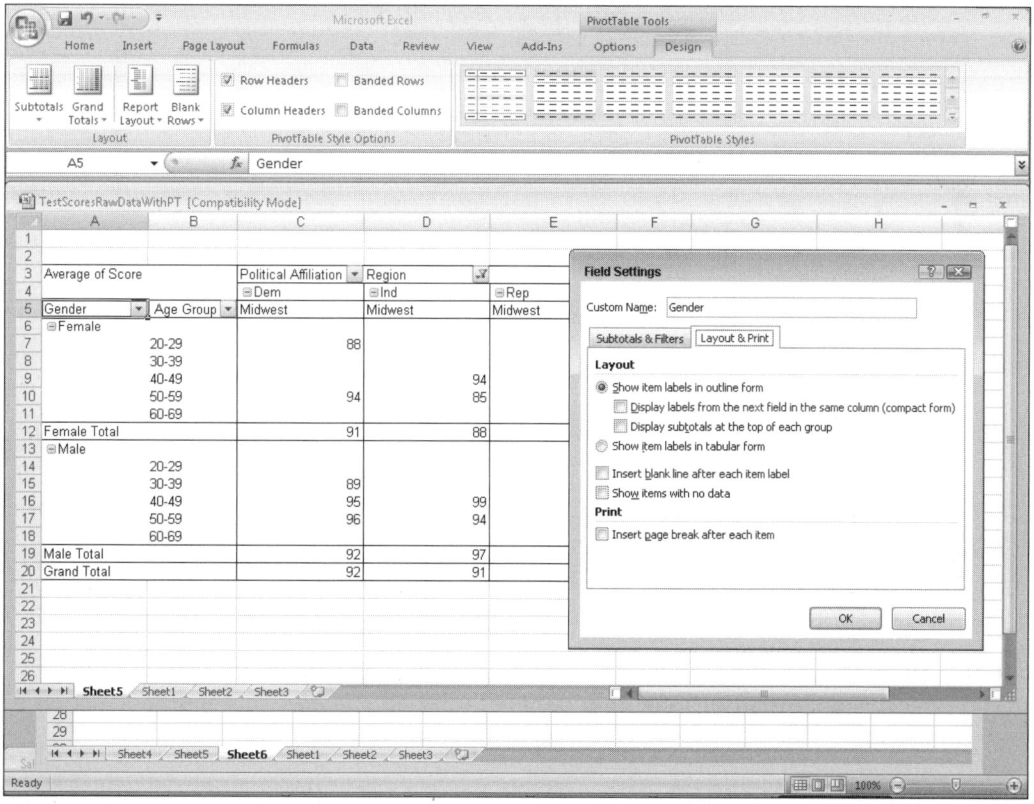

Figure 4-44: The effects of the row field layout option settings, part 1.

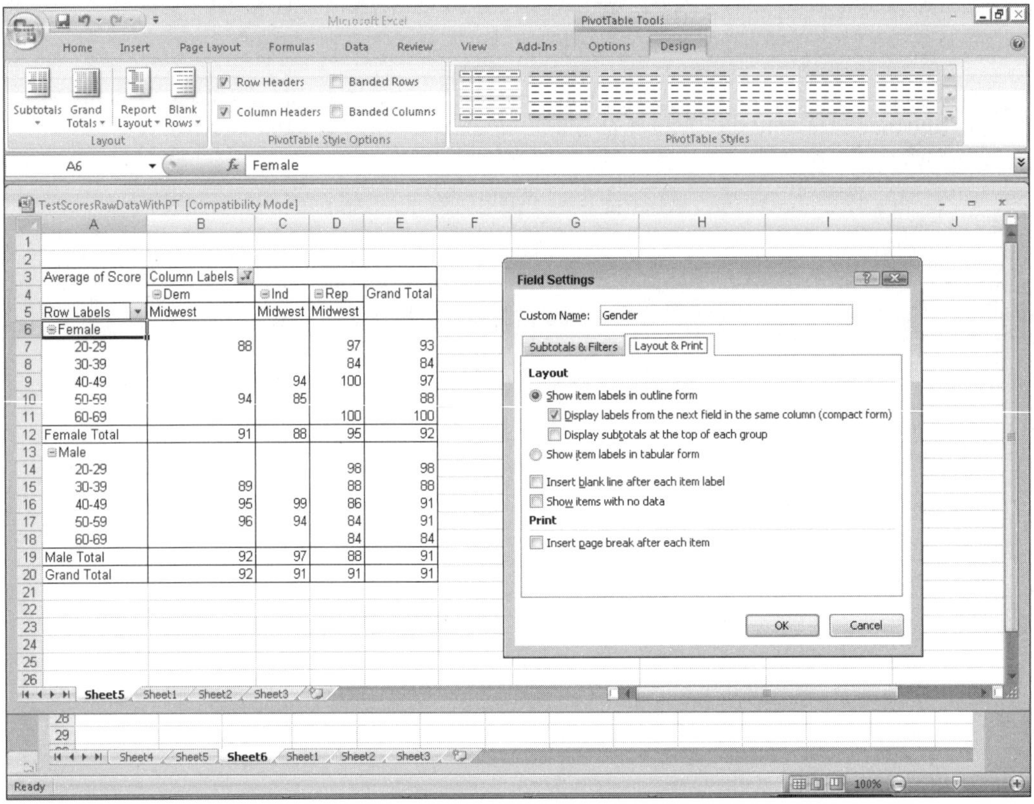

Figure 4-45: The effects of the row field layout option settings, part 2.

The other options on the Layout & Print tab are:

- **Insert blank line after each item label**—If selected, a blank line is inserted after each item label.

- **Show items with no data**—If selected, row items for which there is no data are displayed in the report.

- **Insert page break after each item**—If selected, each item starts on a new page when the report is printed.

Be aware that certain of the layout options, such as Insert blank line, may not seem to have an effect on the report unless you have multiple row fields and you are setting properties for the outer field.

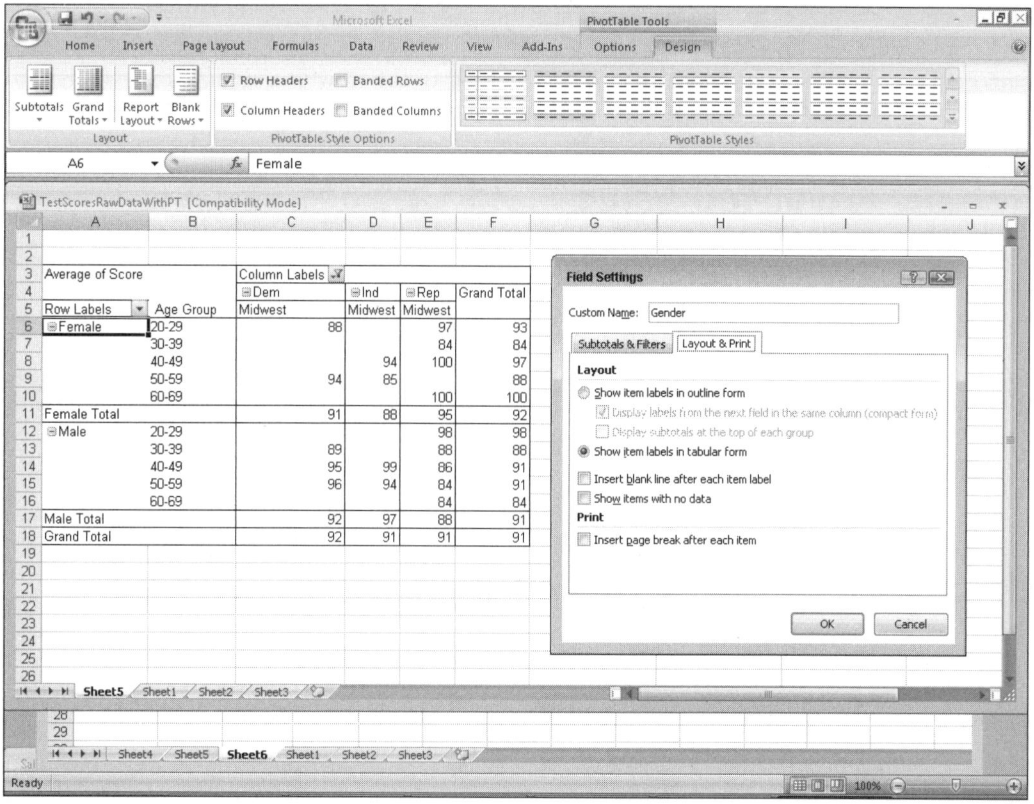

Figure 4-46: The effects of the row field layout option settings, part 3.

Working with Settings for Report Filter Fields

When you open the Field Settings dialog box for a report filter field (see Figure 4-42), it looks like the PivotTable Field dialog box for a row or column field. In fact, the field settings are precisely the same for report filter fields and for row and column fields. However, most of these settings will have no effect on a filter field, so what's the point?

The point lies in the fact that you can move fields between the row or column area and the filter area. When you move a field from the filter area to the row area, then these settings will come into play. When you move a field from the row area to the filter area, the settings become irrelevant. To simplify things, the same set of options is used for fields in both locations.

For example, when you change the Subtotals option for a report filter field you may wonder why the PivotTable report does not change. This setting takes effect only for row and column fields. If you pivot the table by moving the field to the Row or Column area, you'll see the effect of the Subtotals option you selected.

Setting Advanced Value Field Options

In an earlier section, I mentioned the Show values as tab in the Value Field Settings dialog box. This tab, shown in Figure 4-47, lets you access some advanced options that control some of the most sophisticated capabilities of PivotTable reports.

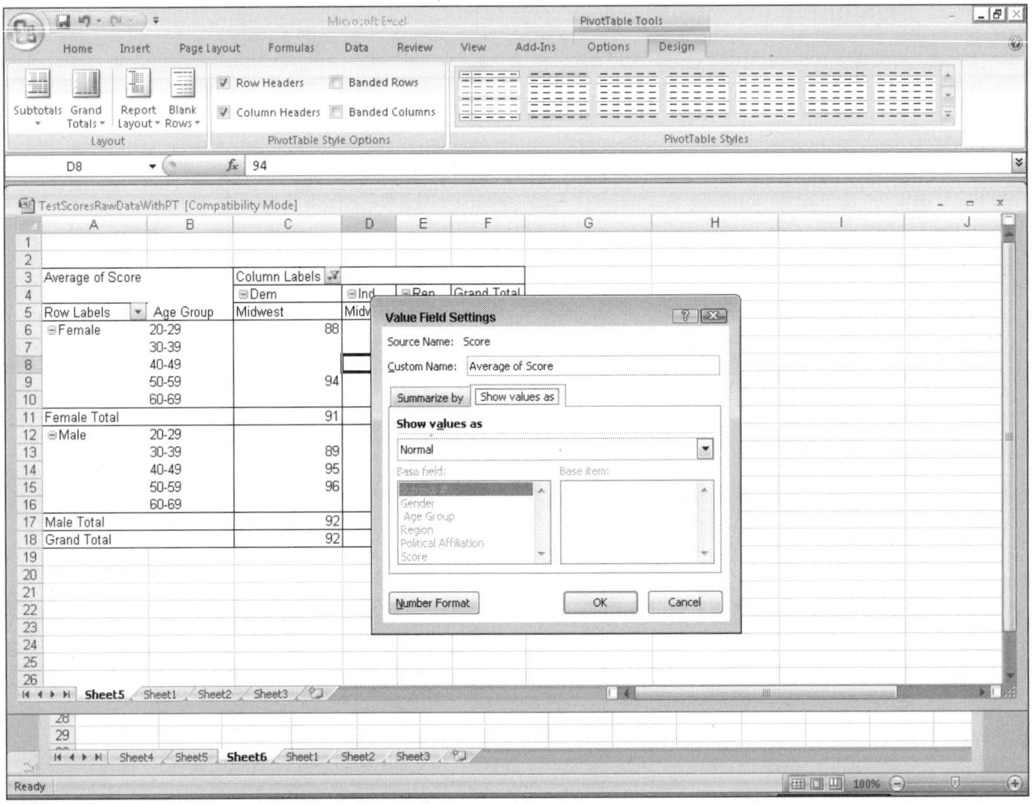

Figure 4-47: The Show values as tab of the Value Field Settings dialog box.

The default setting in this part of the dialog box is Normal in the Show Values As drop-down list, as shown in Figure 4-47. With this option, which you'll probably use most of the time, the field is summarized by means of the calculation that you select in the Summarize by list — for example, a straightforward sum, count, or average. If you pull down the Show values as list, however, you'll see several different ways in which the field data can be summarized. Just to give one example, a data item could be displayed as the percentage of the total of all data items in that row.

Watch Where You Click

Double-clicking a field button brings up the PivotTable Field dialog box for that field, but double-clicking a data cell activates drill-down, which displays the underlying data for the cell in a new worksheet. If you do this by mistake you'll have to delete the drill-down worksheet and return to the sheet where the PivotTable is located.

The following table shows some raw data that gives the number of each of three items that were sold, plus the overall total.

	Widgets	Doohickeys	Dinguses	Total
Number sold	55	24	66	145

Suppose you are not interested in the actual number but in percentages. For example, you want to know what percentage of items sold were widgets, what percentage were doohickeys, and so on. You can do this in a PivotTable report. The result is that, instead of displaying the value 55 in the Widgets column, Excel divides that number by 145 (the value in the Total column) and then multiplies by 100 to get the percentage value. The resulting PivotTable will look like this:

	Widgets	Doohickeys	Dinguses	Total
Number sold	38%	17%	46%	100%

When you set up a field to show data as something other than the default Normal, the first choice you must make is from the Show values as list. Then, for some of these selections, you must also make a selection in the Base field or Base item lists. It's essential that you understand what these choices mean, because it's not that uncommon for Excel users to set up a summary that displays something different from what they intended.

The simplest options in the Show data as list—simple because they do not require Base field or Base item selections—are as follows:

- **% of Row**—The data value as a percentage of the total for that row.
- **% of Column**—The data value as a percentage of the total for that column.
- **% of Total**—The data value as a percentage of the total for the entire report.

When you select Running Total in the Show values as list, you must also select a base field. The resulting display will be a running total of the base field; in other words, the display for the current item will be the actual data value for the current item added to the total values for all preceding data items.

For an example, look at these raw data:

Month	Totals
Jan	123
Feb	95
Mar	141
Apr	77
May	90
Jun	122

If these data were displayed as a running total you would see the following:

Month	Running Totals
Jan	123
Feb	218
Mar	359
Apr	436
May	526
Jun	648

The value displayed for Jan is the same as the raw data because there is no previous item. The value displayed for Feb is the Feb value plus the Jan value: (123+95)=218. The value displayed for Mar is Mar's raw value plus the value displayed for Feb: (141+218)=359. And so on.

The remaining Show data as options require you to specify both a base field and a base item:

- The Base field is one of the fields in the PivotTable. This includes fields that have been added to the PivotTable as well as those that have not (that is, those that are in the Field List but not the PivotTable itself).

- The Base item is a value for the column field. It can also be either of the special values (previous) or (next), which use the previous or next item, respectively, for the calculation.

The calculations available to you are:

- **Difference from**—Displays the difference between the raw value and the value of the base field/base item data.

- **% of**—Displays the raw value as a percentage of the value of the base field/base item data.

- **% difference from**—Displays, as a percentage, the difference between the raw value and the value of the base field/base item data.

The final option available in the Show data as list is Index. It calculates the display value as follows:

```
((value in cell) x (Grand Table Total)) / ((Grand Row Total) x (Grand Column
Total))
```

The options available here are very powerful but are a bit difficult to understand. Be careful when using them to make sure your result is actually what you want it to be.

Using Value and Label Filters

In a PivotTable report, row and column fields give you the option of applying value or label filters to the report data. Rather than just filtering based on values in the field, these filters let you define your own criteria.

Let's look at an example. The worksheet in Figure 4-48 shows data that gives sales information for your company's sales representatives.

	A	B	C	D	E	F	G
2	Date	Sales Rep	Item	Cost each	Quantity	Sale total	
3	13-Nov-06	Rosenstein, F.	Q00345B $	39.00	5 $	195.00	
4	13-Nov-06	Carver, W.	Q00345B $	39.00	17 $	663.00	
5	13-Nov-06	McBride, O.	C55440D $	16.75	5 $	83.75	
6	14-Nov-06	Baker, J.T.	Q00345B $	39.00	13 $	507.00	
7	14-Nov-06	Ackerman, Q.	Q00345B $	39.00	20 $	780.00	
8	14-Nov-06	Atkins, G.	C55440D $	16.75	8 $	134.00	
9	15-Nov-06	McBride, O.	J21344A $	19.50	9 $	175.50	
10	15-Nov-06	Yamamoto, A.	J21344A $	19.50	7 $	136.50	
11	15-Nov-06	Sanchez, L.	C55440D $	16.75	5 $	83.75	
12	15-Nov-06	Muller, S.	L98700F $	8.25	6 $	49.50	
13	15-Nov-06	Yamamoto, A.	L98700F $	8.25	14 $	115.50	
14	16-Nov-06	Wilson, J.	C55440D $	16.75	4 $	67.00	
15	16-Nov-06	Wilson, J.	Q00345B $	39.00	11 $	429.00	
16	17-Nov-06	Atkins, G.	J21344A $	19.50	4 $	78.00	
17	17-Nov-06	Ackerman, Q.	B20011A $	22.15	16 $	354.40	
18	17-Nov-06	Wilson, J.	C55440D $	16.75	16 $	268.00	
19	17-Nov-06	Baker, J.T.	L98700F $	8.25	5 $	41.25	
20	17-Nov-06	Sanchez, L.	C55440D $	16.75	16 $	268.00	
21	17-Nov-06	Baxter, X.	B20011A $	22.15	12 $	265.80	
22	18-Nov-06	Ackerman, Q.	Q00345B $	39.00	19 $	741.00	
23	18-Nov-06	Wilson, J.	Q00345B $	39.00	18 $	702.00	
24	18-Nov-06	McBride, O.	J21344A $	19.50	9 $	175.50	
25	18-Nov-06	D.F. Chang	C55440D $	16.75	7 $	117.25	
26	18-Nov-06	Sanchez, L.	B20011A $	22.15	8 $	177.20	
27	19-Nov-06	Carver, W.	B20011A $	22.15	3 $	66.45	
28	19-Nov-06	Baxter, X.	B20011A $	22.15	16 $	354.40	

Figure 4-48: The raw sales data.

You create a PivotTable report that shows the total sales for each person, as shown in Figure 4-49. This is fine as far as it goes, but using value or label filters will permit you to do things such as:

- Display only those sales reps whose last names begin with A.
- Display only those sales reps whose sales totals were over $4,000.
- Display the top five sales reps in terms of total sales.

	A	B	C
1			
2			
3	Sales Rep	Sum of Sale total	
4	Ackerman, Q.	$3,929	
5	Atkins, G.	$212	
6	Baker, J.T.	$1,816	
7	Baxter, X.	$620	
8	Carver, W.	$4,138	
9	D.F. Chang	$982	
10	McBride, O.	$1,188	
11	McSnee, A.	$227	
12	Muller, S.	$1,384	
13	Rosenstein, F.	$5,309	
14	Sanchez, L.	$2,547	
15	Wilson, J.	$2,738	
16	Yamamoto, A.	$3,022	
17	**Grand Total**	**$28,112**	
18			
19			

Figure 4-49: A PivotTable report that summarizes sales for each sales representative.

To apply a value or label filter, click the down arrow next to the field name in the PivotTable—SalesRep in this example—then select either Value Filters or Label Filters from the menu. The next menu, shown for Value Filters in Figure 4-50, lists the various types of filters you can define.

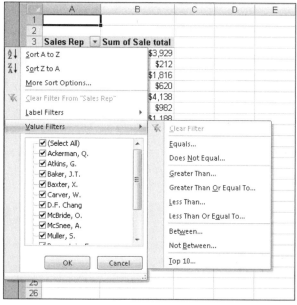

Figure 4-50: Selecting a value filter from the menu.

The selections on this menu, except for the last one, Top 10, are self-explanatory. Select one and the Value Filter dialog box opens, as shown in Figure 4-51. Make entries as follows:

- The list on the left lets you select the value field on which to base the filter. This list will include all of the value fields that have been added to the PivotTable.

- In the middle, select the comparison to use. The comparison you selected on the menu will be automatically entered here, but you can change it if you like.

- On the right, enter the comparison value. If you selected either Between or Not Between as the comparison, there will be two boxes for you to enter the upper and lower values.

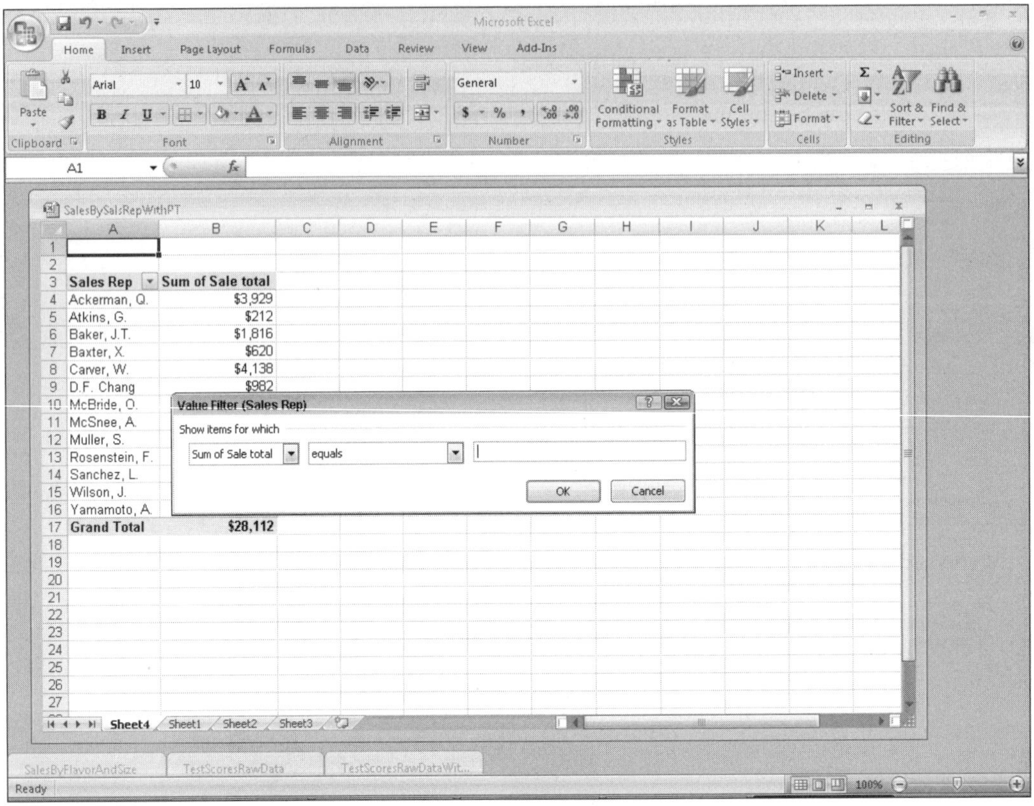

Figure 4-51: Defining a value filter in the Value Filter dialog box.

When you choose Labels Filter, the menu has a few more choices as shown in Figure 4-52. Some of the filter choices are the same as those for value filters. Note that for labels, Greater Than, Between, and so on are interpreted in terms of alphabetical order. Other filter choices, such as Begins With and Contains, are self-explanatory.

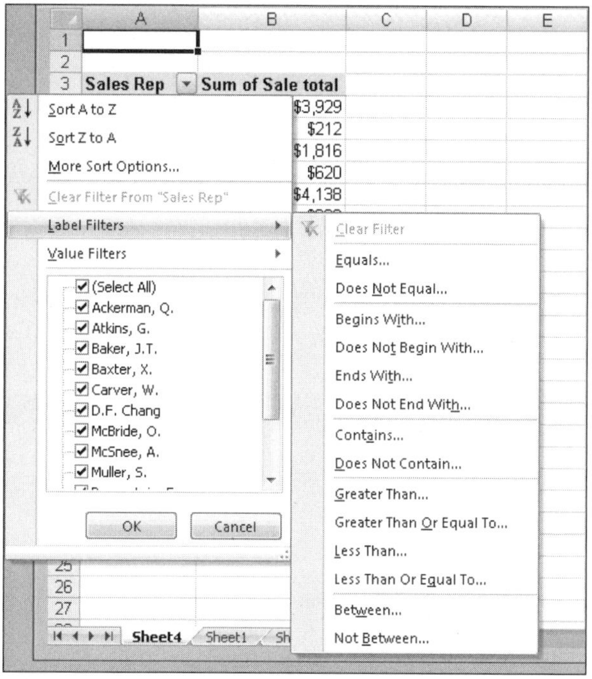

Figure 4-52: Selecting a label filter from the menu.

The value filters menu has one additional choice, Top 10, that can be very useful. With this filter you can display only the top or bottom *n* items based on data in the report—for example, the 10 sales reps with the highest sales or the 5 students with the lowest test score.

When you select this filter, the dialog box shown in Figure 4-53 opens. Make your filter entries as follows (left to right):

- Select Top or Bottom.
- Specify the number of items to display.
- Select what to display: items, percent, or sum.
- Select the value field to base the filter on.

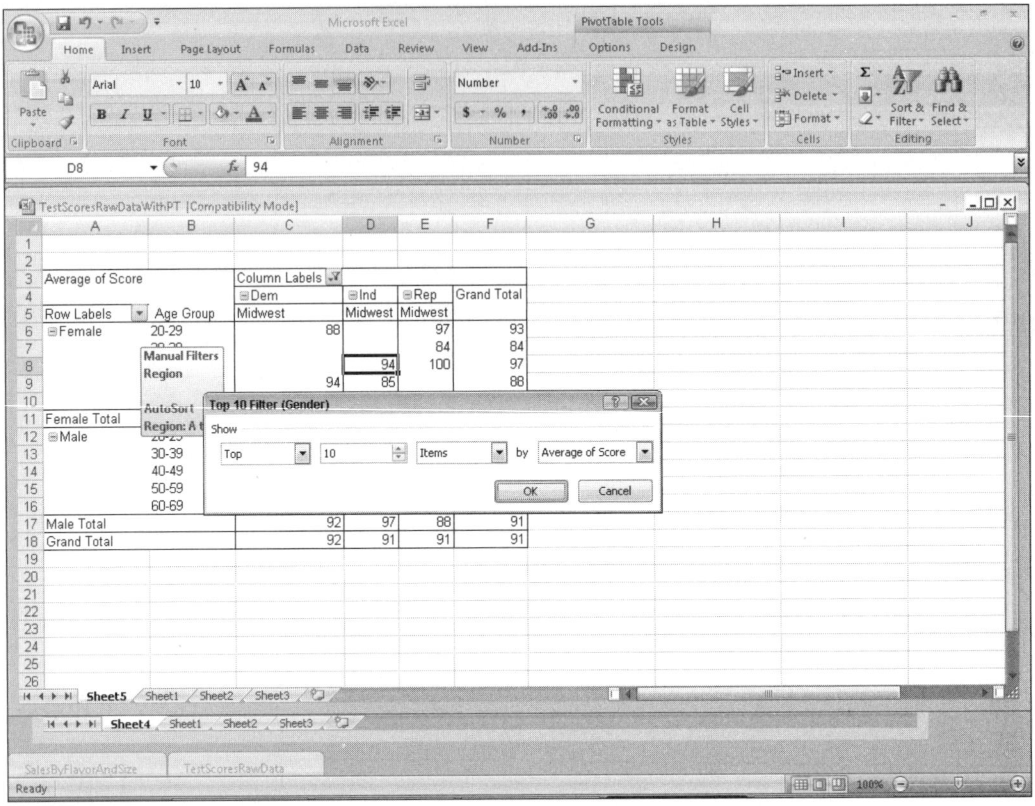

Figure 4-53: Defining a Top 10 filter.

You can clear a value or label filter from a field by selecting Clear Filter from the corresponding menu.

Using a Value Filter and Custom Sort

This section shows you how to use the value filter and sort options to change the way a PivotTable report is displayed. It uses the raw data shown earlier in Figure 4-48. The data are a list of individual sales, with each record giving the sales rep's name, the item sold, the cost per item, the quantity, and the total cost. These data are in the workbook SalesBySalesRep.xlsx.

First, create the basic PivotTable:

1. Put the cell pointer on any cell in the data range A2:F120.

2. Click the PivotTable button on the Insert ribbon to open the Create PivotTable dialog box.

3. Click OK to create the blank PivotTable report.

4. Add the Sale Total field to the Values area.

5. Add the Sales Rep field to the Row Labels area.

6. Format the Sum of Sale Total field to display as Currency with no decimal places.

At this point the PivotTable looks like Figure 4-54.

	A	B	C
1			
2			
3	**Sales Rep** ▼	**Sum of Sale total**	
4	Ackerman, Q.	$3,929	
5	Atkins, G.	$212	
6	Baker, J.T.	$1,816	
7	Baxter, X.	$620	
8	Carver, W.	$4,138	
9	D.F. Chang	$982	
10	McBride, O.	$1,188	
11	McSnee, A.	$227	
12	Muller, S.	$1,384	
13	Rosenstein, F.	$5,309	
14	Sanchez, L.	$2,547	
15	Wilson, J.	$2,738	
16	Yamamoto, A.	$3,022	
17	**Grand Total**	**$28,112**	
18			
19			

Figure 4-54: The default PivotTable before applying a filter and sort.

The next step is to apply a Top 10 filter so the report shows the top 10 sales reps based on sales:

1. Click the arrow next to the Sales Rep field label in the PivotTable report.

2. Select Value Filter from the menu.

3. Select Top 10 from the next menu to open the Top 10 Filter dialog box.

4. The default settings for the filter are what you want, so click OK to create the filter.

Now the PivotTable displays only the top 10 sales reps, but they are still sorted in alphabetic order by name. The following steps tell you how to define this sort in order by total sales:

1. Click the arrow next to the Sales Rep field label in the PivotTable report.

2. Click More Sort Options to display the Sort dialog box (see Figure 4-55).

3. Select the Descending option.

4. From the list, select Sum of Sale Total.

5. Click OK.

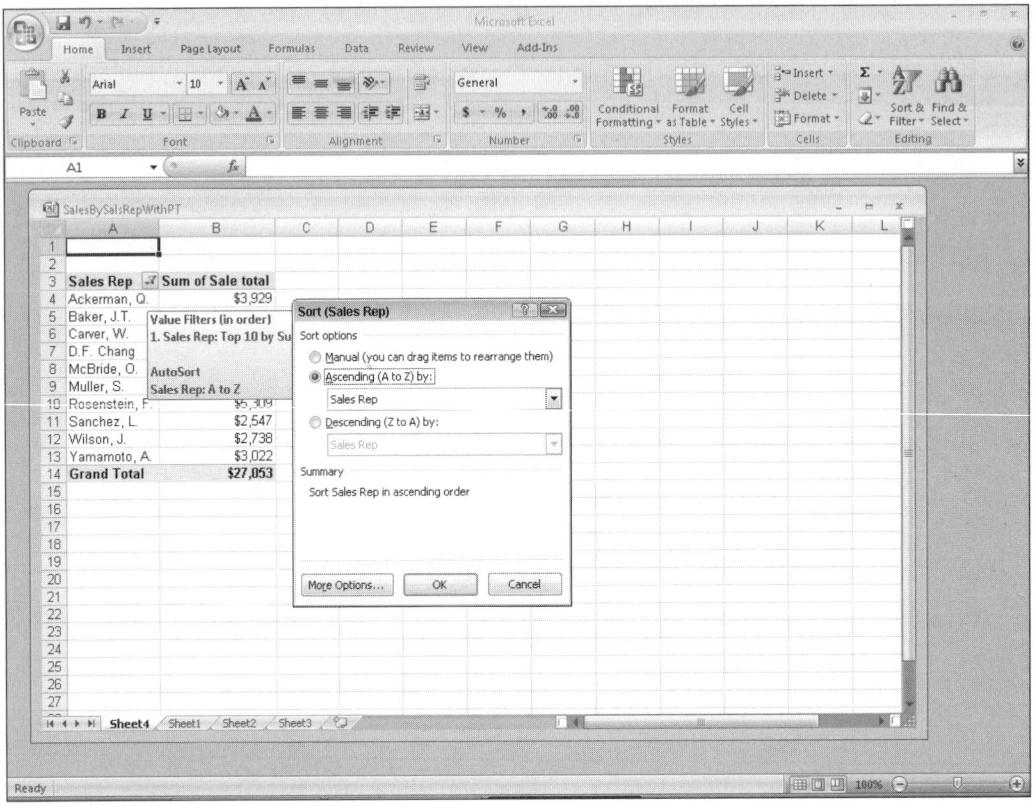

Figure 4-55: The Sort dialog box.

Now the PivotTable report is complete (see Figure 4-56). Only the top 10 sales reps are shown, and they are sorted from highest to lowest sales amount.

	A	B	C
1			
2			
3	**Sales Rep**	**Sum of Sale total**	
4	Rosenstein, F.	$5,309	
5	Carver, W.	$4,138	
6	Ackerman, Q.	$3,929	
7	Yamamoto, A.	$3,022	
8	Wilson, J.	$2,738	
9	Sanchez, L.	$2,547	
10	Baker, J.T.	$1,816	
11	Muller, S.	$1,384	
12	McBride, O.	$1,188	
13	D.F. Chang	$982	
14	**Grand Total**	**$27,053**	
15			
16			

Figure 4-56: The completed PivotTable report.

Chapter 5

More About PivotTable Components

Chapter 4 discusses how PivotTable components provide you with a lot of flexibility and power in designing your PivotTable reports. This chapter continues the exploration of PivotTable components, showing you how to create calculated items and fields, show and hide detail, and group data.

In This Chapter

- ◆ Using calculated fields and items
- ◆ Showing and hiding detail
- ◆ Grouping and ungrouping your PivotTable display

Working with Calculated Fields and Items

Calculated fields and calculated items are often confused with each other, and for good reason. Not only are the names similar; they are similar in concept. You need to understand the differences to use them effectively.

Calculated Fields

A calculated field acts like any other field in your PivotTable. Its name appears in the Field List and you can add it to the PivotTable just as you would any other field. It exists only in the PivotTable, however, and only for the duration of the PivotTable. In other words, it is not part of the data source.

Suppose your data source contains the total annual sales for each of your company's sales reps. The annual bonus for each rep is calculated as 2 percent of his or her total annual sales, but the data source doesn't contain the bonus amount. You can create a calculated field in your PivotTable to do this. It calculates total annual sales times 2 percent for each rep and lets you use this field in your PivotTable.

To create a calculated field, follow these steps:

1. Click anywhere in the PivotTable report to make sure it is active.

2. Click the Formulas button on the Options ribbon.

3. Select Calculated Field from the menu. Excel will display the Insert Calculated Field dialog box (see Figure 5-1).

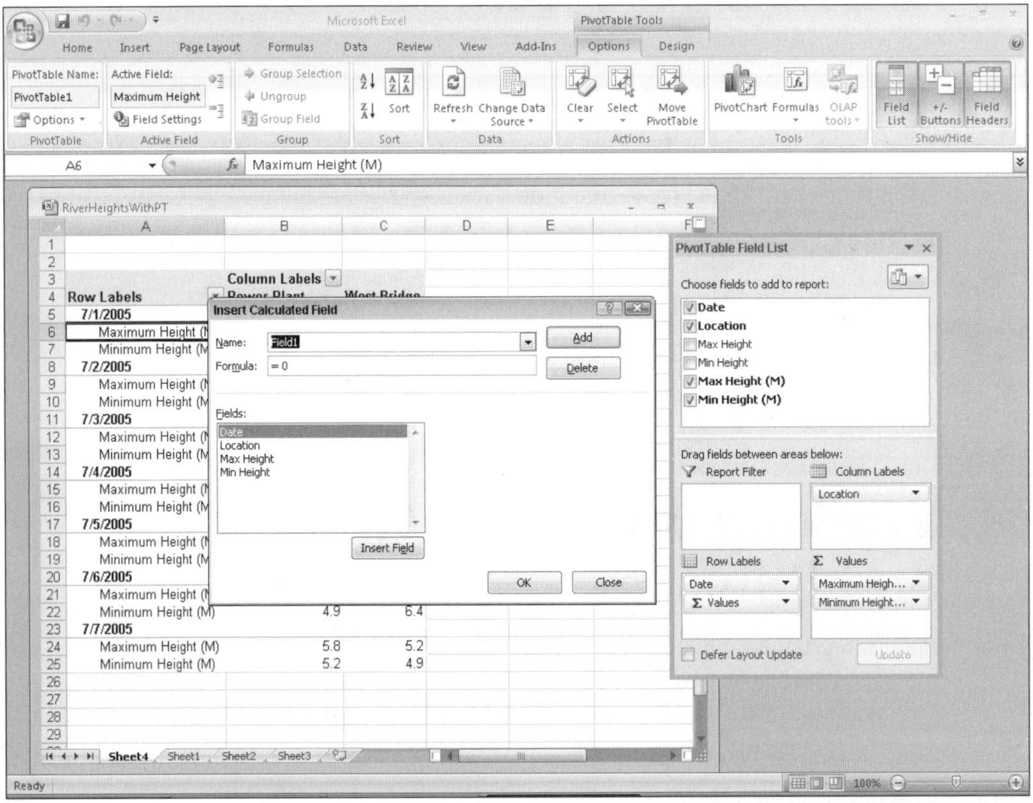

Figure 5-1: You use the Insert Calculated Field dialog box to define a calculated field.

OLAP data source? Sorry, no calculated fields for you.

If your PivotTable is based on an external Online Analytical Processing (OLAP) data source, you will not be able to create calculated fields or items.

4. Enter the name for the calculated field in the Name box. It's a good idea to use a descriptive name.

5. Enter the formula for the calculation in the Formula box:

   - The formula must start with an equal sign.

   - It can contain numbers, parentheses in pairs, and the operators + (addition), - (subtraction), * (multiplication), / (division), and ^ (exponentiation).

   - To add an existing field to the formula, click the field name in the Fields list and then click Insert Field.

6. When the formula is complete, click the OK button to add the calculated field to the Field List.

7. Click OK to close the dialog box. The new calculated field will now be included in the Field List and also automatically added to the PivotTable's Values area.

A calculated field can be based on any fields in the data source as well as on other calculated fields that have already been defined. For example, look at this formula for a calculated field:

```
=(ProductTotal+ServiceTotal)*.1
```

The formula adds the values in the ProductTotal and ServiceTotal fields and multiplies the sum by 0.1. ProductTotal and ServiceTotal can each be a field in the data source or another calculated field.

You also use the Insert Calculated Field dialog box to add and delete calculated fields. Display the dialog box as described previously; then select an existing calculated field in the Name list. Then perform one of these actions:

- To delete the selected calculated field, click the Delete button.

- To modify the formula of the selected calculated field, edit the formula, click the Modify button to save your changes, and then click the OK button.

Creating and Using a Calculated Field

For this section you will use the data shown in Figure 5-2. These data contain the measurements of the maximum and minimum heights of a river over a week, as measured at two locations. These data are in the workbook RiverHeights.xlsx. The measurements are in feet, and we want to create a PivotTable report that displays them in meters.

	A	B	C	D	E
1					
2	Date	Location	Max Height	Min Height	
3	7/1/2005	West Bridge	22	19	
4	7/2/2005	West Bridge	21	19	
5	7/3/2005	West Bridge	20	18	
6	7/4/2005	West Bridge	24	21	
7	7/5/2005	West Bridge	23	22	
8	7/6/2005	West Bridge	22	21	
9	7/7/2005	West Bridge	17	16	
10	7/1/2005	Power Plant	19	17	
11	7/2/2005	Power Plant	23	21	
12	7/3/2005	Power Plant	24	23	
13	7/4/2005	Power Plant	22	21	
14	7/5/2005	Power Plant	20	17	
15	7/6/2005	Power Plant	17	16	
16	7/7/2005	Power Plant	19	17	
17					
18					

Figure 5-2: The sample river height data.

The first step in creating a calculated field is to create a basic PivotTable report, as follows:

1. Place the cell pointer on any cell in the data range A2:D16.

2. Click the PivotTable button on the Insert ribbon to open the Create PivotTable dialog box.

3. Click OK to close the dialog box and create the blank PivotTable.

4. Click the Formulas button on the Options ribbon, then select Calculated Field from the menu. Excel opens the Insert Calculated Field dialog box.

5. Enter **Max Height (M)** in the Name box.

6. Press Tab to move to the Formula box.

7. Enter = 0.305*.

8. In the Fields list, click Max Height.

9. Click Insert Field. The Insert Calculated Field dialog box should now look like Figure 5-3.

10. Click OK to add the calculated field to the Field List and to the Values area of the PivotTable.

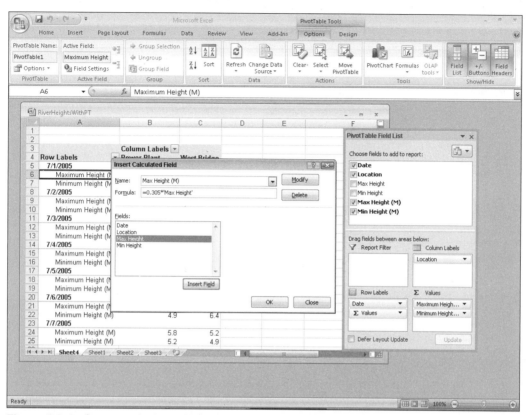

Figure 5-3: Defining a calculated field to display Max Height in meters.

You also need a calculated field for Min Height in meters. Follow the previous steps to define this field—enter **Min Height (M)** in the Name box, and use the formula **=0.305*'Min Height'**.

At this point, your Field List and PivotTable report will look like Figure 5-4. You can see that the two calculated fields are listed and have been added to the Values area. Note also that a field called Values has been added to the Row Labels area—you'll see how this is used soon.

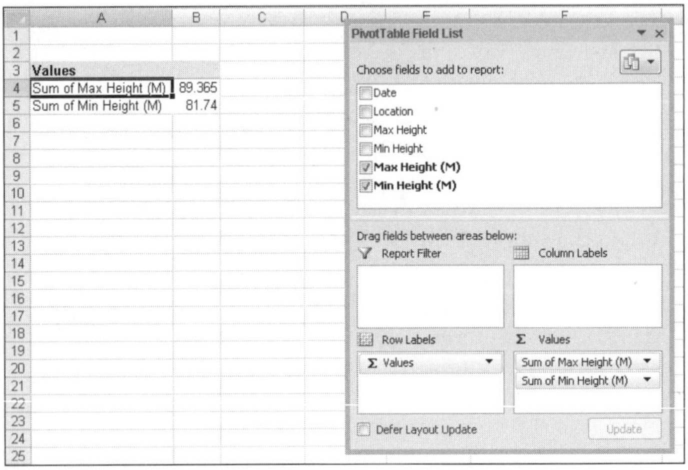

Figure 5-4: The Field List and PivotTable report after defining the two calculated fields.

To complete the PivotTable report, follow these steps:

1. Add the Location field to the Column Labels area.

2. Add the Date field to the Row Labels area.

3. If necessary, move the Values field from outer to the inner position in the Row Labels area.

At this point, your PivotTable will look like Figure 5-5.

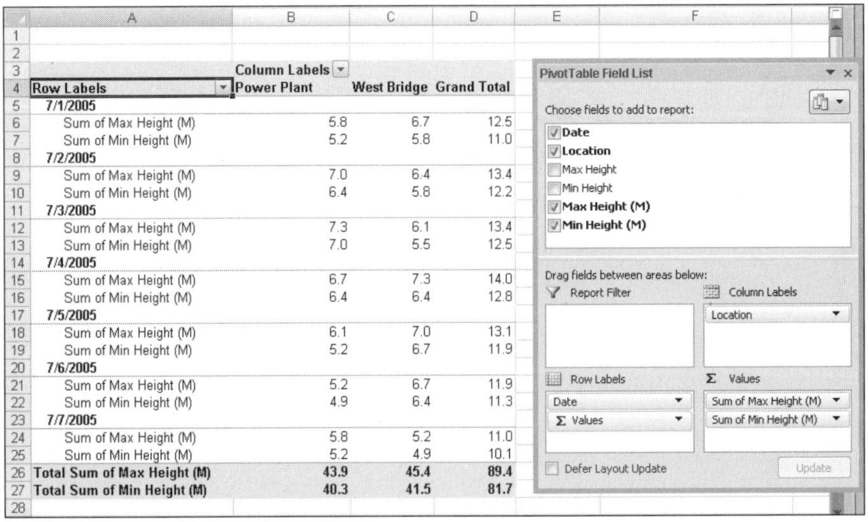

Figure 5-5: The PivotTable after adding fields to the various areas.

The data is arranged the way we want it, but there's still some work to be done: changing the display names of the two calculated fields, displaying the data with only 1 decimal point, and getting rid of the totals. Here are the steps to follow:

1. Right-click any cell in the PivotTable corresponding to the Sum of Max Height (M) field and select Value Field Settings from the popup menu.

2. Change the Custom Name to **Maximum Height (M)**.

3. Click the Number Format button to open the Format Cells dialog box.

4. Select the Number format with 1 decimal place.

5. Click OK twice to return to the PivotTable report.

6. Repeat steps 1 through 5 for the Sum of Min Height (M) field, renaming it to **Minimum Height (M)**.

7. Click the Grand Totals button on the Design ribbon.

8. Select Off for Rows and Columns.

Now the PivotTable report is finished and should look as shown in Figure 5-6.

	A	B	C
1			
2			
3		Column Labels ▾	
4	Row Labels ▾	Power Plant	West Bridge
5	7/1/2005		
6	Maximum Height (M)	5.8	6.7
7	Minimum Height (M)	5.2	5.8
8	7/2/2005		
9	Maximum Height (M)	7.0	6.4
10	Minimum Height (M)	6.4	5.8
11	7/3/2005		
12	Maximum Height (M)	7.3	6.1
13	Minimum Height (M)	7.0	5.5
14	7/4/2005		
15	Maximum Height (M)	6.7	7.3
16	Minimum Height (M)	6.4	6.4
17	7/5/2005		
18	Maximum Height (M)	6.1	7.0
19	Minimum Height (M)	5.2	6.7
20	7/6/2005		
21	Maximum Height (M)	5.2	6.7
22	Minimum Height (M)	4.9	6.4
23	7/7/2005		
24	Maximum Height (M)	5.8	5.2
25	Minimum Height (M)	5.2	4.9
26			

Figure 5-6: The completed PivotTable report showing river heights in meters.

Part II

Working with Calculated Items

As you have seen, a calculated field performs a calculation on the data in an existing field. A calculated item, on the other hand, performs a calculation on one or more items within a field. So what's the difference? An item is an individual data value in a field. In your data source, you might have a field named Department and within that field you might have the items Accounting, Design, Maintenance, and so on.

To create a calculated item, make sure the PivotTable is active. Click a cell that belongs to the field that the calculated item will be based on. The calculated item will be inserted in the row below where you click. Then click the Formulas button on the Options toolbar and select Calculated Item from the menu. Excel displays the Insert Calculated Item dialog box, shown in Figure 5-7. Note that the title of the dialog box indicates the field you are using, Month in this case.

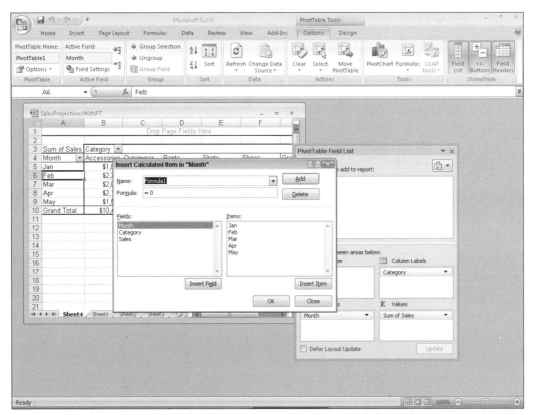

Figure 5-7: You use the Insert Calculated Item dialog box to define a calculated item.

Ungroup First

If the items in a field are grouped (grouping is covered later in this chapter), you should ungroup them before creating a calculated item:

1. Right-click the group.

2. Click Ungroup on the popup menu.

You can regroup the items after the calculated item has been created, if you wish.

 NOTE
If the Calculated Item menu command is not available, it is probably because you clicked, in the PivotTable, a field that cannot be used to create a calculated item.

The Fields list in the lower part of the dialog box lists the PivotTable fields. When you select a field in this list, the Items list displays the names of the items for that field. This can be confusing because the dialog box lets you insert (or try to insert) things in the formula that cannot be used. For example, you will never use the Insert Field button because calculated items are not based on fields but on items. Likewise, you cannot insert items from fields other than the selected one (the one you clicked in the PivotTable before displaying this dialog box). Fortunately Excel prevents you from entering incorrect items in the formula by displaying an error message, either when you try to add the item or when you try to close the dialog box.

To complete the calculated item, follow these steps. They are similar in many ways to the procedure for creating a calculated field.

1. In the Name box, enter the name for the calculated item. This is the name that will be displayed in the PivotTable.

2. Enter the formula for the item in the Formula box:

   • The formula must start with an equals sign.

   • It can contain numbers, parentheses in pairs, and the operators + (addition), - (subtraction), * (multiplication), / (division), and ^ (exponentiation).

   • To add an item to the formula, click the item name in the Items list and then click Insert Item.

3. When the formula is complete, click the OK button to add the calculated item to the PivotTable.

Creating and Using a Calculated Item

This section uses the data shown in Figure 5-8. These data, found in the workbook `SalesProjections.xlsx`, are sales totals for different categories over five months, January through May. In this section you will create a PivotTable that uses a calculated item to display a projected sales amount for June.

	A	B	C
1			
2	**Month**	**Category**	**Sales**
3	Jan	Shoes $	1,769
4	Jan	Shirts $	2,397
5	Jan	Pants $	2,150
6	Jan	Outerwear $	2,820
7	Jan	Accessories $	1,845
8	Feb	Shoes $	2,192
9	Feb	Shirts $	2,846
10	Feb	Pants $	2,814
11	Feb	Outerwear $	2,606
12	Feb	Accessories $	2,718
13	Mar	Shoes $	1,055
14	Mar	Shirts $	2,319
15	Mar	Pants $	1,187
16	Mar	Outerwear $	1,606
17	Mar	Accessories $	2,078
18	Apr	Shoes $	2,919
19	Apr	Shirts $	2,648
20	Apr	Pants $	1,873
21	Apr	Outerwear $	2,255
22	Apr	Accessories $	2,195
23	May	Shoes $	2,742
24	May	Shirts $	2,798
25	May	Pants $	1,880
26	May	Outerwear $	1,714
27	May	Accessories $	1,590
28			

Figure 5-8: The sample sales data.

The first step is to create the basic PivotTable report, as follows:

1. Place the cell pointer on any cell in the data range A2:C27.

2. Click the PivotTable button on the Insert ribbon to open the Create PivotTable dialog box.

3. Click OK to close the dialog box and create the blank PivotTable.

4. Add the Month field to the Row Labels area.

5. Add the Sales field to the Values area.

6. Double-click the Sum of Sales heading in the PivotTable to open the Field Settings dialog box for that field.

7. Click the Number button to display the Format Cells dialog box.

8. Select the Currency format and specify no decimal places.

9. Click OK twice.

At this point, the PivotTable will look like the one shown in Figure 5-9.

	A	B	C
1			
2			
3	Month ▼	Sum of Sales	
4	Jan	$10,981	
5	Feb	$13,176	
6	Mar	$8,245	
7	Apr	$11,890	
8	May	$10,724	
9	Grand Total	$55,016	
10			
11			

Figure 5-9: The basic PivotTable report displays the sum of sales for each month.

The next step is to define a calculated item to display projected sales for June. In past years you have found that sales in June tend to be 120 percent of the average sales for the previous two months, April and May. Here's how to define that calculated item:

1. Click any cell in the Month column in the PivotTable.

2. Click the Formulas button on the Options ribbon and select Calculated Item from the menu to display the Insert Calculated Item dialog box.

3. Enter **June (projected)** in the Name box.

4. Click in the Formula field and erase the 0 (leaving the equals sign in place).

5. Enter .5*(after the equals sign).

6. Click Month in the Fields list.

7. Click May in the Items list.

8. Click Insert Item to insert May into the formula.

9. Enter a plus sign.

10. Click Apr in the Items list.

11. Click Insert Item to insert Apr in the formula.

12. Enter)*1.2. The dialog box should now appear as shown in Figure 5-10.

13. Click Add; then click OK.

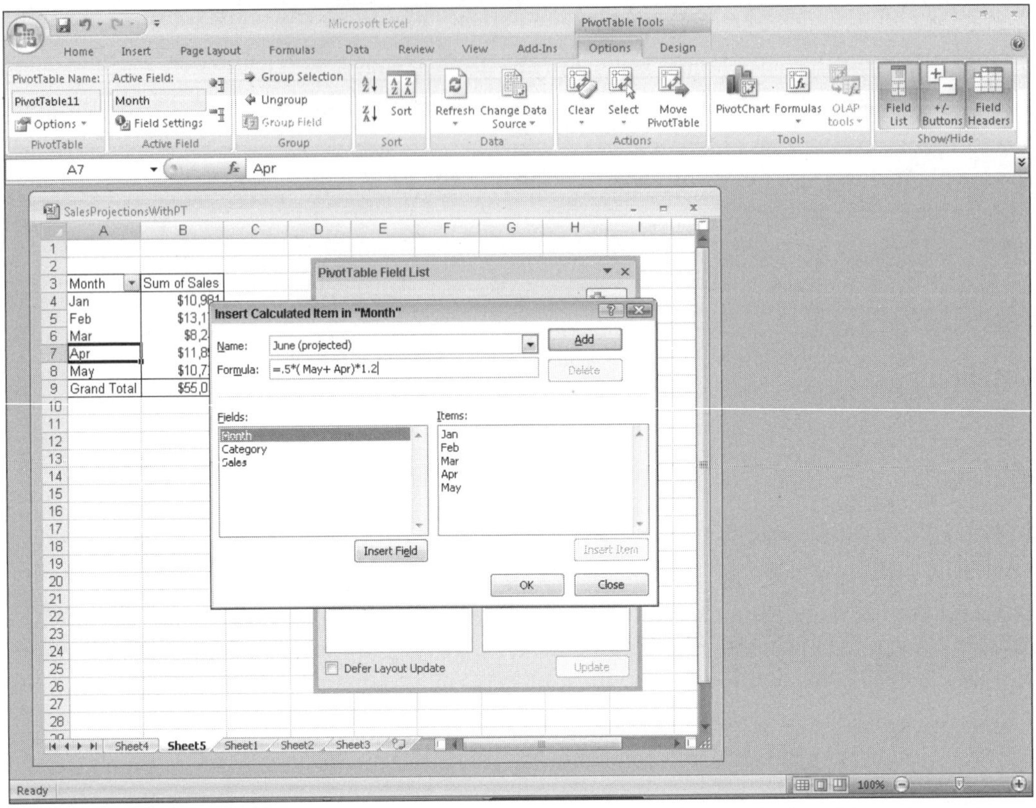

Figure 5-10: The Insert Calculated Item dialog box after you define a calculated item for projected June sales.

Excel adds the calculated item to the PivotTable report at the bottom of the Month column, as shown in Figure 5-11.

Figure 5-11: The calculated item displayed in the PivotTable report.

Before you finish with this section, look at some additional features of calculated items. In the PivotTable report used in the previous example, the Category field was not used and the PivotTable simply summed all values across categories for each month. What happens when you add the Category field to the PivotTable? Go ahead. All you need to do is add the Category field to the Column Labels area. Now the PivotTable looks like what you see in Figure 5-12. The calculated item is automatically extended across all columns.

	A	B	C	D	E	F	G
1							
2							
3	Sum of Sales	Category					
4	Month	Accessories	Outerwear	Pants	Shirts	Shoes	Grand Total
5	Jan	$1,845	$2,820	$2,150	$2,397	$1,769	$10,981
6	Feb	$2,718	$2,606	$2,814	$2,846	$2,192	$13,176
7	Mar	$2,078	$1,606	$1,187	$2,319	$1,055	$8,245
8	Apr	$2,195	$2,255	$1,873	$2,648	$2,919	$11,890
9	May	$1,590	$1,714	$1,880	$2,798	$2,742	$10,724
10	June (projected)	$2,271	$2,381	$2,252	$3,268	$3,397	$13,568
11	Grand Total	$12,697	$13,382	$12,156	$16,276	$14,074	$68,584
12							

Figure 5-12: When you add the Category field to the Column Label area, the calculated item is automatically entered in each column.

In a situation like this, where a calculated item is displayed in more than one cell, you can modify the calculated item for individual cells. Move the Excel pointer onto any one of the calculated item cells in the PivotTable, cells B10 to F10. The formula bar shows that each cell contains the formula you specified for the calculated item:

```
=.5*(May+Apr)*1.2
```

Suppose you know that while this projection formula is accurate overall, you would get a more accurate projection for the Pants category if you were to use a factor of 1.4 instead of 1.2. All you need to do is move the pointer to cell D10, where the calculated projection for Pants is located, press F2 to edit the formula, and make the desired change. However, this kind of ad hoc change to a PivotTable is generally considered to be bad practice because it is so hard to trace.

Showing and Hiding Detail

PivotTable reports give you the ability to view a greater or lesser amount of detail depending on your current needs.

Viewing Detail for Value Items

Viewing detail for data items is sometimes referred to as *drilling down* or *expanding to detail*. When you drill down, Excel displays the raw data records that underlie the selected value item. To use this feature, you must ensure that the Enable Show Details option is turned on in the PivotTable Options dialog box.

To drill down, simply double-click the value cell of interest. Excel places the underlying raw data in a new worksheet and displays them. Figure 5-13 shows an example from the PivotTable you created earlier in this chapter from the data in `SalesBySalesRep.xlsx`. Double-clicking the data cell for Baker, J.T. creates the detail worksheet shown on the right. You can see that this contains all the raw data for Baker, J.T.

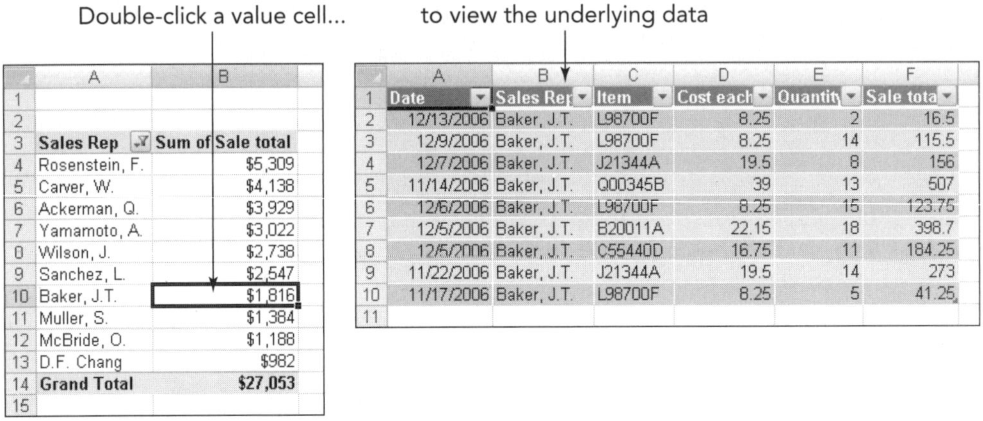

Double-click a value cell...   to view the underlying data

Figure 5-13: Double-clicking a value cell in the PivotTable (left) drills down to the underlying raw data (right).

To remove detail data, simply delete the worksheet they are on (click Delete on the Home tab and then select Delete Sheet).

Viewing Details for Field Items

To control how much detail is shown for a field, right-click the field button, select Expand/Collapse from the menu, and select the Expand or Collapse from the next menu.

Expanding and collapsing detail for a field item has different effects depending on the field position in the PivotTable. If the PivotTable has two or more row fields and the field of interest is not the inner field, collapsing detail for a field works by collapsing any fields that are more "inner." I am speaking here of row fields but it works the same way for column fields.

An example will help clarify this. The top part of Figure 5-14 shows the PivotTable you created earlier from the data in `TestScores.xls`. If you hide the details for the Gender field, the result is that the inner field, Age Group, is collapsed and the PivotTable looks like the lower part of Figure 5-14. Expanding the Gender field returns the PivotTable to its original display.

Sum of Score		Political A▼	Region ▼								
		⊟Dem					⊟Ind				
Gender ▼	Age Group ▼	Midwest	NorthEast	NorthWest	South	SouthWest	Midwest	NorthEast	NorthWest	South	So
⊟Female	20-29	88		100	83	189			82		
	30-39			434		252			94	98	
	40-49		81	98		99	94		278		
	50-59	94		333		80	169				
	60-69		99			195			279		
Female Total		182	180	965	83	815	263		733	98	
⊟Male	20-29		92	177		179		94			
	30-39	177	94	363	171	86					
	40-49	95	180	89	91	91	90	94	83	81	
	50-59	96		96			94				
	60-69			95							
Male Total		368	366	820	262	356	184	188	83	81	
Grand Total		550	546	1785	345	1171	447	188	816	179	

Sum of Score		Political Affiliation ▼	Region	▼			
		⊟Dem					⊟Ind
Gender ▼	Age Group ▼	Midwest	NorthEast	NorthWest	South	SouthWest	Midwest
⊞Female		182	180	965	83	815	
⊞Male		368	366	820	262	356	
Grand Total		550	546	1785	345	1171	

Figure 5-14: The PivotTable report before (top) and after (bottom) the detail for the Gender field is hidden.

In Figure 5-14 the details for Age Group are hidden, but the Field button is still displayed. You can still pull down this list and filter the PivotTable based on Age Group.

In other situations the Collapse command has the following effects:

- If the field is the inner field, hiding its details has the same effect as collapsing its parent field (as in the previous example). To show the details again you must execute the Expand command on the parent field.
- If the field is the only row field, the Collapse command has no effect.

NOTE

Note that the effect of collapsing/expanding a field seems to be the same as using the expand/collapse (+ and -) buttons in the PivotTable report. The difference is that the + and - buttons expand or collapse individual items, while the expand/collapse commands on the menu operate on all items for that field.

When you select Expand for an inner or only field, Excel displays a list of available fields, including those that are already part of the PivotTable and any that have not been added to the PivotTable. It does not, however, list fields that are already added to the region (row or column) where the field of interest is located. This is shown for the TestScores PivotTable in Figure 5-15.

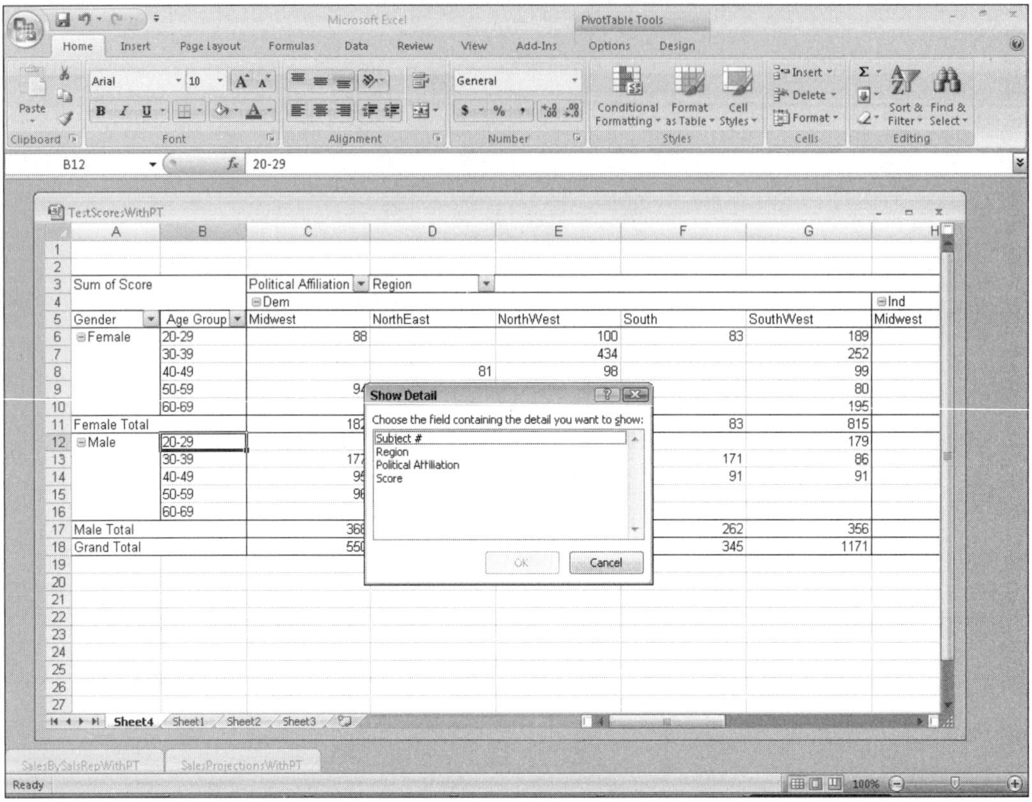

Figure 5-15: Showing detail for an inner or only field means adding a field to the Row or Column area.

When you select a field from this list and click OK, Excel adds the field as an inner field to the Row Labels area:

- If the field was already part of the PivotTable, the effect is the same as that of pivoting the table; the field is moved from its current location (for example, the Column Labels area) to the new location as the inner field in the Row Labels area.

- If the field was not already part of the PivotTable it is simply added as the inner field.

This is shown in Figure 5-16. At the top is the original PivotTable. At the bottom is the PivotTable after you have shown detail for the Age Group field and selected the column Subject #.

	A	B	C	D
1				
2				
3	Sum of Score		Political Affiliation ▼	Region ▼
4			⊟Dem	
5	Gender ▼	Age Group ▼	Midwest	NorthEast
6	⊟Female	20-29	88	
7		30-39		
8		40-49		81
9		50-59	94	
10		60-69		99
11	Female Total		182	180
12	⊟Male	20-29		92
13		30-39	177	94
14		40-49	95	180
15		50-59	96	
16		60-69		
17	Male Total		368	366
18	Grand Total		550	546
19				

	A	B	C	D	E
1					
2					
3	Sum of Score			Political Affiliation ▼	Region ▼
4				⊟Dem	
5	Gender ▼	Age Group ▼	Subject # ▼	Midwest	NorthEast
6	⊟Female	⊟20-29	20		
7			27		
8			32		
9			37		
10			51	88	
11			56		
12			67		
13			83		
14			85		
15			90		
16			100		
17		20-29 Total		88	
18		⊟30-39	6		
19			24		
20			30		
21			39		
22			45		
23			48		
24			53		
25			63		
26			64		
27			66		

Figure 5-16: Showing detail for an inner or only field means adding a field to the Row or Column area.

Grouping PivotTable Items

Excel gives you the ability to group items in a PivotTable report, providing another level of analysis that can be very useful in some situations. Suppose, for example, that your raw data are about individual people and one of the data items is Age. This value will range from, say, 18 to 65.

Using the Group command you can define three groups:

Group 1: 18 to 35

Group 2: 36 to 49

Group 3: 50 to 65

The resulting PivotTable summarizes data according to the groups you define. You can also group non-numeric data. Suppose your sales data include the city of the branch that is reporting, and you want to analyze by region. You can define groups that contain specified cities, such as:

Northeast: Boston, Hartford, New York

South: Atlanta, Miami, Charleston

Midwest: Chicago, Toledo, Omaha

The details for grouping depend on the kind of data being grouped, as explained in the following sections. For any field, you group or ungroup items by selecting the field in the PivotTable report and using the commands in the Group section of the Options ribbon.

Grouping Numeric Items

When a field contains numeric data, you can group the items by numeric value. To illustrate, I will use the data shown in Figure 5-17, which includes a row for each respondent.

Subject #	Age	Gender	Date of Survey	Race	Question 1	Question 2	Question 3
1	50	M	9/1/2005	Black	No	Yes	Yes
2	19	M	9/3/2005	Hispanic	No	Unsure	Unsure
3	31	F	9/2/2005	White	Yes	Yes	No
4	51	M	9/2/2005	Asian	Yes	No	Yes
5	24	F	9/1/2005	White	No	Unsure	Yes
6	58	F	9/3/2005	Other	No	Unsure	Yes
7	21	F	9/1/2005	Black	No	No	No
8	36	M	9/3/2005	White	Unsure	No	Yes
9	49	M	9/2/2005	White	Yes	Unsure	No
10	55	F	9/2/2005	Asian	No	Unsure	No
11	31	M	9/1/2005	White	No	Yes	Unsure
12	18	F	9/3/2005	Other	Unsure	Unsure	Unsure
13	44	M	9/1/2005	Black	No	Yes	Unsure
14	45	M	9/3/2005	White	Yes	Yes	Yes
15	39	M	9/2/2005	Black	Unsure	Unsure	No
16	52	F	9/2/2005	Hispanic	No	Yes	Unsure
17	65	M	9/1/2005	White	No	Yes	No
18	42	F	9/3/2005	Asian	Yes	Unsure	No
19	19	F	9/1/2005	White	Yes	No	Unsure
20	41	F	9/3/2005	Other	No	Yes	Yes
21	18	M	9/2/2005	Black	Yes	No	No
22	61	M	9/2/2005	White	Yes	Unsure	No
23	23	F	9/1/2005	White	No	Yes	Yes
24	58	M	9/3/2005	Asian	Yes	No	Yes
25	45	F	9/1/2005	White	No	No	No
26	35	M	9/3/2005	Other	No	No	Yes
27	56	M	9/2/2005	Black	Yes	Yes	No

Figure 5-17: The raw survey data.

If you are interested in responses as a function of age, you might create the PivotTable report shown in Figure 5-18. This report does what you want, technically at least, but the fact that age is broken down one year per row makes the data impossible to interpret. This is a perfect situation in which to use grouping.

Count of Question 1	Question 1	Gender								
	No		No Total	Unsure		Unsure Total	Yes		Yes Total	Grand Total
Age	F	M		F	M		F	M		
18		1	1	1	2	3	1	2	3	7
19		2	2	1		1	2		2	5
20	1	1	2	2		2	1	2	3	7
21	1	2	3							3
22	1	1	2	1	1		2		1	5
23	2		2	3		3	3	2	5	10
24	2	4	6	1	3	4	1	1	2	12
25				2	1	3		2	2	5
26	3	1	4		1	1	1		1	6
27		3	3					1	1	4
28	5		5	1	1	2	2	1	3	10
29	1	1	2	1		1	2		2	5
30				2	2	4		1	1	5
31	1		1	2		2	2	3	5	8
32	1		1		1	1	1	2	3	5
33	1		1	2	1	3		1	1	5
34	1	2	3		2	2	1	1	2	7
35	1	2	3		1	1	1	1	2	6
36	1	1	2		2	2		1	1	5
37	1	2	3		2	2	3	2	5	10
38		2	2		1	1	1	3	4	7
39	1	3	4	1	2	3		2	2	9
40	2		2		1	1		1	1	4
41	2		3					1	1	4

Figure 5-18: A PivotTable report created from the survey data.

To group a numeric field, click the field button—Age in this case—then click the Group Field button on the Options ribbon. Excel opens the Grouping dialog box, shown in Figure 5-19. Note the following:

- The Starting At and Ending At boxes are automatically filled in with the lowest and highest values that are present in this field—18 and 65 in this example.

- The By box contains 10 by default—this is the size of each group.

You can change any of these values to suit your needs; then click OK to create the groups. The resulting PivotTable is shown in Figure 5-20, and I think you'll agree that it is a lot easier to interpret.

Part II

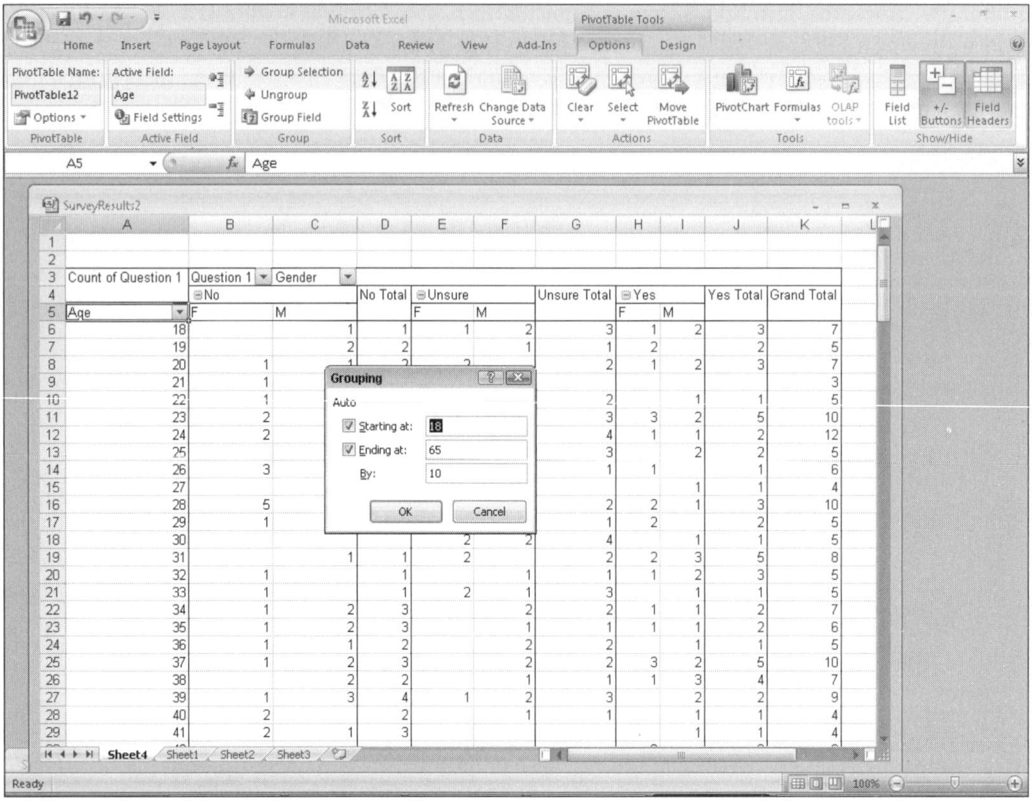

Figure 5-19: The Grouping dialog box for a numeric field.

	A	B	C	D	E	F	G	H	I	J	K
1											
2											
3	Count of Question 1	Question 1	Gender								
4		No		No Total	Unsure		Unsure Total	Yes		Yes Total	Grand Total
5	Age	F	M		F	M		F	M		
6	18-27	10	15	25	10	9	19	9	11	20	64
7	28-37	12	9	21	8	12	20	12	13	25	66
8	38-47	11	13	24	2	8	10	9	10	19	53
9	48-57	7	4	11	12	20	32	6	11	17	60
10	58-67	11	10	21	12	7	19	6	9	15	55
11	Grand Total	51	51	102	44	56	100	42	54	96	298
12											

Figure 5-20: The PivotTable report after grouping the Age field.

Suppose, however, you want the groups to be by decade—20–29, 30–39, and so on, rather than 18–27, 28–37, and so on as in the previous example. Then you set the Starting At and Ending At options manually:

1. Turn both the Starting At and Ending At options off.

2. Enter **20** in the Starting At box.

3. Enter **59** in the Ending At box.

Figure 5-21 shows what the dialog box now looks like.

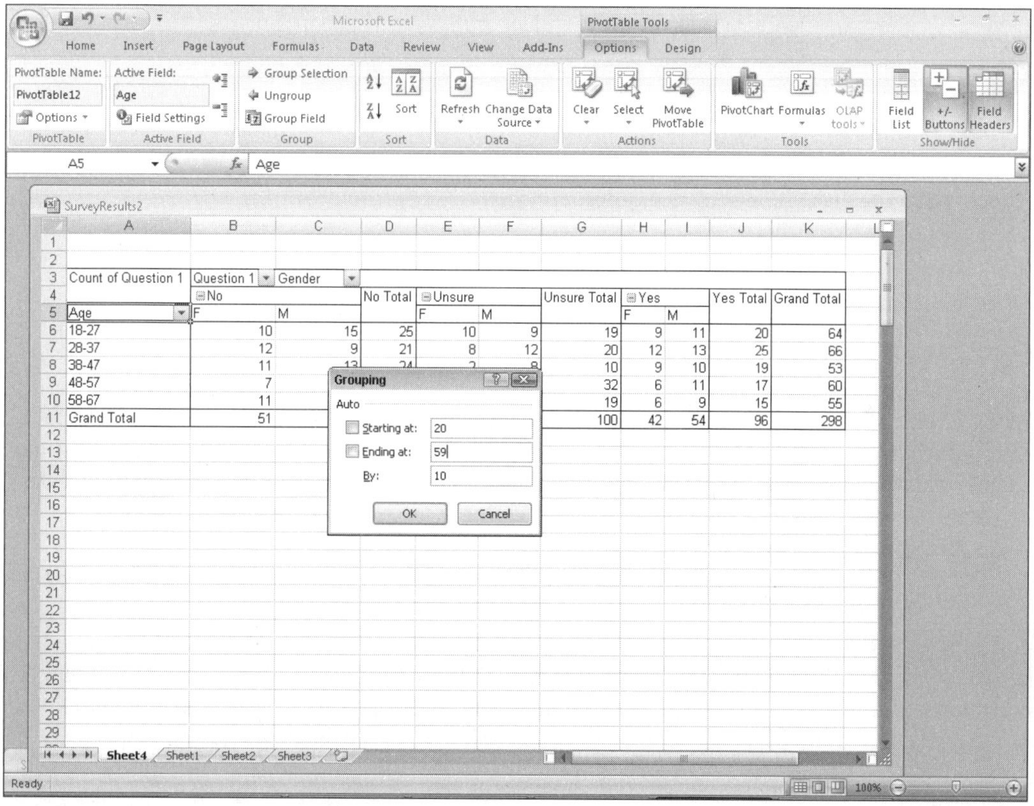

Figure 5-21: Setting numeric field group options manually.

When you click OK, the PivotTable changes, as shown in Figure 5-22. The PivotTable now displays six groups:

- One group labeled <20 for all ages below the Starting At value.

- Four groups for the age groups 20–29, 30–39, and so on.

- One group labeled >60 for all data above the Ending At value.

	A	B	C	D	E	F	G	H	I	J	K
1											
2											
3	Count of Question 1	Question 1	Gender								
4		No		No Total	Unsure		Unsure Total	Yes		Yes Total	Grand Total
5	Age	F	M		F	M		F	M		
6	<20		3	3	1	3	4	3	2	5	12
7	20-29	16	13	29	11	7	18	10	10	20	67
8	30-39	7	13	20	7	14	21	9	17	26	67
9	40-49	10	8	18	1	7	8	8	6	14	40
10	50-59	11	5	16	13	21	34	7	15	22	72
11	>60	7	9	16	11	4	15	5	4	9	40
12	Grand Total	51	51	102	44	56	100	42	54	96	298
13											

Figure 5-22: The PivotTable after the group options have been set manually.

Grouping Dates

When a field contains dates, you can define groups based on essentially any measurement ranging from seconds up to years. Remember, in Excel the term *date* refers to data that can specify a date, a time, or both. You can create a single grouping, such as by grouping dates by weeks, or you can create more than one level of grouping, such as by grouping dates by years and then within years by quarters.

When a field contains date data, the Grouping dialog box looks as it does in Figure 5-23.

At the top of this dialog box are Starting At and Ending At options. These options are turned on by default and, as with numeric data, the starting and ending dates (or times) are determined automatically by Excel. In most instances you will leave these unchanged.

The By list contains all the intervals by which you can group: seconds through years. Click an interval to select it; click again to deselect. You can select one or more intervals.

Depending on the interval or intervals selected, the Number Of option may be available. When it is, you enter a value to determine the size of the grouping. For example, if you select Days as the interval you can enter **5** to create groups of five days.

For an illustration, look at the PivotTable report in Figure 5-24. It shows survey data organized by date in the Row area. The survey was administered on three days in 2005 and again, to different people, on three days about a year later.

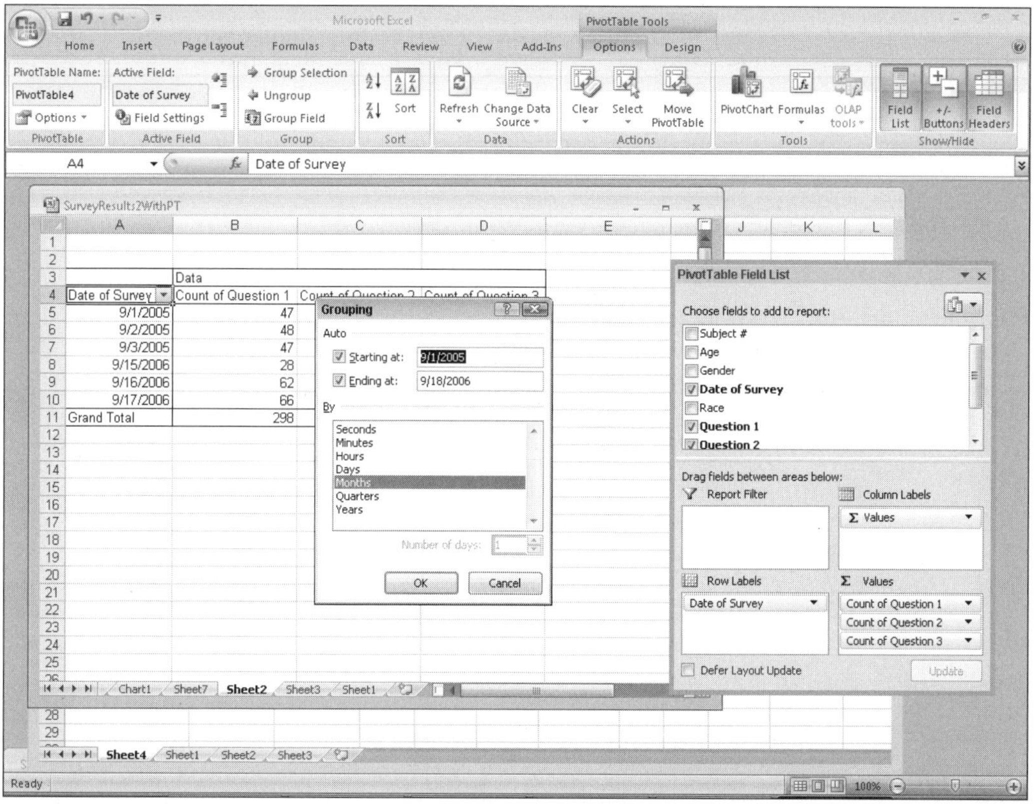

Figure 5-23: Setting grouping options for a field that contains date data.

Count of Question 1	Question 1			
Date of Survey	No	Unsure	Yes	Grand Total
9/1/2005	22	15	10	47
9/2/2005	12	18	18	48
9/3/2005	16	13	18	47
9/15/2006	9	13	6	28
9/16/2006	21	20	21	62
9/17/2006	22	21	23	66
Grand Total	102	100	96	298

Figure 5-24: Survey data organized by date.

To create groups for these data, display the Grouping dialog box for the Date of Survey field, select Years as the interval. The resulting grouped PivotTable is shown in Figure 5-25, and is certainly easier to read that when the dates are not grouped.

	A	B	C	D	E	F
1						
2						
3	Count of Question 1		Question 1 ▾			
4	Years ▾	Date of Survey ▾	No	Unsure	Yes	Grand Total
5	⊟2005	Sep	50	46	46	142
6	⊟2006	Sep	52	54	50	156
7	Grand Total		102	100	96	298
8						

Figure 5-25: The Date of Survey field after being grouped.

You can use the Starting At and Ending At options to change the way groups are formed. They work like these same options for numeric data, as described in the previous section. By turning off the Starting At option you create a group for all dates that are before the specified date, and by turning off the Ending At option you create a group for all dates that are after the specified date. These groups will not appear, however, if there are no dates before or after the cutoffs.

Grouping Other Items

The category *other items* refers to any data that are not numbers or dates. States, department names, product descriptions, colors, and flavors are just a few examples of this kind of data (sometimes called *category data*). To group this kind of data, click each individual item while holding down Ctrl. When all the items to be grouped have been selected, click the Group Selection button on the Options toolbar. Repeat for additional groups. You'll see how in the next section—you will also see how to create subtotals for the groups you define.

Grouping Category Data

This section shows you how to group category data as well as how to create subtotals for a group, something that Excel does not do automatically. You'll use the data shown in Figure 5-26, which is located in the workbook `SurveyResults2.xlsx`.

The first task is to create the basic PivotTable:

1. Place the cell pointer on any cell in the data range A2:H300.

2. Click the PivotTable button on the Insert ribbon to open the Create PivotTable dialog box.

3. Click OK to close the dialog box and create the blank PivotTable.

4. Add the Race field to the Row Labels area.

5. Add the Question 1 field to the Column Labels area.

6. Drag the Question 1 field to the Values area.

	A	B	C	D	E	F	G	H
2	Subject #	Age	Gender	Date of Survey	Race	Question 1	Question 2	Question 3
3	1	50	M	9/1/2005	Black	No	Yes	Yes
4	2	19	M	9/3/2005	Hispanic	No	Unsure	Unsure
5	3	31	F	9/2/2005	White	Yes	Yes	No
6	4	51	M	9/2/2005	Asian	Yes	No	Yes
7	5	24	F	9/1/2005	White	No	Unsure	Yes
8	6	58	F	9/3/2005	Other	No	Unsure	Yes
9	7	21	F	9/1/2005	Black	No	No	No
10	8	36	M	9/3/2005	White	Unsure	No	Yes
11	9	49	M	9/2/2005	White	Yes	Unsure	No
12	10	55	F	9/2/2005	Asian	No	Unsure	No
13	11	31	M	9/1/2005	White	No	Yes	Unsure
14	12	18	F	9/3/2005	Other	Unsure	Unsure	Unsure
15	13	44	M	9/1/2005	Black	No	Yes	Unsure
16	14	45	M	9/3/2005	White	Yes	Yes	Yes
17	15	39	M	9/2/2005	Black	Unsure	Unsure	No
18	16	52	F	9/2/2005	Hispanic	No	Yes	Unsure
19	17	65	M	9/1/2005	White	No	Yes	No
20	18	42	F	9/3/2005	Asian	Yes	Unsure	No
21	19	19	F	9/1/2005	White	Yes	No	Unsure
22	20	41	F	9/3/2005	Other	No	Yes	Yes
23	21	18	M	9/2/2005	Black	Yes	No	No
24	22	61	M	9/2/2005	White	Yes	Unsure	No
25	23	23	F	9/1/2005	White	No	Yes	Yes
26	24	58	M	9/3/2005	Asian	Yes	No	Yes
27	25	45	F	9/1/2005	White	No	No	No
28	26	35	M	9/3/2005	Other	No	No	Yes
29	27	56	M	9/2/2005	Black	Yes	Yes	No
30	28	30	M	9/2/2005	White	Unsure	Yes	Unsure

Figure 5-26: The survey data that will be used for the PivotTable report.

At this point your PivotTable will look like the one in Figure 5-27. Note how putting the Question 1 field in both the Column Labels and Values areas has given you the desired result—a count of the number of people in each category giving answers of Yes, No, and Unsure.

	A	B	C	D	E
1					
2					
3	Count of Question 1	Question 1 ▾			
4	Race ▾	No	Unsure	Yes	Grand Total
5	Asian	14	20	16	50
6	Black	15	15	16	46
7	Hispanic	11	4	5	20
8	Other	20	13	15	48
9	White	42	48	44	134
10	Grand Total	102	100	96	298
11					

Figure 5-27: The basic PivotTable report displays count totals.

But now you want to look at the data in a new way; you want to compare the results for the White group to the total results for all other groups. This is an ideal situation for grouping: you create a group that contains the Asian, Black, Hispanic, and Other categories. Here's how:

1. Drag the mouse over the cells that contain the labels Asian, Black, Hispanic, and Other to select them. The PivotTable should look like Figure 5-28.

2. Click the Group Selection button on the Options ribbon. Excel groups the selected fields, as shown in Figure 5-29.

	A	B	C	D	E
1					
2					
3	Count of Question 1	Question 1 ▼			
4	Race ▼	No	Unsure	Yes	Grand Total
5	Asian	14	20	16	50
6	Black	15	15	16	46
7	Hispanic	11	4	5	20
8	Other	20	13	15	48
9	White	42	48	44	134
10	Grand Total	102	100	96	298
11					

Figure 5-28: After selecting the fields to be grouped together.

	A	B	C	D	E	F
1						
2						
3	Count of Question 1		Question 1 ▼			
4	Race2 ▼	Race ▼	No	Unsure	Yes	Grand Total
5	⊟Group1	Asian	14	20	16	50
6		Black	15	15	16	46
7		Hispanic	11	4	5	20
8		Other	20	13	15	48
9	⊟White	White	42	48	44	134
10	Grand Total		102	100	96	298
11						

Figure 5-29: The PivotTable after grouping four of the Race items together.

You can see that a group named Group1 has been created, containing the four categories you selected. Note also that another field, called Race2, has in effect been created. This field contains two items: Group1 and White. You can use the Race2 field button to filter the report on these values.

This is okay as far as it goes, but you also want to rename Group1 to something more meaningful and to display subtotals for this group as well. To change the name, click the cell that says Group 1 and type in the new name. You may also want to change the label Race2 by right-clicking the heading, selecting Field Settings from the popup menu, and entering the desired name in the Custom Name box.

To display subtotals, right-click the field Race2 (or whatever you have renamed it to) and select Subtotal Race2 from the popup menu. Now the PivotTable looks like Figure 5-30, with subtotals for each category in the Race2 field.

	A	B	C	D	E	F
1						
2						
3	**Count of Question 1**		Question 1 ⌄			
4	**Race Group** ⌄	Race ⌄	No	Unsure	Yes	Grand Total
5	⊟ Other	Asian	14	20	16	50
6		Black	15	15	16	46
7		Hispanic	11	4	5	20
8		Other	20	13	15	48
9	**Other Total**		60	52	52	164
10	⊟ White	White	42	48	44	134
11	**White Total**		42	48	44	134
12	**Grand Total**		102	100	96	298
13						

Figure 5-30: The PivotTable report with subtotals for the groups.

There's one more thing to do. For this kind of data it is usually better to display percentages. Because the different groups contain different numbers of people, the raw numbers do not tell you much. Each value should show the percentage of people in that category with a particular answer. Here's how to set this up:

1. Right-click a data cell and select Value Field Settings from the pop-up menu to display the Value Field Settings dialog box.

2. On the Show Values As tab, select % of Row.

3. Click the Number Format button and specify no decimal places.

4. Click OK twice.

Finally, click the Grand Totals button on the design ribbon and select On For Columns Only (since the row totals, which are all 100%, are meaningless). The final PivotTable report is shown in Figure 5-31.

	A	B	C	D	E	F
1						
2						
3	**Count of Question 1**		Question 1 ⌄			
4	**Race Group** ⌄	Race ⌄	No	Unsure	Yes	
5	⊟ Other	Asian	28%	40%	32%	
6		Black	33%	33%	35%	
7		Hispanic	55%	20%	25%	
8		Other	42%	27%	31%	
9	**Other Total**		37%	32%	32%	
10	⊟ White	White	31%	36%	33%	
11	**White Total**		31%	36%	33%	
12	**Grand Total**		34%	34%	32%	
13						
14						

Figure 5-31: The PivotTable report with data displayed as the percentage of the row total.

Chapter 6

Understanding and Using PivotCharts

One of the strong points Excel is its charting capabilities. If you can chart regular data in Excel, why not the data in a PivotTable? Indeed you can, and the result is called, appropriately enough, a PivotChart. In many respects, a PivotChart is like any other Excel chart. In some ways, however, it is special, reflecting its link to PivotTable data. In this chapter, you learn to create and use PivotCharts.

In This Chapter

- ◆ Learning about PivotCharts
- ◆ How to create a PivotChart
- ◆ The parts of a PivotChart
- ◆ Using 3-D PivotCharts

Understanding PivotCharts

A PivotChart is a graphical representation of the data in a PivotTable report. Excel has long been known for its excellent charting capabilities. The value of charts is that they let you see trends and relationships that may not be obvious when looking at the data in a tabular form. PivotTables are no different and the data they contain can also benefit from graphical display.

A PivotChart is always based on a PivotTable report. Although you can create a PivotTable without a PivotChart, you cannot do the reverse. They are linked so that changes in the report are always reflected in the chart. In fact, the way to make many changes to a PivotChart is to change the underlying PivotTable report.

Remember that a PivotChart is for the most part just a regular Excel chart that happens to be linked to a PivotTable report. Essentially, anything you can do with a regular chart you can also do with a PivotTable chart, including formatting. This chapter does not describe all of the Excel charting features, just the ones that apply to PivotCharts. If you need a refresher course of Excel chart basics, turn to Appendix C.

Creating a PivotChart

You can create a PivotChart from an existing PivotTable or you can create the PivotChart at the same time you create the PivotTable.

Creating a PivotChart from an Existing PivotTable

If you have already created the PivotTable report, creating a PivotChart is almost a one-click operation. With the PivotTable report active, simply click the PivotChart button on the Options ribbon. Excel displays the Insert Chart dialog box, shown in Figure 6-1. Select the desired chart type and style and click OK. The new PivotChart will be added to the same worksheet where the PivotTable is located.

Figure 6-1: Selecting the chart type and style for a PivotChart.

Creating a PivotChart from Scratch

If you have not created the PivotTable yet, you can create the PivotChart from scratch. To be more precise, you create the PivotTable and PivotChart at the same time. To do so, click the arrow below the PivotTable button on the Insert ribbon and select PivotChart to open the Create PivotTable with PivotChart dialog box, shown in Figure 6-2.

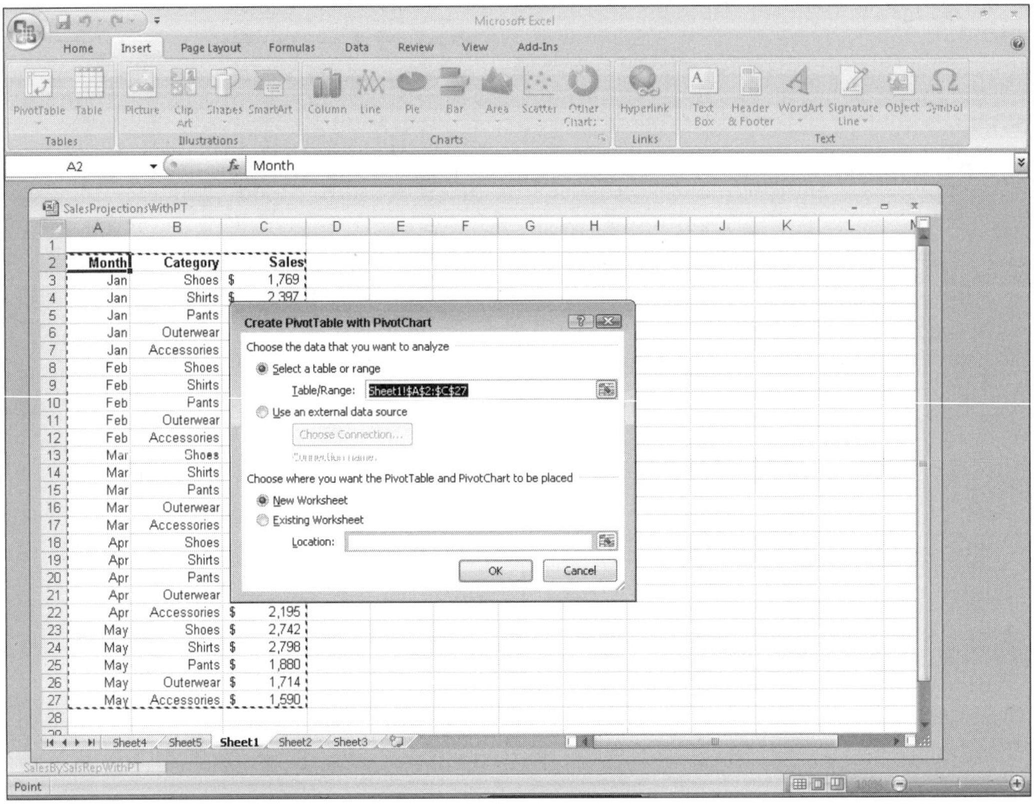

Figure 6-2: Creating a PivotTable and PivotChart at the same time.

Except for its title, this dialog box is exactly the same as the Create PivotTable dialog box discussed in Chapter 2. Specify the data source and the location for the PivotTable and click OK—the PivotTable is created as usual and the PivotChart is created in the same worksheet. Both are initially blank, and the PivotChart Filter Pane is displayed as shown in Figure 6-3. You'll learn how to use the PivotChart Filter Pane later in this chapter.

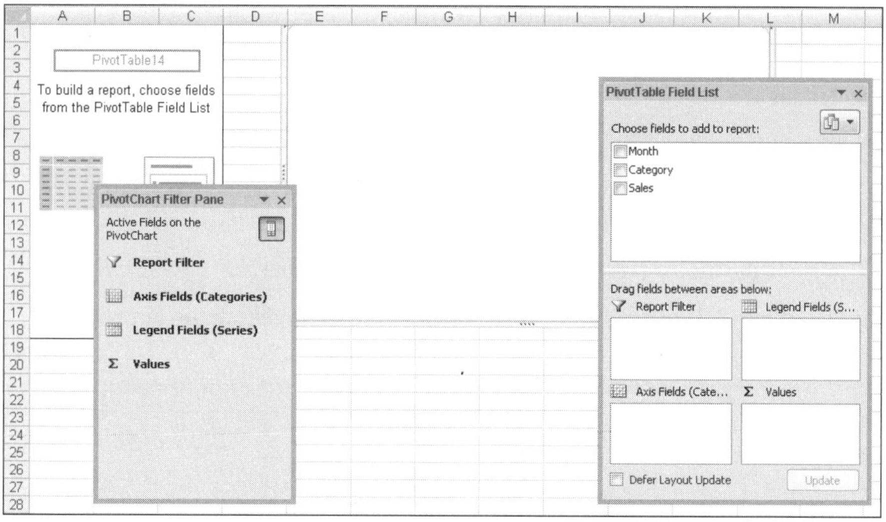

Figure 6-3: After creating a new PivotTable and PivotChart together.

Creating a PivotTable and PivotChart Together

This section takes you through the steps of creating a PivotTable and PivotChart at the same time, without an existing PivotTable. You use the data in SportingGoodsRawData.xlsx. You used these data in Chapter 5; they are shown again in Figure 6-4.

Store	Region	Date	Customers	Total Sales	Camping	Fitness	Soccer	Baseball	Fishing	Football
2134	Northeast	01-Mar-07	207	$ 6,581	$ 326	$ 1,284	$ 970	$ 1,270	$ 1,488	$ 1,243
2134	Northeast	02-Mar-07	162	$ 3,584	$ 901	$ 247	$ 765	$ 1,251	$ 228	$ 192
2134	Northeast	03-Mar-07	188	$ 4,713	$ 837	$ 1,260	$ 959	$ 765	$ 179	$ 713
2134	Northeast	04-Mar-07	171	$ 5,263	$ 553	$ 1,134	$ 236	$ 1,353	$ 1,011	$ 976
2134	Northeast	05-Mar-07	64	$ 4,731	$ 775	$ 294	$ 1,480	$ 160	$ 864	$ 1,158
2134	Northeast	06-Mar-07	246	$ 3,853	$ 429	$ 853	$ 773	$ 760	$ 739	$ 299
2134	Northeast	07-Mar-07	63	$ 6,077	$ 1,075	$ 1,418	$ 659	$ 1,445	$ 1,340	$ 140
2918	Northeast	01-Mar-07	89	$ 775	$ 294	$ 1,480	$ 160	$ 864	$ 1,158	$ 990
2918	Northeast	02-Mar-07	132	$ 429	$ 853	$ 773	$ 760	$ 739	$ 299	$ 659
2918	Northeast	03-Mar-07	90	$ 1,075	$ 1,418	$ 659	$ 1,445	$ 1,340	$ 140	$ 325
2918	Northeast	04-Mar-07	145	$ 1,330	$ 459	$ 314	$ 1,119	$ 149	$ 447	$ 343
2918	Northeast	05-Mar-07	213	$ 456	$ 426	$ 368	$ 1,045	$ 1,453	$ 1,175	$ 254
2918	Northeast	06-Mar-07	98	$ 1,061	$ 729	$ 211	$ 939	$ 939	$ 1,205	$ 645
2918	Northeast	07-Mar-07	78	$ 1,191	$ 341	$ 123	$ 1,293	$ 300	$ 269	$ 126
2298	Midwest	01-Mar-07	86	$ 4,075	$ 866	$ 399	$ 270	$ 690	$ 418	$ 1,432
2298	Midwest	02-Mar-07	234	$ 3,933	$ 1,056	$ 266	$ 781	$ 131	$ 1,376	$ 323
2298	Midwest	03-Mar-07	286	$ 3,818	$ 1,330	$ 459	$ 314	$ 1,119	$ 149	$ 447
2298	Midwest	04-Mar-07	99	$ 4,923	$ 456	$ 426	$ 368	$ 1,045	$ 1,453	$ 1,175
2298	Midwest	05-Mar-07	85	$ 5,084	$ 1,061	$ 729	$ 211	$ 939	$ 939	$ 1,205
2298	Midwest	06-Mar-07	218	$ 3,517	$ 1,191	$ 341	$ 123	$ 1,293	$ 300	$ 269
2298	Midwest	07-Mar-07	124	$ 4,435	$ 998	$ 581	$ 350	$ 1,249	$ 295	$ 962
2300	Midwest	01-Mar-07	132	$ 1,995	$ 615	$ 1,623	$ 370	$ 2,065	$ 8,625	$ 1,957
2300	Midwest	02-Mar-07	90	$ 612	$ 709	$ 878	$ 1,218	$ 656	$ 5,902	$ 1,829
2300	Midwest	03-Mar-07	145	$ 1,099	$ 1,804	$ 1,005	$ 1,509	$ 771	$ 8,032	$ 1,844
2300	Midwest	04-Mar-07	213	$ 1,470	$ 1,430	$ 787	$ 2,074	$ 1,114	$ 7,786	$ 911
2300	Midwest	05-Mar-07	98	$ 2,092	$ 364	$ 1,793	$ 502	$ 1,541	$ 7,669	$ 1,377
2300	Midwest	06-Mar-07	78	$ 360	$ 655	$ 522	$ 559	$ 1,914	$ 5,211	$ 1,201

Figure 6-4: The raw data on sporting goods sales.

Follow these steps to simultaneously create the PivotTable and PivotChart:

1. Place the cell pointer on any cell in the data range.

2. Click the arrow below the PivotTable button on the Insert ribbon.

3. Select PivotChart from the menu to open the Create PivotTable with PivotChart dialog box.

4. Click OK to close the dialog box and create the blank PivotTable and PivotChart.

5. Close the PivotChart Filter Pane by clicking the X in the top right corner. Your screen should now resemble Figure 6-5.

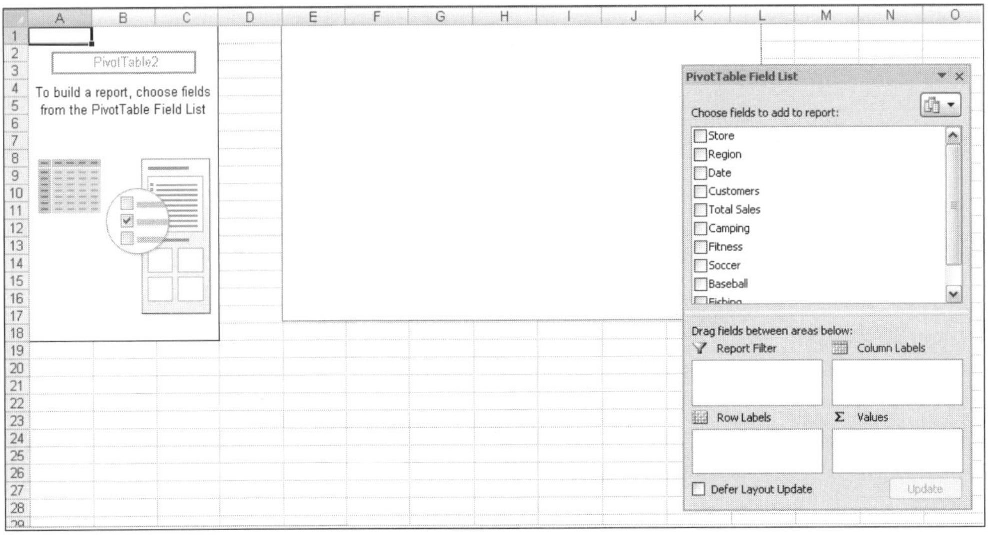

Figure 6-5: The blank PivotTable and PivotChart before any fields are added.

6. Click the blank PivotTable to make sure it is active.

7. Add the Camping field to the Values area.

8. Add the Date field to the Row Labels area.

9. Add the Region field to the Column Labels area.

At this point the PivotChart will look like Figure 6-6. I have hidden the Field List to make the entire chart visible, and I have dragged the PivotChart so that it does not overlap the PivotTable.

Changing a PivotChart to a Static Chart

To change a PivotChart to a static chart, one that is no longer linked to the data source, delete the underlying PivotTable report. To delete the PivotTable:

1. Drag over the PivotTable to select all its cells.

2. Press Delete.

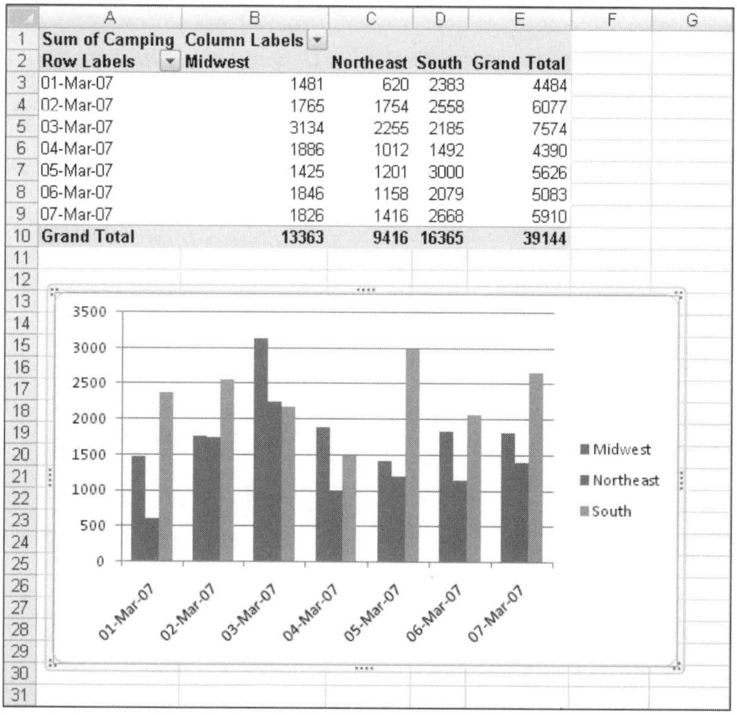

	A	B	C	D	E	F	G
1	Sum of Camping	Column Labels ▾					
2	Row Labels ▾	Midwest	Northeast	South	Grand Total		
3	01-Mar-07	1481	620	2383	4484		
4	02-Mar-07	1765	1754	2558	6077		
5	03-Mar-07	3134	2255	2185	7574		
6	04-Mar-07	1886	1012	1492	4390		
7	05-Mar-07	1425	1201	3000	5626		
8	06-Mar-07	1846	1158	2079	5083		
9	07-Mar-07	1826	1416	2668	5910		
10	Grand Total	13363	9416	16365	39144		

Figure 6-6: After creating the PivotTable and PivotChart.

After you create a PivotChart, you must always remember that it is linked to the PivotTable report. Changes that you make to the report will be reflected in the chart. For example, if you change the number display format of a value field in the report, that format change will carry over to the labels in the PivotChart.

NOTE

In previous versions of Excel, PivotCharts had a lot of the same customization features as did PivotTables. You could work on the chart and see the changes reflected in the PivotTable, or vice versa. In Excel 2007, things have been simplified. Except for applying filters and grouping, which you can do on the chart or on the report, all changes are made to the PivotTable and are then reflected in the chart automatically.

Understanding the Parts of a Chart

Before I go into more detail about creating and using PivotCharts, you should be sure you understand the Excel chart terminology. Let's look at the following frequently used terms, which are referenced in the chart shown in Figure 6-7:

- **Plot area**—Where the actual data are displayed.

- **Data series**—The chart elements corresponding to one related group of numbers. In a PivotChart, this refers to a column of numbers, although in regular (non-pivot) charts it can also refer to a row.

- **Category axis**—Lists the values of the data categories.

- **Data series axis**—Identifies the individual data series. Relevant only for 3-D charts.

- **Value axis**—Displays a scale of values for the data points.

- **Chart title**—The title of the chart.

- **Axis labels**—Titles for the individual axes.

- **Legend**—Identifies the data series by color and/or pattern.

Some of these chart elements are options and are not present in all charts, namely the chart and axis titles and the legend.

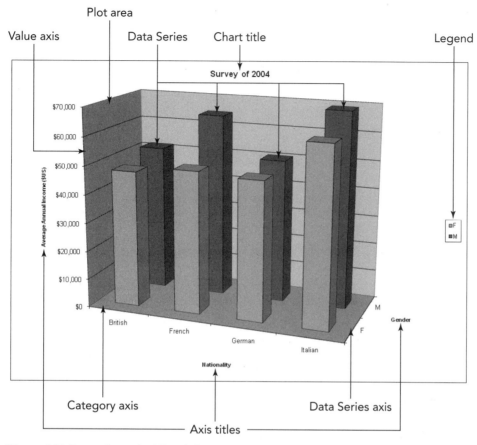

Figure 6-7: Parts of a typical Excel chart.

Working with the PivotChart Ribbon

When a PivotChart is active, Excel displays four ribbons that you use to work with the chart. Three of these ribbons, Design, Layout, and Format, are related to all Excel charts, not just PivotCharts. You use them to do things such as change the chart type, apply chart styles, work with axis titles, and change fonts used on the chart. Because these tools are not PivotChart-specific, they are for the most part not covered in this chapter. Please refer to Appendix C if you want to brush up on Excel chart basics.

The fourth ribbon is the Analyze ribbon, and it is displayed only when a PivotChart is active. This ribbon is shown in Figure 6-8. The elements on the ribbon are:

- **Active Field**—Lists the name of the currently active field (if there is one).

- **Expand/Collapse Entire Field**—Used to show or hide detail in the chart. This has the same effect has expanding or collapsing fields in the PivotTable report as was covered in Chapter 5.

- **Refresh**—Displays a menu from which you can refresh the PivotTable and PivotChart, refresh all PivotTables in the workbook, view refresh status, or cancel the refresh.

- **Clear**—Displays a menu from which you can select one of the following commands:

  - **Clear All**—Removes all fields from the PivotTable (and PivotChart), the PivotTable is then ready to add new fields from the Pivot Table Field List.

  - **Clear Filters**—Removes any filters that have been applied to the PivotTable and PivotChart.

- **Field List**—Click to hide or display the Field List.

- **PivotChart Filter**—Click to hide or display the PivotChart Filter dialog box.

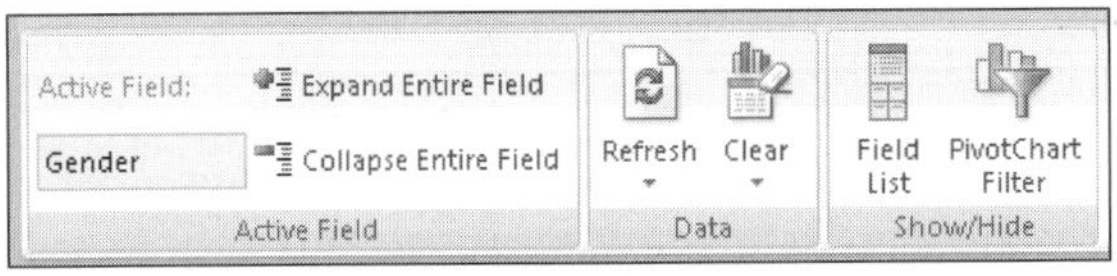

Figure 6-8: The Analyze ribbon contains PivotChart-specific commands.

Understanding and Changing PivotChart Types

Unless you changed the default settings, Excel is set to create a new PivotChart as a column chart. After the chart has been created, you can change its type to almost any one of Excel chart types, and you can also use the program's capability to define your own custom types. (One restriction is that the XY (Scatter), Bubble, and Stock types cannot be used for PivotCharts.) It's easy to try out the different chart types and see which one best suits your data.

To change the chart type of a PivotChart:

1. Right-click the chart and select Change Chart Type from the popup menu. Excel displays the Change Chart Type dialog box (see Figure 6-9). You can also display this dialog box by clicking the Change Chart Type button on the Design ribbon.

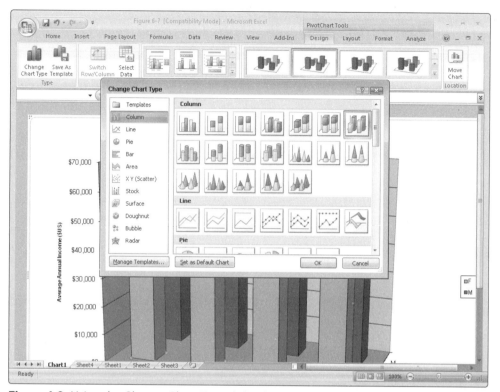

Figure 6-9: Using the Change Chart Type dialog box to change the type of a PivotChart.

2. Click the desired chart type in the list on the left.

3. Click the desired subtype in the gallery on the right. (Some custom charts do not offer subtypes.)

4. Click OK to accept the selected type and apply it to the PivotChart.

You can change a chart's type as many times as you want without affecting its data or other formatting.

Returning to Default Formatting

Certain aspects of a chart's formatting, such as colors and patterns, can be changed independently of the chart type. Such format changes are normally retained when you change the chart type. If you want to discard any custom formatting and return the chart to the default formatting, right-click the chart and select Reset to Match Style from the popup menu.

> ### Changing the Default Chart Type
>
> You can change the default Excel chart type from stacked column to another type by displaying the Chart Type dialog box, selecting the desired chart type and subtype, and clicking the Set as Default Chart button.

Understanding a PivotChart's Structure

Excel follows certain rules when creating a PivotChart. These rules determine how the PivotTable data are arranged in the chart—which categories are placed on which axis, how data series are defined, and so on. You want to have a good understanding of these rules to create PivotCharts with the structure you want. In this section you look at some examples.

A Simple PivotChart

The PivotTable shown in Figure 6-10 is about as simple as it gets. It consists of only one row field and one column of data (the value field).

3		
4	Sum of Value	Column ▼
5	Row ▼	Students
6	Biology	258
7	Chemistry	173
8	Ecology	159
9	Geology	269
10	Marine Biology	227
11	Physics	342
12	Grand Total	1428
13		

Figure 6-10: A PivotTable that contains one row field and one value field.

When you create a PivotChart from this table you get a chart like the one shown in Figure 6-11. You can see that each data value in the row field becomes an item on the chart's horizontal (category) axis.

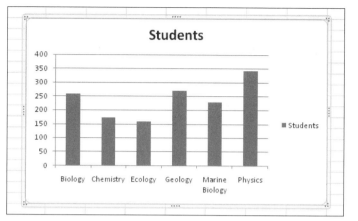

Figure 6-11: A PivotChart created from the PivotTable in Figure 6-10.

Suppose you had created the PivotTable with a column field instead of a row field. The PivotTable and PivotChart would now look as shown in Figure 6-12. Now there is only one item on the horizontal axis and the different column fields are represented by different colored bars. In Excel chart terminology, each column field is a data series in the chart.

	A	B	C	D	E	F	G	H
1								
2								
3								
4		Column ▾	Row ▾					
5		⊟Students						Students Total
6		Biology	Chemistry	Ecology	Geology	Marine Biology	Physics	
7	Sum of Value	258	173	159	269	227	342	1428
8								
9								

Figure 6-12: The same PivotTable as in Figure 6-10 with a column field instead of a row field, and the resulting PivotChart.

You see from this example that a PivotChart plots row fields as categories and column fields as data series.

PivotCharts and Moving Fields

When a PivotChart is active, you can still move data fields between the various areas using the Field List. However, the areas in the Field List and the menu that Excel displays when you click a field name are slightly different when a PivotChart is active. The Move to Column Labels command is replaced by the Move to Legend Fields command, and the Move to Row Labels command is replaced by the Move to Axis Fields command. This makes perfect sense because, in the PivotChart, column fields are represented as legend fields (data series) row fields are represented as axis fields. The end result is exactly the same.

A PivotChart with Two Row Fields

The PivotTable shown in Figure 6-13 has some added complexity, with its two row fields. The data themselves are simple, consisting only of a single number for each row.

	A	B	C
1			
2			
3	Gender	Values	
4	Female	Average	85.3
5		Maximum	99
6		Minimum	70
7	Male	Average	84.4
8		Maximum	98
9		Minimum	70
10			

Figure 6-13: A PivotTable that contains two row fields.

A PivotChart created from this PivotTable is shown in Figure 6-14. Note how the PivotChart handles the two row fields. The outer row field, Gender, has two values, Male and Female. These values are represented on the lower level of the horizontal axis. The inner row field, Data, has three values: Average, Maximum, and Minimum, which are represented on the upper level of the horizontal axis. The result is two groups of three bars: one for males and one for females.

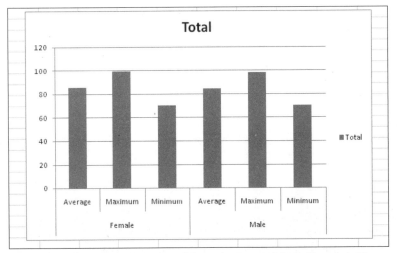

Figure 6-14: A PivotChart created from the PivotTable in Figure 6-13.

Suppose you want to reorganize the chart to make it easier to compare the results for males and females for each of the three measures. You need to go to the underlying PivotTable and move the Gender field to the inner row position. The PivotTable will then look like Figure 6-15.

	A	B	C
1			
2			
3	Values	Gender ▾	
4	Average	Female	85.3
5		Male	84.4
6	Maximum	Female	99
7		Male	98
8	Minimum	Female	70
9		Male	70
10			

Figure 6-15: The PivotTable with the Gender field in the inner row position.

Because the PivotChart is linked, it automatically updates to reflect the change and will now appear as in Figure 6-16.

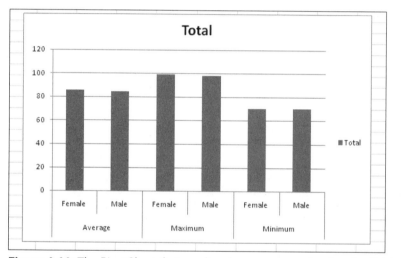

Figure 6-16: The PivotChart that results when you move the Gender field to the inner row position.

Another possibility with this PivotTable report is to make the Gender field a column field and leave Values as the row field. The resulting PivotTable and PivotChart are shown in Figures 6-17 and 6-18 respectively. The PivotChart now lists only the Data field on the horizontal axis and represents the Gender field by separate bar—that is, separate data series. I do not think that this arrangement is particularly useful for these data, but it does illustrate another way in which a PivotChart changes when you modify the underlying PivotTable.

⊿	A	B	C
1			
2			
3		Gender ▾	
4	**Values**	**Female**	**Male**
5	Average	85.3	84.4
6	Maximum	99	98
7	Minimum	70	70
8			

Figure 6-17: The PivotTable with the Gender field in the Column Labels area.

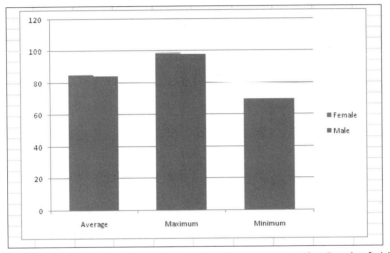

Figure 6-18: The PivotChart that results when you move the Gender field to the Column Labels area.

A PivotChart with Two Column Fields

When a PivotTable has more than one column field, the PivotChart handles it a bit differ-ently from when there are multiple row fields. Whereas row fields become items on the horizontal axis, column fields become data series. When there are two column fields, Excel creates a data series for each combination of field values.

Figure 6-19 shows a PivotTable report with two column fields. One field has two values: M and F. The other field has three values: Yes, No, and Unsure.

	A	B	C	D	E	F	G	H	I	J
1										
2										
3	Count of Question 1	Question 1	Gender							
4		No		No Total	Unsure		Unsure Total	Yes		Yes Total
5	Age	F	M		F	M		F	M	
6	<20		3	3	1	3	4	3	2	5
7	20-29	16	13	29	11	7	18	10	10	20
8	30-39	7	13	20	7	14	21	9	17	26
9	40-49	10	8	18	1	7	8	8	6	14
10	50-59	11	5	16	13	21	34	7	15	22
11	>60	7	9	16	11	4	15	5	4	9
12										

Figure 6-19: A PivotTable report with two column fields.

When you create a PivotChart from this report, as shown in Figure 6-20, Excel creates six data series: M-Yes, M-No, M-Unsure, and so on. The single row field, Age, is represented by categories on the horizontal axis, as you would expect.

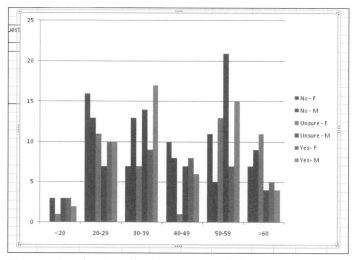

Figure 6-20: The PivotChart based on the PivotTable report in Figure 6-19.

When your PivotTable gets relatively complex, you can take advantage of Excel's three-dimensional chart types, which have features for clearly displaying more fields. The next section provides a step-by-step example of creating this kind of PivotChart.

Creating a 3-D PivotChart

The extra visual dimension that 3-D charts provide is often just what you need to create a clear graphical presentation of your PivotTable data. In this section, you work through an example of creating a 3-D PivotChart. The source data, which are the results of a survey about educational level and income, are shown in Figure 6-21. You'll find them in the workbook SurveyResults3.xlsx.

	A	B	C	D	E	F
2	ID	Gender	Nationality	Years Education	Annual Income	
3	1	M	German	17	$ 76,955	
4	2	F	British	18	$ 84,863	
5	3	M	Italian	19	$ 32,546	
6	4	M	German	9	$ 63,833	
7	5	F	French	19	$ 89,371	
8	6	F	British	6	$ 46,177	
9	7	F	French	6	$ 19,492	
10	8	M	Italian	13	$ 69,064	
11	9	F	German	12	$ 26,478	
12	10	F	British	9	$ 82,230	
13	11	M	Italian	6	$ 83,753	
14	12	M	German	12	$ 96,387	
15	13	M	French	11	$ 63,572	
16	14	F	British	6	$ 54,008	
17	15	M	French	9	$ 61,860	
18	16	M	Italian	10	$ 30,326	
19	17	F	Italian	16	$ 63,316	
20	18	F	German	16	$ 54,966	
21	19	F	French	9	$ 41,126	
22	20	M	British	14	$ 34,301	
23	21	F	French	8	$ 87,024	
24	22	M	Italian	8	$ 46,174	
25	23	M	German	20	$ 47,924	
26	24	F	British	11	$ 98,430	
27	25	F	Italian	17	$ 64,973	
28	26	F	German	14	$ 80,141	
29	27	M	French	11	$ 49,985	
30	28	F	British	10	$ 30,334	

Sheet4 / Sheet6 / **Sheet1** / Sheet2 / Sheet3

Figure 6-21: The survey data that will be used for this example.

Follow these steps to begin the example exercise:

1. Put the cell pointer on any cell in the data range.

2. Click the arrow below the PivotTable button on the insert menu and select PivotChart from the menu. Excel opens the Create PivotTable with PivotChart dialog box.

3. Click OK to close the dialog box and create the blank PivotTable and PivotChart.

4. Add the Gender field to the Row Labels (Axis Fields) area.

5. Add the Nationality field to the Column Labels (Legend Fields) area.

6. Add the Annual Income field to the Values area.

At this point the PivotTable and PivotChart look like Figure 6-22. There are three problems with it. First, the data show the sum of Annual Income, not the average, which is what you want. Second, the data are not displayed with currency format. Finally, the chart is still in 2-D format.

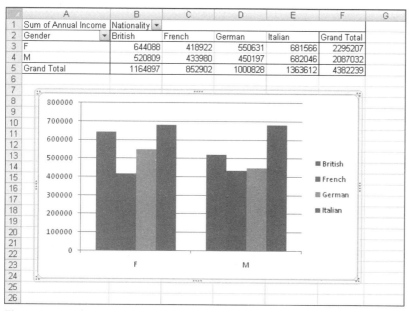

	A	B	C	D	E	F	G
1	Sum of Annual Income	Nationality ▼					
2	Gender ▼	British	French	German	Italian	Grand Total	
3	F	644088	418922	550631	681566	2295207	
4	M	520809	433980	450197	682046	2087032	
5	Grand Total	1164897	852902	1000828	1363612	4382239	
6							

Figure 6-22: The initial PivotTable and PivotChart.

Follow these steps to fix things:

1. Right-click the Sum of Annual Income cell in the PivotTable report and select Value Field Settings from the popup menu. Excel opens the Value Field Settings dialog box.

2. In the Summarize value field by list, click Average.

3. Click the Number Format button to display the Format Cells dialog box.

4. Select Currency format with no decimal places.

5. Click OK twice to return to the worksheet.

6. Right-click the PivotChart and select Change Chart Type from the popup menu. Excel opens the Change Chart Type dialog box.

7. Select the 3-D column chart sub-type as shown in Figure 6-23.

8. Click OK.

Select this sub-type

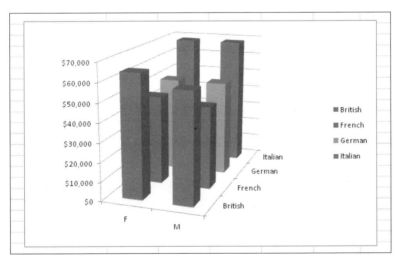

Figure 6-23: Selecting the 3-D column chart sub-type.

At this point, the PivotChart correctly displays the average of Annual Income, and the vertical axis numbers are formatted as currency (see Figure 6-24). The 3-D chart style makes it easier to interpret the data than if a 2-D style had been used.

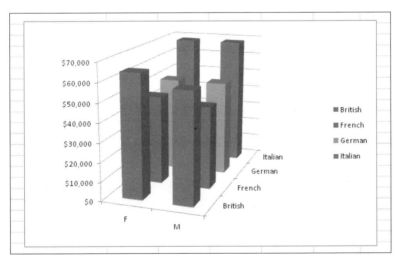

Figure 6-24: The 3-D column PivotChart displaying average income.

This looks pretty good, but there are a few cosmetic improvements that can still be made. For example, the legend is not needed because the nationality groups are identified on the 3-D chart axis. Also, it would be nice to have an axis label identifying the data that are plotted. Here are the steps to follow:

1. Click the PivotChart to make sure it is active.

2. Display the Layout ribbon.

3. Click the Legend button and select None from the menu.

4. Click the Axis Titles button and select Primary Vertical Axis Title from the menu.

5. On the next menu, select Rotated Title. Excel inserts a title that says Axis Title next to the vertical axis.

6. Click the title and enter the title **Average Annual Income**.

7. Click anywhere outside the title to accept your edits.

The final PivotChart is shown in Figure 6-25. By arranging the PivotTable fields correctly—one row field and one column field—and by using a 3-D chart type, you were able to create a PivotChart that displays the data in a clear and concise manner.

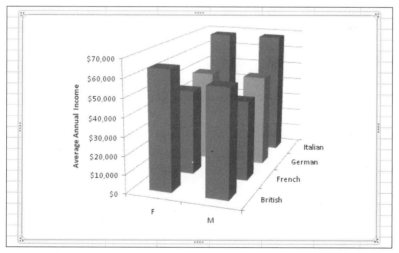

Figure 6-25: The completed 3-D PivotChart.

Using the PivotChart Filter Pane

When a PivotChart is active, you can display the PivotChart Filter Pane by clicking the PivotChart Filter button on the Analyze ribbon. The Filter Pane is shown in Figure 6-26. It lists the axis fields (that is, row fields), legend fields (column fields), and value fields. It also lists report filter fields if any are defined for the PivotTable.

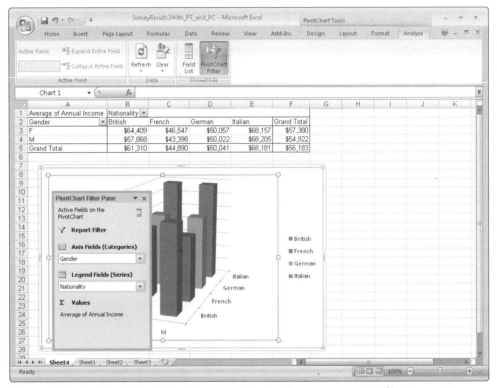

Figure 6-26: The PivotChart Filter Pane provides quick access to report filtering options.

The filtering and sorting capabilities that the Filter Pane provides are exactly the same as those available in the PivotTable report itself. When you are working on a PivotChart, using the Filter Pane may be more convenient. Click the arrow next to an axis, legend, or report filter field and you'll see the menu shown in Figure 6-27. For a detailed explanation of the commands on this menu, refer to Chapter 4.

Figure 6-27: Filtering and sorting options available from the Filter Pane.

Part II

Part III

Getting the Most out of PivotTables and Charts

Chapter 7

Using PivotTables with Multidimensional Data

Excel PivotTables give you the ability to work with multidimensional data. In fact, it is not uncommon to come across analysis tasks that require multidimensional data; there's just no other way to approach them. To truly master PivotTables, you must understand what multidimensional data are and how they are used. These are the topics of this chapter.

In This Chapter

- ◆ Understanding multidimensional data
- ◆ Creating a PivotTable from an online cube file
- ◆ Creating an offline cube file
- ◆ Working with OLAP-based PivotTables

Using Multidimensional Data

Before getting to the *what* of multidimensional data, you will find it useful to look at the *why*. So far this book has used small data sources that consisted of a single table in an Excel worksheet (or in some cases an Access database). For clarity of presentation, I have deliberately kept these data sources small— consisting of maybe a hundred rows of data at most. Of course real-world data are almost always a lot larger, but Excel can handle it—right? Let's take a look.

Some Other Terms

Multidimensional data are sometimes referred to as *hierarchical data* or *OLAP data* even though these terms don't mean precisely the same thing. Multidimensional data may or may not actually contain hierarchies and they may or may not reside on an OLAP server or data warehouse. When you come across the other two terms, it's a good idea to determine precisely what they mean.

Excel used to be limited to 65,535 rows and 256 columns of data in a single worksheet. With Excel 2007 those limits have increased to 1,048,576 rows and 16,384 columns. It sounds like a lot, but it really isn't. Compared with the data needs of modern businesses and organizations, it's a drop in the bucket. Databases consisting of millions of records are not uncommon, and PivotTables can be a useful tool for analyzing them. Consider sales records for a large online retailer, inventory for a major manufacturing concern, or demographic data kept by an insurance company. These and other data sources are well beyond the capabilities of Excel.

PivotTables and PivotCharts themselves also have some limitations:

- 256 page fields
- 256 value fields
- 256 data series in a PivotChart

These limitations would seem to put the analysis of large data sets beyond the realm of Excel and PivotTables. The fact is that huge data sets place severe demands on any analysis tool and can result in processing times of several hours or more. To deal with this challenge, programmers have developed a set of tools called Online Analytical Processing, or OLAP. OLAP is designed to work with hierarchical raw data, organizing and summarizing them in a multidimensional form. When your analysis program, such as Excel, accesses the data it is actually accessing the OLAP summaries and not the raw data themselves. In other words, OLAP does most of the analysis grunt work so that the final analysis program—Excel or whatever—doesn't have to.

Understanding Multidimensional Data

Before you can start using Excel PivotTables with multidimensional data, you need to understand exactly what they are. You can best do this by looking at multidimensional data in relation to two other kinds of data, flat data and relational data. Multidimensional data are the most complex of these types. Let's start with the simplest and work up.

Flat Data

Flat data, sometimes called *non-relational data*, are the kind of data that most people are accustomed to working with. For example, the raw data used in all the previous parts are flat data. The defining characteristic of flat data is that all the information is contained in a single table—one set of rows (records) and columns (fields). Figure 7-1 shows an example of a flat parts inventory database. Each record contains full information for a particular part—the part name and number, its wholesale cost, and the name and address of the supplier.

	A	B	C	D	E	F	G	H	I
1	Part_Num	Description	WholesaleCost	Supplier_Name	Supplier Address	Supplier_City	Supplier_Stat	Supplier_Phone	
2	Q123	Cotter pin	$ 0.56	Wilson Mfg.	12 Oak Street	Cleveland	OH	555-666-7777	
3	L12-45	Hex nut	$ 0.90	Trumbill Machine	1244 Park Way	Atlanta	GA	111-222-3333	
4	ZS-5667	Axle bolt	$ 1.25	Parts Unltd.	15-A West End Ave.	Albany	NY	333-444-5555	
5	F-445566	Washer Asst	$ 2.50	Wilson Mfg.	12 Oak Street	Cleveland	OH	555-666-7777	
6	LK-13224	Allen bolt	$ 1.78	Parts Unltd.	15-A West End Ave.	Albany	NY	333-444-5555	
7	D-990-a	Punch	$ 4.55	Parts Unltd.	15-A West End Ave.	Albany	NY	333-444-5555	
8	S-4500	Hinge	$ 0.98	Trumbill Machine	1244 Park Way	Atlanta	GA	111-222-3333	
9	DF-555-g	Pulley	$ 3.38	Wilson Mfg.	12 Oak Street	Cleveland	OH	555-666-7777	
10									

Figure 7-1: A flat data source contains all the information in one table.

In Figure 7-1 each supplier's information is present more than once. This causes several problems. First it is an inefficient use of storage space to keep the same information in more than one location. Second, updating a supplier's information—for example, if the address changes—will require changes in multiple locations and introduce the possibility of errors. Finally, there is the possibility of completely deleting a supplier from the database when you do not want to, if, for example, all of that supplier's parts are deleted. To avoid these problems, *relational databases* were devised.

Relational Data

A relational database keeps related data in separate tables. Records in the two tables are linked by a *key field* that defines which record(s) in one table are associated with which record(s) in the other table. Figure 7-2 shows the same data from Figure 7-1 in a relational database.

	A	B	C	D	E	F	G
1	Part_Num	Description	WholesaleCost	Supplier_ID			
2	Q123	Cotter pin	$ 0.56	1			
3	L12-45	Hex nut	$ 0.90	2			
4	ZS-5667	Axle bolt	$ 1.25	3			
5	F-445566	Washer Asst	$ 2.50	1			
6	LK-13224	Allen bolt	$ 1.78	3			
7	D-990-a	Punch	$ 4.55	3			
8	S-4500	Hinge	$ 0.98	2			
9	DF-555-g	Pulley	$ 3.38	1			
10							
11							
12							
13							
14							
15	Supplier_ID	Name	Address	City	State	Phone	
16	1	Wilson Mfg.	12 Oak Street	Cleveland	OH	555-666-7777	
17	2	Trumbill Machin	1244 Park Way	Atlanta	GA	111-222-3333	
18	3	Parts Unltd.	15-A West End Ave.	Albany	NY	333-444-5555	
19							
20							

Figure 7-2: A relational data source contains two or more tables that are related to one another.

Part III

But Not in Excel

Although I have used Excel in Figures 7-1 and 7-2 to illustrate what relational data look like, you should be aware that Excel does not have the capability to actually work with relational data, at least not directly. You need a dedicated database program such as Microsoft Access for that.

This time there is a table of suppliers with one record for each. Each supplier record is identified by a unique Supplier_ID number. There is also a table of parts with one record for each part. Each part record also has a Supplier_ID field that identifies the supplier for that part in the Suppliers table. For example, in the first record in the Parts table, the Supplier_ID field contains the value 1. If you go to the linked Suppliers table, you can see that this key is associated with Wilson Manufacturing, therefore identifying the supplier for this part. The problems described earlier for a flat database have been solved:

- Each supplier's information is present only once.

- Modifying a supplier's information requires a change in only one location, the single record for that supplier.

- Deleting part records cannot delete supplier information.

Relational databases are the mainstay of almost all modern data storage systems. Despite their great flexibility and power, they do not, however, solve all problems. Particularly when it comes to detailed analysis of large amounts of data, relational databases do not really simplify or speed up the process. Multidimensional data is the preferred solution for these challenges.

Multidimensional Data

As its name implies, *multidimensional data* have more than one dimension. But what exactly does the word *multidimensional* mean in this context? It is not used in the same sense as in geometry, as, for example, in a three-dimensional Excel chart. It will perhaps be easiest to understand if you work through the same data from flat to relational to multidimensional.

Figure 7-3 shows a sales database that is flat. In other words, each record contains all the relevant information. In this case, each record includes a field named Sale_ID that contains a unique numeric ID for each record. This is called the *primary key* and is used in all database tables, although it is not directly relevant to our exploration of multidimensional data. This database also contains the customer name, the salesman's name, the year, month, and day of the week of the sale, and finally the amount of the sale.

	A	B	C	D	E	F	G	H
1	Sale_ID	Customer	Salesman	Year	Month	Day	Amount	
2	1	Acme Metal Works	Jackson	2002	Jan	Tues	$ 12,312.00	
3	2	S&Q Manufacturing	Anderson	2003	Mar	Wed	$ 34,543.00	
4	3	East End Inc.	Gomez	2004	Feb	Mon	$ 12,134.00	
5	4	Acme Metal Works	Anderson	2002	Feb	Fri	$ 45,324.00	
6	5	S&Q Manufacturing	Jackson	2004	Jan	Thu	$ 12,435.00	
7	6	TechWiz Corp.	Gomez	2002	Mar	Fri	$ 12,546.00	
8	7	S&Q Manufacturing	Chang	2003	Feb	Wed	$ 76,567.00	
9	8	East End Inc.	Jackson	2004	Mar	Mon	$ 34,567.00	
10	9	TechWiz Corp.	Chang	2002	Jan	Fri	$ 12,435.00	
11	10	Acme Metal Works	Gomez	2004	Feb	Thu	$ 87,980.00	
12	11	TechWiz Corp.	Anderson	2002	Mar	Fri	$ 25,432.00	
13	12	Acme Metal Works	Chang	2003	Feb	Tues	$ 12,435.00	
14	13	East End Inc.	Anderson	2004	Jan	Fri	$ 23,546.00	
15	14	TechWiz Corp.	Chang	2004	Mar	Mon	$ 65,780.00	
16	15	S&Q Manufacturing	Gomez	2002	Feb	Wed	$ 32,456.00	
17								
18								

Figure 7-3: The sales data arranged as a flat database.

NOTE

I should point out that these data are greatly simplified from what you would find in the real world. For example, any actual sales database would include the address and phone number of each customer as well as more details about each salesman. I am trying to minimize details in order to more clearly illustrate the principles of multidimensional data.

One way to make this database more usable is to convert it to a relational structure with separate tables for customers, salesmen, days, months, and years. These are called *primary tables* because they do not depend on any other tables; for example, the Customers table contains all the information about each customer. A *master table*, called Sales, links to all these other tables as and contains the Amount data. The Sales table is a *dependent table* because it gets some of its information by means of relational links to the primary tables.

Figures 7-4 and 7-5 show the tables in this new relational database with the five primary tables shown in Figure 7-4 and the dependent Sales table in Figure 7-5. You can see that the data in most of the fields of the Sales table actually consist of links to data in the other tables. Note that any database program displays the actual data and not the link number— for example, Jackson instead of the not-very-useful 1. I have shown the numbers here for purposes of illustration.

Part III

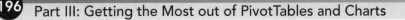
DayOfWeek : Table	
Day_ID	Day
1	Mon
2	Tues
3	Wed
4	Thurs
5	Fri
(AutoNumber)	

Record: 1

Months : Table	
Month_ID	Month
1	Jan
2	Feb
3	Mar
4	Apr
5	May
6	Jun
7	Jul
8	Aug
9	Sep
10	Oct
11	Nov
12	Dec
(AutoNumber)	

Record: 1

Customers : Table	
Customer_ID	Customer_Name
1	Acme Metal Works
2	S&Q Manufacturing
3	East End Inc.
4	TechWiz Corp.
(AutoNumber)	

Record: 1 of

Years : Table	
Year_ID	Year
1	2001
2	2002
3	2003
4	2004
5	2005
(AutoNumber)	0

Record: 1

SalesMen : Table	
Salesman_ID	Salesman_Nam
1	Jackson
2	Anderson
3	Gomez
4	Chang
(AutoNumber)	

Record: 1

Figure 7-4: The primary tables in the relational Sales database.

Sales : Table						
Sale_ID	Customer_ID	Salesman_ID	Year_ID	Month_ID	Day_ID	Amount
1	1	1	2	1	2	$12,312.00
2	2	2	3	3	3	$34,543.00
3	3	3	4	2	1	$12,134.00
4	1	2	2	2	5	$45,324.00
5	2	2	4	1	4	$12,435.00
6	4	3	2	3	5	$12,546.00
7	2	4	3	2	3	$76,567.00
8	3	1	4	3	1	$34,567.00
9	4	4	2	1	5	$12,435.00
10	1	3	4	2	4	$87,980.00
11	4	2	4	2	4	$25,432.00
12	1	4	2	3	5	$25,432.00
13	3	2	4	1	5	$23,546.00
14	4	4	4	3	1	$65,780.00
15	2	3	2	2	3	$32,456.00
(AutoNumber)	0	0	0	0	0	$0.00

Figure 7-5: The dependent table in the relational Sales database.

As you may have guessed, a relational database does not consist of only primary and dependent tables; it also requires that you define the links, or relationships, between the tables. For example, you must specify that the Customer_ID field in the Sales table is linked to the Customer_ID field in the Customers table. This enables the database to know that the value 1 means Acme Metal Works, that 2 means S&Q Manufacturing, and so on. A database program always provides a method for defining these relationships and usually also provides a way to display them. Figure 7-6 shows the relationships in the Sales database as displayed in Microsoft Access. (Excel does not have the ability to work directly with relational databases.)

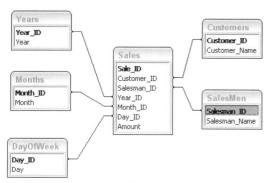

Figure 7-6: The defined relationships in the Sales database.

At this point the relational Sales database is complete and ready to use. You will find many databases essentially just like this one in use in the real world, and for many purposes they are just fine. However, for certain types of analysis with a really large database, this sort of structure is not ideal. Here's where the idea of multidimensional data comes into play. Let's take a look as this relates to the sample data.

As designed, the database includes a table for salesmen and another for customers. But perhaps you want to analyze the relationship between salesmen and customers. You may think that certain salespeople do better with certain customers. Perhaps Gomez does really well selling to Acme Metal Works but not so well with East End Inc. This kind of analysis is possible with the relational database just described, but it can be slow and cumbersome with large data sets. By adding another dimension to the data you can enable faster and more robust data analysis.

But what will this dimension be? Look at the existing data—each sales record has a Customer value and a Salesman value, currently separate. What if you combine them? In other words, instead of having a Salesman value of Gomez and a Customer value of Acme Metal Works, the record had a Salesman_Customer value of Gomez-Acme Metal Works. This will be the new dimension.

The database will still be relational. All you are doing is inserting an extra level, or dimension, of data between the dependent Sales table and the primary Customer and Salesmen tables. This new table, called Salesman_Customers, is also a dependent table because it links to the Customers and Salesmen tables. The Sales table links to the new Salesmen_Customers table rather than to the Customers and Salesmen tables individually.

To make these changes you must first remove the Customer_ID and Salesman_ID fields from the Sales table and add the Salesman_Customer_ID field. The resulting table is shown in Figure 7-7, although the Salesman_Customer_ID data have not been entered yet.

Sale_ID	Salesman_Customer_ID	Year_ID	Month_ID	Day_ID	Amount
1		2	1	2	$12,312.00
2		3	3	3	$34,543.00
3		4	2	1	$12,134.00
4		2	2	5	$45,324.00
5		4	1	4	$12,435.00
6		2	3	5	$12,546.00
7		3	2	3	$76,567.00
8		4	3	1	$34,567.00
9		2	1	5	$12,435.00
10		4	2	4	$87,980.00
11		4	2	4	$25,432.00
12		2	3	5	$25,432.00
13		4	1	5	$23,546.00
14		4	3	1	$65,780.00
15		2	2	3	$32,456.00
* (toNumber)	0	0	0	0	$0.00

Figure 7-7: The Sales table after the field layout is changed.

Next you need the Salesman_Customer table. This table will have three fields:

- **Salesman_Customer_ID**—The table's primary key, which will be used by the Sales table to link to salesman/customer combinations.

- **Salesman_ID**—This table will link to the primary Salesmen table.

- **Customer_ID**—This table will link to the primary Customers table.

Finally, the database needs some new relationships, as follows:

- A link between the Salesman_Customer_ID field in the Sales table to the Salesman_Customer_ID field in the Salesman_Customer table.

- A link between the Customer_ID field in the Salesman_Customer table to the Customer_ID field in the Customers table.

- A link between the Salesman_ID field in the Salesman_Customer table to the Salesman_ID field in the Salesmen table.

Figure 7-8 shows the new Salesman_Customer table after it has been populated with data. It contains one record for every possible combination of the four salesmen with the four customers, for a total of 16 records.

Salesman_Cust	Salesman_ID	Customer_ID
1	1	1
2	1	2
3	1	3
4	1	4
5	2	1
6	2	2
7	2	3
8	2	4
9	3	1
10	3	2
11	3	3
12	3	4
13	4	1
14	4	2
15	4	3
16	4	4
(AutoNumber)	0	0

Salesman_Customer : Table

Figure 7-8: The Salesman_Customer table contains one record for every possible combination of salesman and customer.

Figure 7-9 shows the new relationships for the database. The added dimension, namely the Salesman_Customer table, sits between the dependent Sales table and the primary Customers and Salesmen tables.

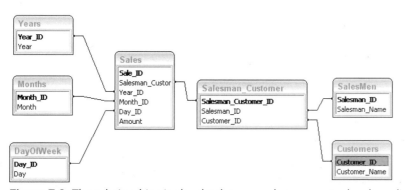

Figure 7-9: The relationships in the database now have an extra level, or dimension, represented by the Salesman_Customer table.

Finally, Figure 7-10 shows the Sales table after the Sales_Customer_ID field has been populated with data. To reiterate, here's how this works, taking the third record in Sales for an example. The Salesman_Customer_ID value for this record is 11. Because this field is linked to the Salesman_Customer table, you look at the record in that table in which the

Part III

Salesman_Customer_ID is also 11. This record has a Customer_ID field with a value of 3 and a Salesman_ID also with a value of 3. Following the links from these two fields to the Customers and Salesmen tables, you find the actual data values East End Inc. and Gomez. Therefore you know that for the sale whose data is in the specified record of the Sales table, the customer was East End Inc. and the salesman was Gomez.

Sale_ID	Salesman_Customer_ID	Year_ID	Month_ID	Day_ID	Amount
1	1	2	1	2	$12,312.00
2	6	3	3	3	$34,543.00
3	11	4	2	1	$12,134.00
4	5	2	2	5	$45,324.00
5	2	4	1	4	$12,435.00
6	12	2	3	5	$12,546.00
7	14	3	2	3	$76,567.00
8	3	4	3	1	$34,567.00
9	16	2	1	5	$12,435.00
10	9	4	2	4	$87,980.00
11	8	4	2	4	$25,432.00
12	13	2	3	5	$25,432.00
13	7	4	1	5	$23,546.00
14	16	4	3	1	$65,780.00
15	10	2	2	3	$32,456.00
(AutoNumber)	0	0	0	0	$0.00

Record: 15 of 15

Figure 7-10: The Sales table after the Salesman_Customer_ID information has been filled in.

At this point you have created a new dimension that condenses the salesman and customer data into a single table. There's more you can do, however. Take a look at the date data. They contain three pieces of information: the month of the sale, the year, and the day of the week. Can these data be condensed into a new dimension? You bet they can. By doing so, you simplify and speed analyses that look at questions such as, "Are more sales made on certain days of the week in January as opposed to June?"

The procedures are essentially the same as for the customer and salesman data, so I will not go into details. Briefly, the result is a new table called DayMonthYear that contains one record for each possible combination of day of the week, month, and year. The Sales table links to this new table through a field named DayMonthYear_ID, and the new table in turn links to the three primary tables DayofWeek, Months, and Years. The new DayMonthYear table—or part of it, because it contains 300 records—is shown in Figure 7-11, and the final relationship structure of the database is shown in Figure 7-12.

DayMonthYear : Table			
DayMonthYear	Day_ID	Month_ID	Year_ID
1	1	1	1
2	2	1	1
3	3	1	1
4	4	1	1
5	5	1	1
6	1	2	1
7	2	2	1
8	3	2	1
9	4	2	1
10	5	2	1
11	1	3	1
12	2	3	1
13	3	3	1
14	4	3	1
15	5	3	1
16	1	4	1
17	2	4	1
18	3	4	1
19	4	4	1
20	5	4	1
21	1	5	1
22	2	5	1
23	3	5	1
24	4	5	1
25	5	5	1
26	1	6	1
27	2	6	1
28	3	6	1

Record: 1 of 300

Figure 7-11: The DayMonthYear table adds another dimension to the database's date data.

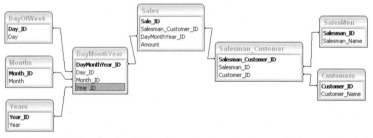

Figure 7-12: The final relationship structure in the multidimensional database.

Where Are Multidimensional Data Stored?

The term *multidimensional* describes the way the data are organized and says nothing specifically about where and how they are stored. As you have seen in the previous example, multidimensional data can be kept in an Access database. But a multidimensional data structure is often used to enable efficient queries and analysis in huge databases that are beyond the capabilities of Access, databases with tens of millions of records. Such huge databases are usually managed with specialized data-warehouse applications such as Microsoft SQL Server Analysis Server or Oracle OLAP Server. These applications are maintained by IT specialists and if you need to work with their data, these specialists will give you information about accessing them.

Multidimensional Data Terminology

When working with multidimensional data and PivotTables you will find that several terms are used in a specialized manner. You need to understand this terminology to work effectively with these tools.

A *dimension* is the highest level grouping. Dimensions are used to group data into hierarchical (parent/child) relationships. Dimensions commonly used in data analysis include people, location, time, products, and similar categories.

Within each dimension are two or more *levels*. A level represents a data element that is part of the specified dimension. For example, in the sample multidimensional database created earlier in this chapter you could define a dimension called People with two levels, Customers and Salesmen. This is illustrated in Figure 7-13.

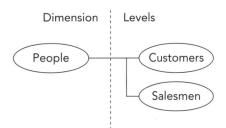

Figure 7-13: A dimension such as People contains two or more levels.

Each level contains one or more items called *members*. The Customers level contains the members Acme Metal Works, S&Q Manufacturing, and so on. Likewise, the Salesmen level contains the members Jackson, Anderson, and so on. This is shown schematically in Figure 7-14.

The example database you have been working with has another potential dimension: time. This dimension would have three levels, DayOfWeek, Month, and Year. Each of these levels would have its own members, for example Mon, Tues, Wed, Thu, and Fri for DayOfWeek.

A *measure* is a summary of a data value. You have actually worked with measures previously, although they were not called that. A sum, average, or count in a PivotTable cell, for example, is a measure. In the current example, the measure would probably be the sum of the Amount values. A cube file can have one or more measures.

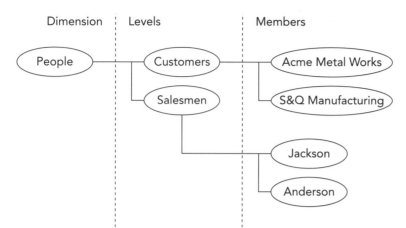

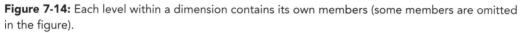

Figure 7-14: Each level within a dimension contains its own members (some members are omitted in the figure).

The term *cube* is applied to the files used to store dimensions, levels, members, and measures. The term comes from the fact that the structure of multidimensional data is sometimes pictured as a three-dimensional cube, with each physical dimension of the cube representing a conceptual dimension in the data. This visualization works only for data with three dimensions, of course, but the image and the name have stuck.

The important thing about cube files is that they contain already summarized data rather than raw data. This relates to something mentioned earlier in this chapter: the ability to analyze huge datasets without overloading your system or experiencing long waits. There's nothing magical about this; the fact is that much of the analysis had already been made when the cube file was created. Your program, in this case Excel, needs only to retrieve the summarized data from the cube file to populate the PivotTable.

Another important thing to be aware of is that you can define multiple cube files for a given data source. When you or someone else creates a cube file, you specify what it will contain—what the dimensions will be as well as the levels and members. A large and complex database is likely to need several cube files, and you must use the one that contains the summary you need.

Finally, a cube file enables you work with your PivotTable when the database itself is unavailable or you are offline.

Creating a PivotTable from an Online Cube

If your IT department has provided you with access to an online cube, you can create a PivotTable from it by following the procedures in this section. You will need to know the name of the server and your logon information (if the server requires a logon). The section assumes that the online cube is based on Microsoft SQL Server Analysis Services. If another database system is in use, the procedures will be somewhat different but should follow the same general pattern.

1. Click the Insert PivotTable button on the Insert ribbon to open the Create PivotTable dialog box.

2. Select the Use External Data Source option.

3. Click the Choose Connection button to open the Existing Connections dialog box.

4. Click the Browse for More button to open the Select Data Source dialog box (see Figure 7-15).

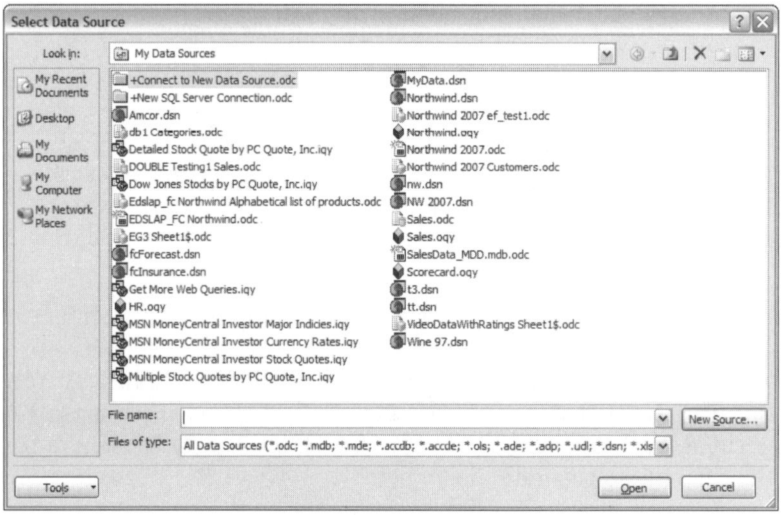

Figure 7-15: The Select Data Source dialog box.

5. In the Select Data Source dialog box, click the New Source button to open the Data Connection Wizard.

6. In the first step, shown in Figure 7-16, select Microsoft SQL Server Analysis Services and then click Next.

7. In the next step, shown in Figure 7-17, enter the server name and your logon credentials; then click Next.

Figure 7-16: In the first step of the wizard, select the database on which the cube is hosted.

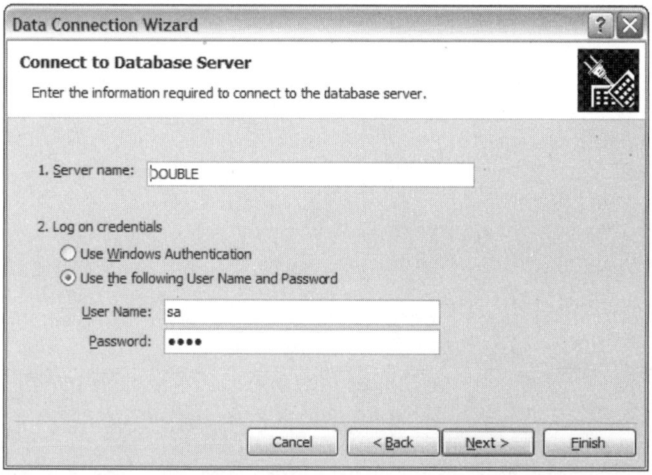

Figure 7-17: In the second step of the wizard, specify the server name and your login credentials.

8. In the next step, shown in Figure 7-18, select the database and cube. In this example, the database is Testing1, and the cube is Sales. Then click Next.

9. The final screen, shown in Figure 7-19, lets you change the data connection file name, the description, and the Friendly Name (the name that is displayed in connection lists), or you can just click Finish to return to the Create PivotTable dialog box.

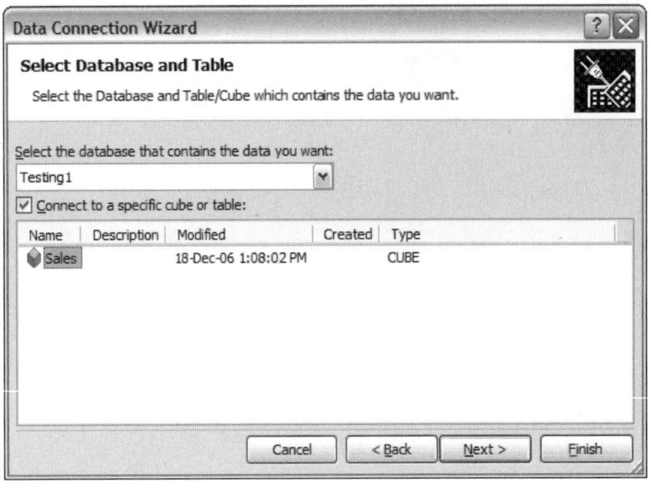

Figure 7-18: In the third step of wizard, select the specific database and cube of interest.

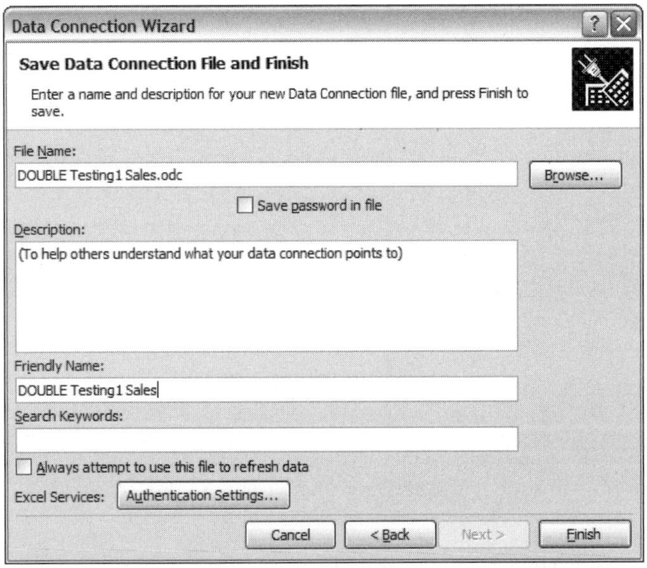

Figure 7-19: The final step of the Data Connection Wizard.

   10. Click OK to close the Create Pivot Table dialog box and create the blank PivotTable. You will see the cube fields displayed in the field list, as shown in Figure 7-20.

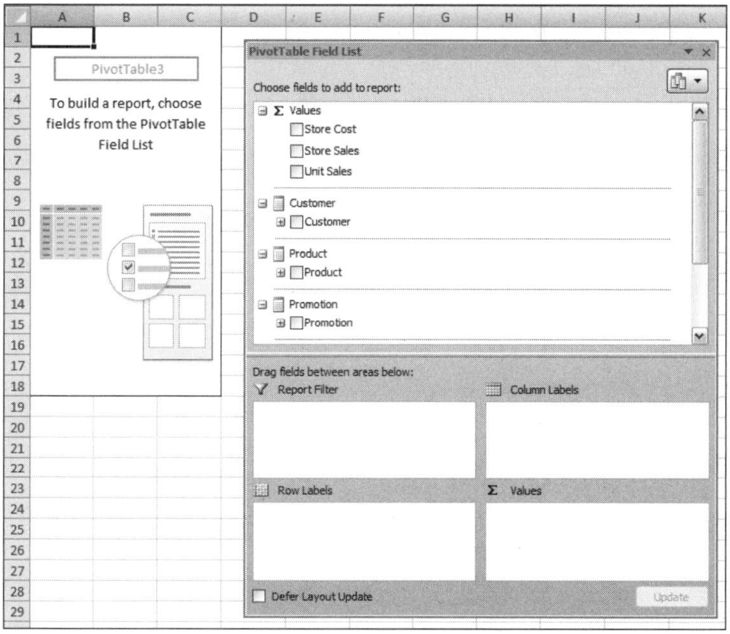

Figure 7-20: When the blank PivotTable is created, the cube fields are displayed in the Field List.

If you look closely at Figure 7-20, you will see that it looks different from the Field List for PivotTables created from non-OLAP data. First of all, what you see here will depend on how the cube was defined. There is a hierarchical arrangement that reflects the dimensions and levels within each dimension. Each dimension—for example, Customer, Product, and Promotion in the figure—is in effect a field and can be added to the PivotTable to define its structure. Each dimension has an adjacent + symbol. Click that symbol to expand the dimension to show its levels. These are not fields, and you can't drag them to the PivotTable. They are listed to show you what each dimension contains. When you add a dimension to the PivotTable, its levels go along automatically.

Several value fields are present as well—Store Cost, Store Sales, and Unit Sales. These are what was specified as the summary data item in the cube when it was created.

Creating an Offline Cube File from an OLAP Server Database

After you have created a PivotTable that is based on an OLAP server database—in other words, an online cube—you can create an offline cube file that resides on the local PC and enables you to work with the data even when not connected to the OLAP server database.

1. Click the OLAP-based PivotTable to make it active.

2. Click the OLAP Tools button on the Options ribbon and select Offline OLAP from the menu. Excel opens the Offline OLAP Settings dialog box (see Figure 7-21).

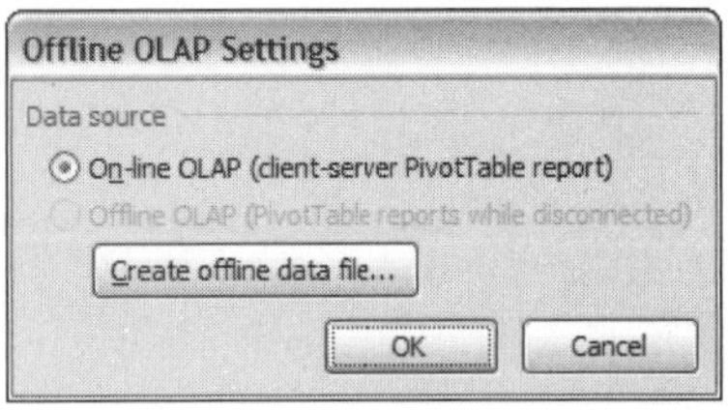

Figure 7-21: The Offline OLAP Settings dialog box.

3. Click the Create Offline Data File button to start the Create Cube File wizard.

4. The first step of the wizard, shown in Figure 7-22, explains what the wizard will do. Read this material if you like; then click Next to continue.

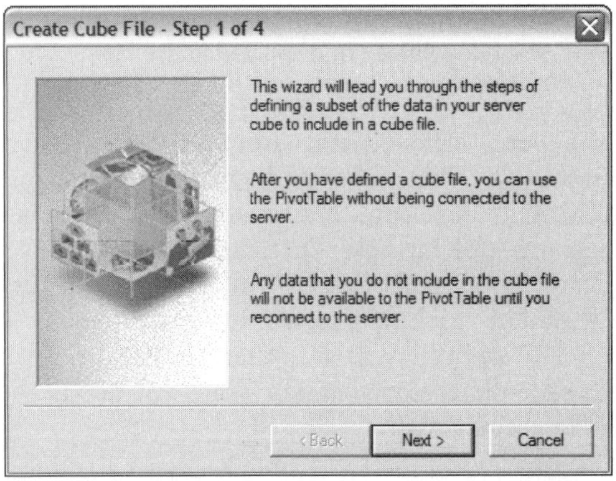

Figure 7-22: The first step of the Create Cube File wizard.

5. The next step, shown in Figure 7-23, displays the dimensions that are available in the data source. Select the dimensions that you want included in your offline cube by clicking the adjacent box. To select specific levels within a dimension, click the adjacent + symbol to display a dimension's levels. When selecting levels, keep the following in mind:

   • Omit lower levels that you do not need in order to reduce the size of the offline cube file.

   • Make sure you include any levels that have grouped items.

- You cannot skip intermediate levels within a dimension.

- If a dimension does not display a + button, it means that you cannot pick and choose levels but must include or exclude the entire dimension.

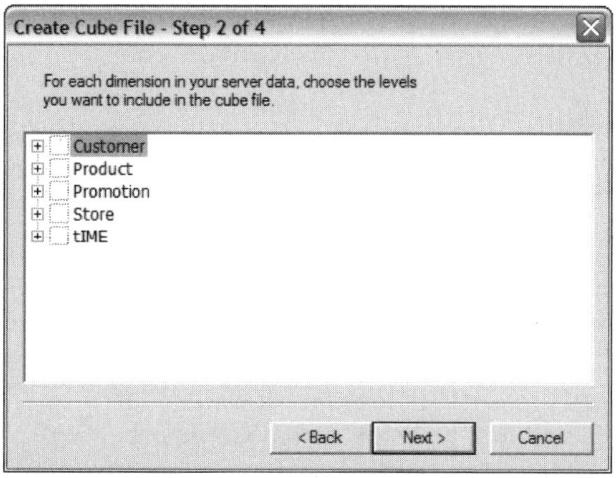

Figure 7-23: In Step 2 of the wizard, select the dimensions and levels to include in the offline cube.

6. Click Next to move to Step 3 of the wizard, shown in Figure 7-24. Here you select the measures that will be available for use as value fields. Select Measures to include them all, or expand the Measures branch to select specific measures.

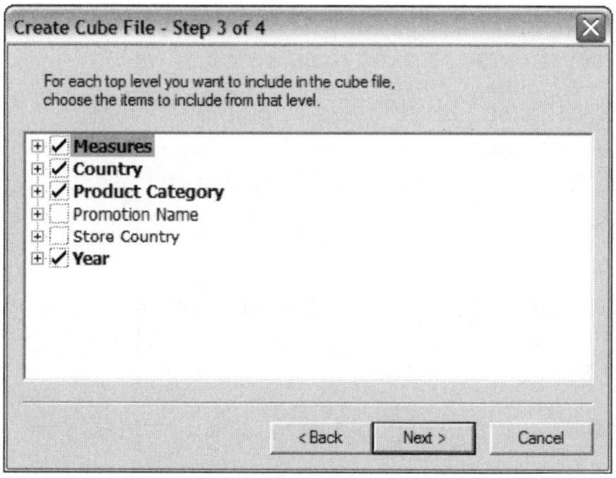

Figure 7-24: In Step 3 of the wizard, select the measures to include in the offline cube.

7. Click Next to go to the final step, shown in Figure 7-25. Enter a name and location for the cube file, and then click Finish.

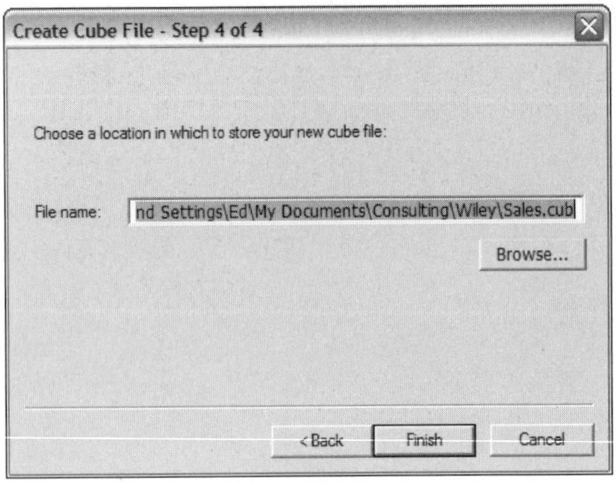

Figure 7-25: In the final step of the wizard, specify the name and location for the new cube file.

At this point the offline cube will be created, a process that may take a while if large amounts of data are involved. The PivotTable will now be linked to the offline cube. You'll be able to work with the data even without a connection to the database, and many operations such as pivoting or filtering may well work a lot faster. Of course, dimensions, levels, and measures from the original data source that you did not include in the offline cube will no longer be available.

Working with OLAP PivotTables

In most respects, a PivotTable created from OLAP data is the same as any other PivotTable. There are some differences, however, and you need to be aware of them.

You cannot drill down in the data of most OLAP-based PivotTables by double-clicking a data cell. In fact, the database administrators can define various actions that a cube supports. Thus, double-clicking may drill-down, it may open a URL, or it may initiate some other custom action. This is all based on the cube and database setup and not something you can change in Excel.

Furthermore, you can't change the calculations used by the measures, such as by changing a sum to an average. The summary calculation is specified and performed when the cube is created and you can't change it from within Excel.

On the Options ribbon, the Formulas commands are not available because a PivotTable based on OLAP data does not permit the use of formulas.

Levels in the data may not be visible in the PivotTable. In fact, those levels are present in the table but initially hidden. You use the Expand/Collapse commands, covered in Chapter 5, to control the display of levels. At present, it seems that the PivotTable has to be in classic PivotTable layout for this to work properly, but this is hopefully something that will be fixed.

Chapter 8

Getting Hard Data from a PivotTable

After you have created your PivotTable report, then what? Of course, many reports are simply viewed or printed, but in other situations you will want to make use of the report data in the worksheet. For example, you may want to use various Excel tools, such as formulas and functions, to perform additional analyses of the PivotTable data including the creation of charts (standard Excel charts as opposed to PivotCharts). How do you make those data available in other parts of the workbook? That's the topic of this chapter.

In This Chapter

◆ About the GETPIVOTDATA function

◆ Analyzing PivotTable data in your worksheet

◆ Copying and moving PivotTables

Understanding the GETPIVOTDATA Function

Suppose that you want to write a formula that references a number in a PivotTable, and that number happens to be in cell G15. Well, you can simply use the cell reference G15 (or perhaps G15), right? Unfortunately, things aren't that simple. Why not? Just think of some of the things you can do with a PivotTable: pivoting it, of course, as well as showing or hiding detail and changing the sort order. These and other manipulations can cause a particular number to change its position. The summary data that were in cell G15 may now be in cell H22! Obviously, you can't reliably retrieve data from a PivotTable using the standard Excel cell references. What to do? Enter the GETPIVOTDATA function.

GETPIVOTDATA Function Basics

The GETPIVOTDATA function is designed specifically to retrieve data from a PivotTable based not on the data's cell address but rather on its logical position in the PivotTable. Let's look at the syntax for this function:

```
GETPIVOTDATA(data_field, pivot_table, field1, item1, field2, item2,...)
```

- data_field is the name of the value field that you want to retrieve—in other words, the name of the field that you added to the Values area of the PivotTable.

- pivot_table is a reference to any cell or range of cells in the PivotTable.

- field1 and item1 are respectively the name of the first field and the first data value associated with the data you want to retrieve.

- field2 and item2 are respectively the name of the second field and the second data value associated with the data you want to retrieve.

You can have as many as 126 field and item pairs, although it is very unlikely you will ever need to use so many. All arguments to GETPIVOTDATA except for the cell reference must be enclosed in quotes. An example will help to clarify how these arguments are used. I will use the PivotTable report shown in Figure 8-1.

	A	B	C	D	E	F	G
1							
2							
3	Sum of Sales	Month					
4	Category	Jan	Feb	Mar	Apr	May	Grand Total
5	Accessories	$1,845	$2,718	$2,078	$2,195	$1,590	$10,426
6	Outerwear	$2,820	$2,606	$1,606	$2,255	$1,714	$11,001
7	Pants	$2,150	$2,814	$1,187	$1,873	$1,880	$9,904
8	Shirts	$2,397	$2,846	$2,319	$2,648	$2,798	$13,008
9	Shoes	$1,769	$2,192	$1,055	$2,919	$2,742	$10,677
10	Grand Total	$10,981	$13,176	$8,245	$11,890	$10,724	$55,016
11							

Figure 8-1: The sample PivotTable report.

Suppose you want to retrieve the sum of sales in the Accessories category for the month of Jan and use that figure elsewhere in the worksheet, outside of the PivotTable. The proper function would be:

```
=GETPIVOTDATA("Sales",$A$3,"Month","Jan","Category","Accessories")
```

Let's dissect these arguments.

- The "Sales" argument is used because the name of the value field in this PivotTable is Sales. That is, when the PivotTable was created, the Sales field was added to the Values area of the PivotTable.

- The A3 argument identifies a cell in the PivotTable. It could be any other cell in the PivotTable.

- The "Month" and "Jan" arguments go together. They specify that you want to retrieve a value where the Month field contains the value Jan.

- The "Category" and "Accessories" arguments also go together. They specify that you want to retrieve a value where the Category field contains the value Accessories.

Looking at the PivotTable in Figure 8-1 you can see that the desired value, where Category=Accessories and Month=Jan, is in cell B5, so the function will return the value 1845.

If you include only a single field/item pair in the argument list, the function returns the corresponding total. For example, the function

```
=GETPIVOTDATA("Sales",$A$3,"Month","Jan")
```

returns the total for all data where Month=Jan, in this case the value 10981. Likewise the function

```
=GETPIVOTDATA("Sales",$A$3,"Category","Pants")
```

returns the sum for all data where Category=Pants, 9904. If you omit any mention of field and item, the GETPIVOTDATA function returns the overall total for the specified data item.

=GETPIVOTDATA("Sales",A3) returns the value 55018, the overall total of Sales items.

The Dreaded #REF

A restriction on using the GETPIVOTDATA function is that the PivotTable cell it references must not be excluded from the table by a filter. In this situation, the GETPIVOTDATA function will return #REF. Unlike with previous versions of Excel, however, the GETPIVOTDATA function works even if the cell it references is hidden (for example, by collapsing detail).

Part III

Copying Formulas That Contain GETPIVOTDATA

You can copy a formula that contains the GETPIVOTDATA function, just as you can any other Excel formula. However, the concept of relative cell addresses does not apply. In other words, the PivotTable cell that the GETPIVOTDATA function refers to will not be adjusted according to where you copy the formula. This makes sense, of course, because the concept of a relative address is meaningless in terms of PivotTable data.

When using the GETPIVOTDATA function, you need to keep the following factors in mind:

- If the pivot_table argument refers to a range that contains two or more PivotTable reports, data are returned from whichever PivotTable was most recently created.

- Calculated fields, calculated items, and custom calculations can all be returned by GETPIVOTDATA.

- If the pivot_table argument refers to a cell or range where no PivotTable is located, the function returns #REF.

- If the field and item arguments refer to data that do not exist in the PivotTable, the function returns #REF.

A GetPivotData Shortcut

Excel makes entering the GETPIVOTDATA function really easy for most situations. All you need to do is to enter an operator in a cell (an equal sign at the beginning of the formula or +−/* as part of a formula) and then click the cell in the PivotTable whose data you want. This cell can be an individual data cell or a total cell. Excel will then automatically enter the correct GETPIVOTDATA function in the formula.

Referencing PivotTable Cells by Address

There may be times when you want to reference a cell in a PivotTable report by its actual cell address rather than by generating a GETPIVOTDATA function. For example, if you are writing some formulas outside of the PivotTable to perform calculations on its data, you may want relative cell addresses to adjust automatically when you copy the formula to other cells. You can set this up simply by typing the address into your formula rather than by clicking the cell. You can also turn off the PivotTable feature that automatically generates GETPIVOTDATA functions when a cell is clicked. To do so, you must add a button to one of your toolbars as follows:

1. Click the Office button at the top left of the Excel screen.

2. Click the Excel Options button at the bottom of the menu to open the Excel Options window.

3. Select Formulas from the list of option categories to display the Excel formula options (see Figure 8-2).

4. In the Working With Formulas section, turn off the Use GetPivotData Functions for PivotTable references.

5. Click OK.

With this option turned off, if you click a PivotTable cell while entering a formula, a regular cell reference is generated instead of a GETPIVOTDATA function.

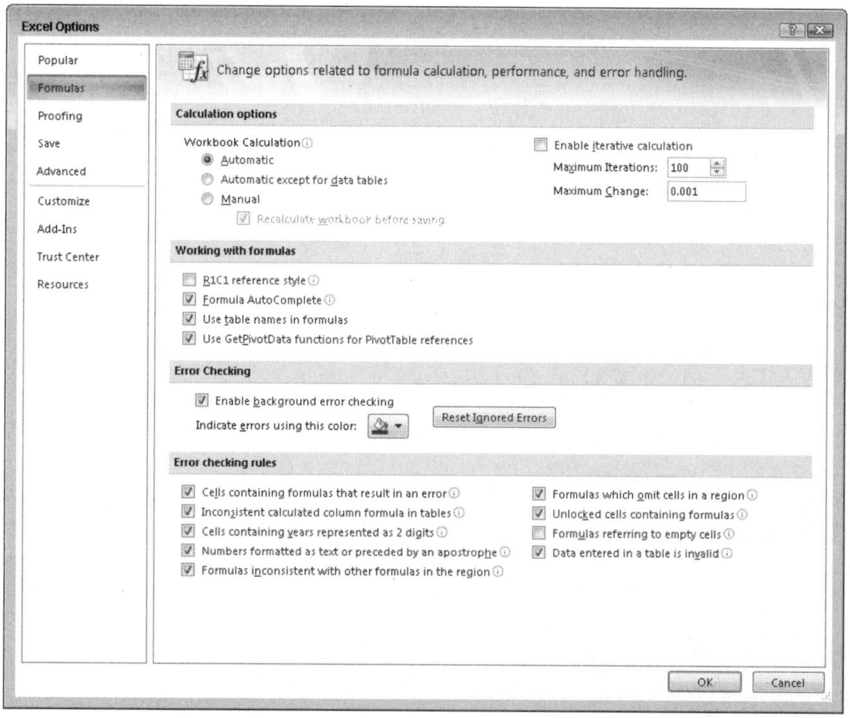

Figure 8-2: Turning off the automatic generation of GetPivotData function references.

Page Fields and the GETPIVOTDATA Function

The GETPIVOTDATA function does not use any reference to the report filter or page fields in a PivotTable report. For example, look at the PivotTable in Figure 8-3, which has three page fields.

	Name Box	B	C	D	E
1	Color	(All) ▼			
2	Item	(All) ▼			
3	Size	Large ▼			
4					
5	Sum of Amount	Month ▼			
6	Store ▼	Jan	Feb	Mar	Grand Total
7	Downtown	$101.64	$68.38	$34.78	$204.80
8	East End	$20.94	$15.88		$36.82
9	Northside		$71.40	$60.12	$131.52
10	South Plaza	$114.96		$41.86	$156.82
11	Grand Total	$237.54	$155.66	$136.76	$529.96
12					

Figure 8-3: A PivotTable report with three page fields.

Suppose you create a GETPIVOTDATA function to retrieve the data in cell D11, the total for March. The function will look like this:

```
=GETPIVOTDATA("Amount",$A$5,"Month","Mar")
```

The function contains no reference to the settings for the three page fields. For example, there is no information relating to the fact that the Size field is filtered on the value Large (as you can see in cell B3 of the PivotTable). This is correct. The report filter fields control which data are summarized in the PivotTable, while the GETPIVOTDATA function returns a specific piece of those data. Changing the report filtering may change the value returned by the GETPIVOTDATA function, of course, and as long as you understand this you can use the GETPIVOTDATA function correctly.

GETPIVOTDATA and OLAP Data

You can use the GETPIVOTDATA function on PivotTable reports based on OLAP data. One difference is that in the function arguments, the item can specify the source name of the dimension as well as the item name itself. Also, arguments are enclosed in brackets. For example, look at this GETPIVOTDATA function that retrieves data from an OLAP-based PivotTable:

```
=GETPIVOTDATA("[Measures].[Sum Of Amount]",
$A$3,"[Date]","[Date].[All].[2001]","[Person]",
"[Person].[All].[Acme Metal Works].[Anderson]")
```

In this example, Date and Person are dimension names and not level names. Because the syntax of GETPIVOTDATA can be rather complex when working with OLAP data, I recommend that you always use the shortcut and let Excel generate the function arguments for you.

GETPIVOTDATA and Expand/Collapse

One of the nice aspects of the GETPIVOTDATA function is that the result it returns does not change when you show additional levels of detail by expanding one or more fields. This is true of all PivotTables, whether they are based on OLAP data or not. Of course, the opposite is not true. If you create a GETPIVOTDATA function that refers to a cell in a PivotTable report and hide that cell with the Collapse command, the function will return #REF.

Using GETPIVOTDATA to Analyze PivotTable Data

For this walkthrough, you use the PivotTable that you created in Chapter 5 that summarized data on river heights. It is shown again in Figure 8-4. Your goal is to create a standard Excel chart (not a PivotChart) that displays the maximum heights at the Power Plant over the time period that the data cover.

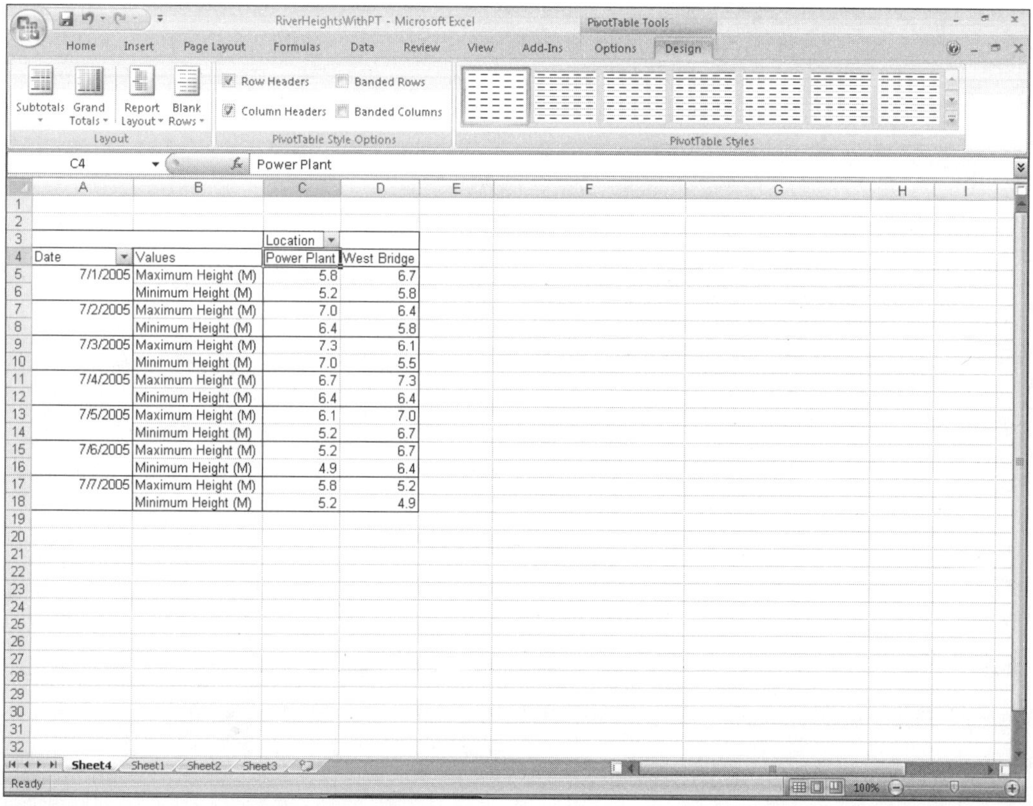

Figure 8-4: The PivotTable for this walkthrough.

The strategy you follow has two parts. The first is to use the GETPIVOTDATA function to pull the required numbers out of the PivotTable and place them in a regular Excel table. The second and easier part is to create a chart from this new table.

1. Open the workbook containing the PivotTable that you created Chapter 5.

2. Decide on a location for the new table. It can be in a new worksheet or the one that contains the PivotTable.

3. Enter a title for the table, **Max River Heights at Power Plant**, in a cell.

4. In the cell below the title, enter **Date**.

5. In the cell to the right of the Date label, enter **Max Height (M)**.

6. In Column below the Date label, enter the seven dates covered, **7/1/2005** to **7/7/2005**.

7. Format all the text you entered as bold. At this point the table will look like Figure 8-5.

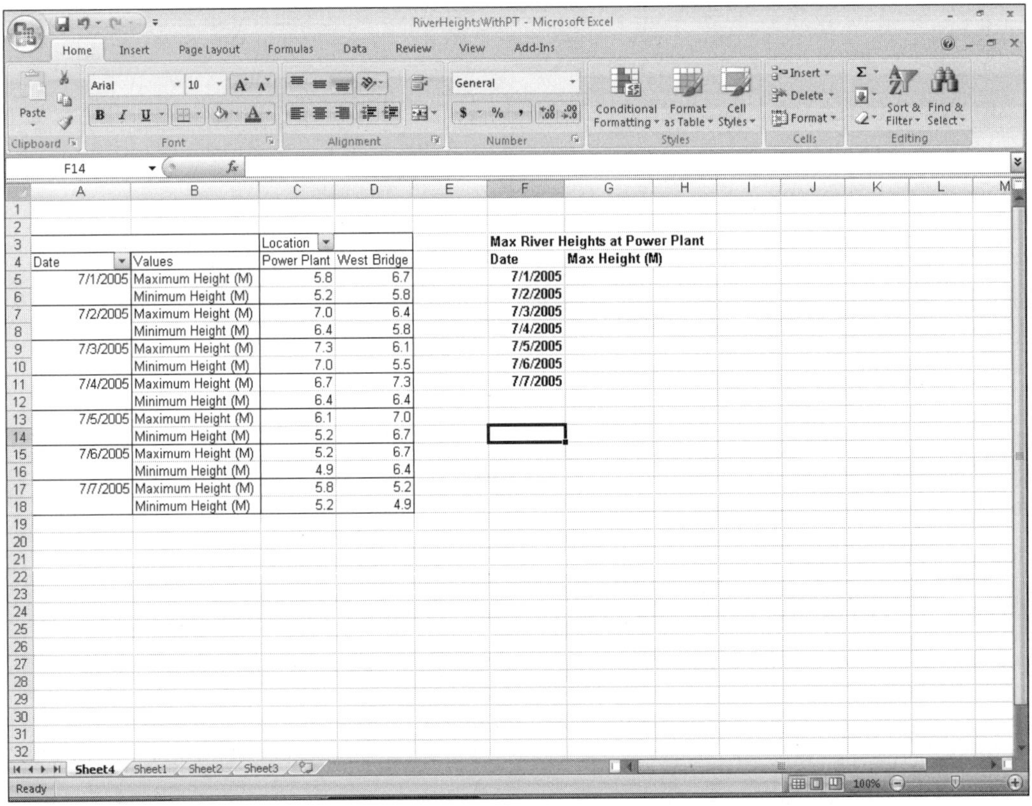

Figure 8-5: The new data table after the row and column headings are entered.

The next step is to enter a GETPIVOTDATA function in the cells of the table that you just created to refer to the proper cells in the PivotTable report. For example, consider the cell in the new table just to the right of the 7/1/2005 label. You want this cell to display the maximum height for the Power Plant for that date, located in cell C5 in the PivotTable. Here's what to do:

1. Place the cell pointer on the cell just to the right of the 7/1/2005 label in your new table (not in the PivotTable). In the figure this is cell G5.

2. Enter an equal sign (=).

3. Click the source cell in the PivotTable, C5 in the figure. Excel enters the appropriate GETPIVOTDATA function in the cell, as shown in Figure 8-6.

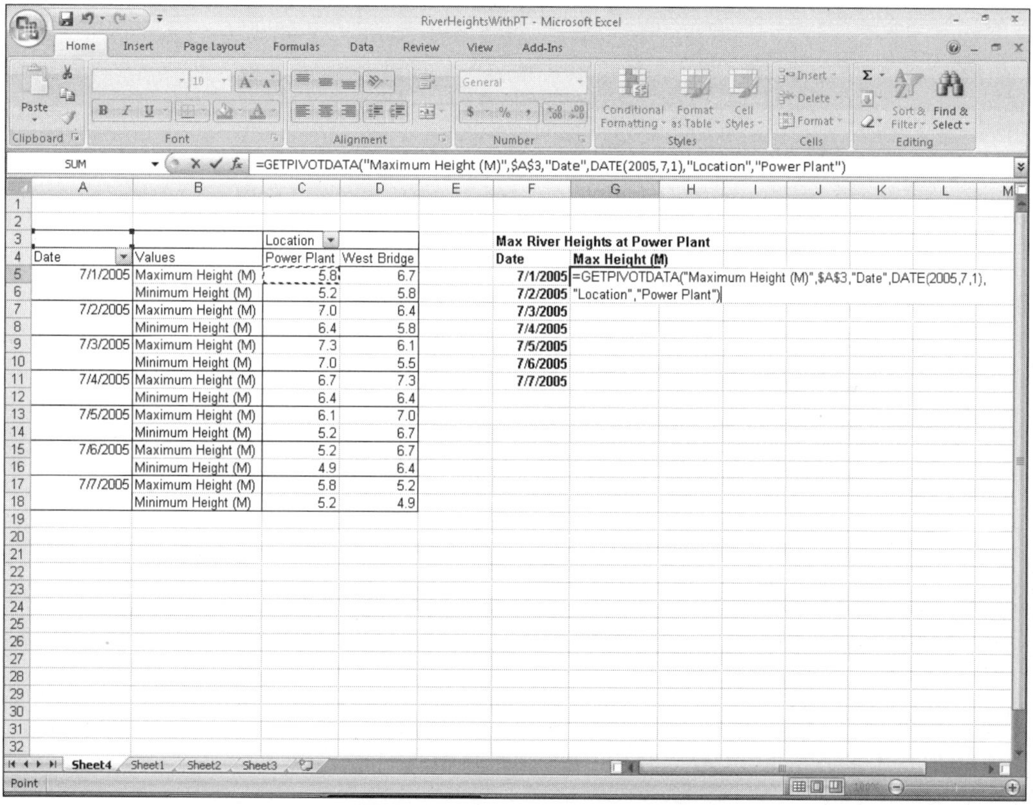

Figure 8-6: The correct GETPIVOTDATA function is generated by Excel.

4. Press Enter to complete entry of the formula. The cell in the new table now displays the data extracted from the PivotTable (although the number of decimal places shown may be different).

5. Repeat these steps to enter the appropriate GETPIVOTDATA function in the remaining cells of the new table.

At this point your table looks like Figure 8-7. The seven data points are all extracted from the PivotTable and displayed in a form that can easily be used as the basis for a chart.

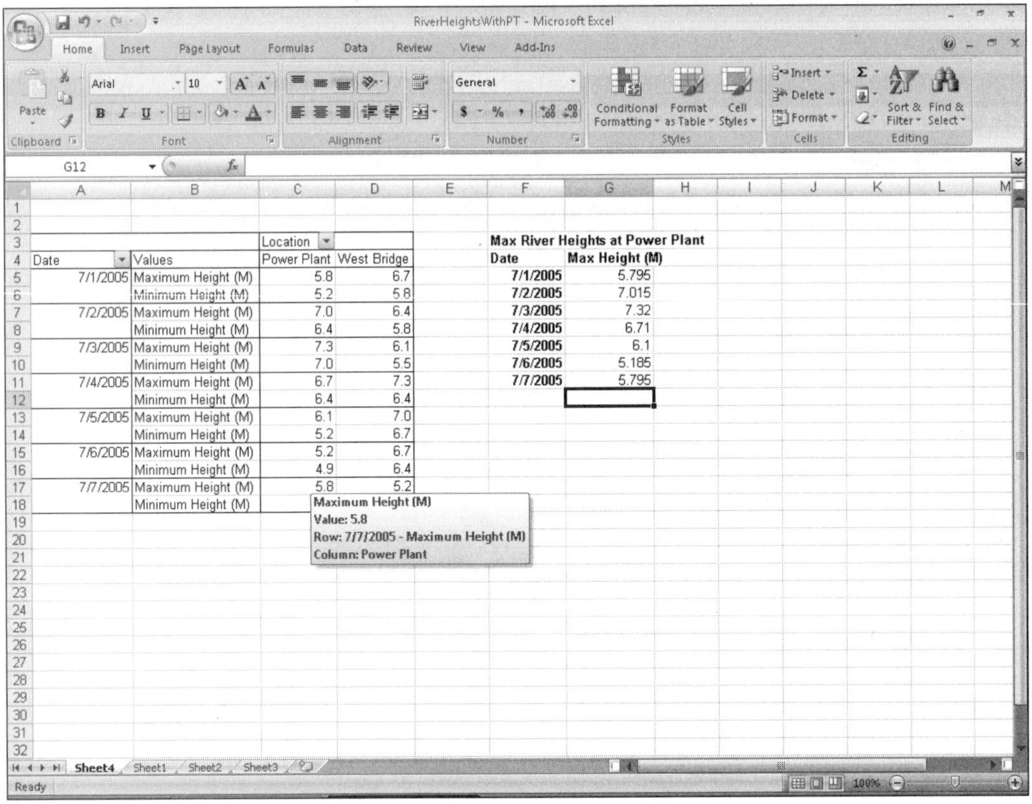

Figure 8-7: The new table after entering all of the required GETPIVOTDATA functions.

The final steps are quite simple and require only that you use the Chart Wizard to make a chart from the new data table you just created.

1. Select the entire data table, excluding the cell with the title in it.

2. Click the Column button in the Charts section of the Insert ribbon.

3. Select the 2-D column sub-type at the top left of the menu.

The resulting chart is shown in Figure 8-8. As with any Excel chart, you can customize it as desired, adding titles and other elements.

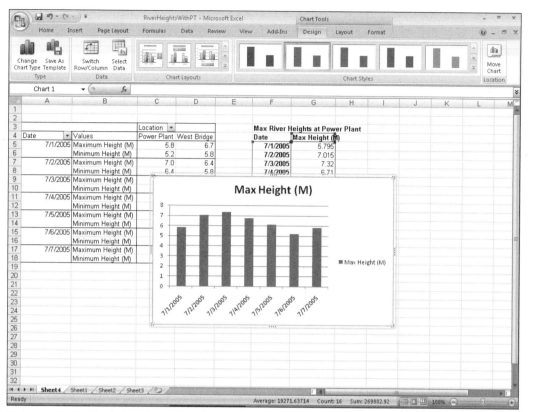

Figure 8-8: The final chart based on the data extracted with the GETPIVOTDATA function.

Think for a moment about what you have accomplished. You started with raw data in a worksheet. You created a PivotTable based on those data and then created an Excel table that summarized certain aspects of the PivotTable data. Finally, you created a chart based on your summary table. If the original data were to change in any way, all you would need to do is refresh the PivotTable to have the changes reflected in all these elements.

Copying and Moving PivotTables

You can copy a PivotTable and paste it in a new location, even in a new workbook, and the copy will continue to function just like the original. You'll be able to refresh data, pivot the table, and so on. If you copy the PivotTable to a new workbook, and the original data are in another Excel workbook, the data reference in the copied PivotTable will still reference the original data location. The copy is partially independent from the original—you can apply a filter or expand/collapse data in one and the other will not be affected.

You can use this ability to copy a PivotTable and retain full functionality to create a master PivotTable workbook that contains multiple PivotTable reports copied from multiple workbooks. PivotTables based on external data, including OLAP cubes, can be copied in the same way. Another reason to create a copy of a PivotTable is that it enables you to pivot or filter the copy differently from the original and display both versions at the same time. To copy a PivotTable, do the following:

1. Click any cell in the PivotTable.

2. Click the Select button on the Options ribbon, and then select Entire Table.

3. Press Ctrl+C or click the Copy button on the Home ribbon.

4. Click the cell in which you want to place the top left of the PivotTable. The cell can be in the same worksheet, in another worksheet in the same workbook, or in another workbook.

5. Press Ctrl+V or select Paste from the Home ribbon.

If the PivotTable is in its final form, you can use Paste Special to copy the displayed data only. The result is plain data, not a PivotTable, just as if you had typed the data in. You cannot refresh or pivot the table. To copy a PivotTable as data, follow these steps:

1. Click any cell in the PivotTable.

2. Click the Select button on the Options ribbon, and then select Entire Table.

3. Press Ctrl+C or click the Copy button on the Home ribbon.

4. Display the Paste menu from the Home ribbon.

5. Select Paste Values.

Of course, you can also use Paste Special to copy any part of a PivotTable, such as a single cell or an entire column or row.

To move a PivotTable:

1. Click any cell in the PivotTable.

2. Click the Move PivotTable button on the Options ribbon. Excel displays the Move PivotTable dialog box (see Figure 8-9).

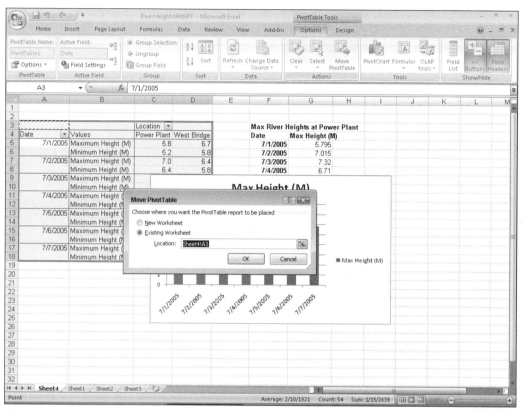

Figure 8-9: Moving a PivotTable to a new location.

3. Select the destination:

   - **New Worksheet**—Excel creates a new worksheet and places the PivotTable at cell A1.

   - **Existing Worksheet**—Excel moves the PivotTable to the location in an existing worksheet that you specify in the Location box.

4. Click OK.

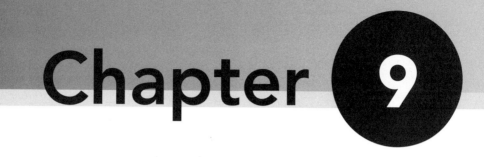

Chapter 9

PivotTable Alternatives

Excel offers a wide range of data analysis tools in addition to PivotTables. It's a good idea to know about these techniques so that when you are faced with a data analysis task, you can choose the best technique. As powerful as PivotTables are, they are not always the best choice—in fact, sometimes they are too powerful and something simpler will serve you better. This chapter provides an overview of some of the other data analysis techniques that perform analysis tasks similar to PivotTables.

In This Chapter

◆ Using subtotals

◆ Working with database functions

◆ Using filters

Working with Subtotals

The Excel subtotal tool makes it easy to generate subtotals based on values in the data. For example, look at the Excel database in Figure 9-1. This database contains data for a video rental chain, specifically the number of titles in stock for each category at each store. This is typical of the kind of data you might analyze with a PivotTable.

	A	B	C	D
1				
2	Popcorn Video Rentals			
3				
4	Store	Category	Titles	
5	Main Street	Action	374	
6	Main Street	Drama	180	
7	Main Street	Childrens	63	
8	Main Street	Sci-Fi	324	
9	Main Street	Classics	203	
10	Main Street	Comedy	145	
11	Northgate	Action	45	
12	Northgate	Drama	287	
13	Northgate	Childrens	320	
14	Northgate	Sci-Fi	36	
15	Northgate	Classics	79	
16	Northgate	Comedy	225	
17	Clarkville	Action	22	
18	Clarkville	Drama	172	
19	Clarkville	Childrens	203	
20	Clarkville	Sci-Fi	324	
21	Clarkville	Classics	251	
22	Clarkville	Comedy	345	
23	West End	Action	310	
24	West End	Drama	369	
25	West End	Childrens	220	
26	West End	Sci-Fi	236	
27	West End	Classics	145	

Figure 9-1: The video store stock data.

Suppose you want titles in stock for each category totaled across all stores. Sure, you can create a PivotTable report for this purpose, as shown in Figure 9-2. But you can also use subtotals.

	A	B	C
1			
2			
3	Category ▾	Sum of Titles	
4	Action	751	
5	Childrens	806	
6	Classics	678	
7	Comedy	1011	
8	Drama	1008	
9	Sci-Fi	920	
10	Grand Total	5174	
11			
12			

Figure 9-2: Using a PivotTable to total the number of titles in each category across all stores.

If you want to use subtotals, the data must be sorted on the field on which you want to subtotal—in this case, Category. To sort the data:

1. Place the cell pointer on any cell in the Category column in the data table.

2. Click the A-Z button in the Sort & Filter section of the Data ribbon.

When the data are sorted by Category, do the following:

1. Place the cell pointer on any cell in the data table.

2. Click the Subtotal button on the Data menu to display the Subtotal dialog box, shown in Figure 9-3.

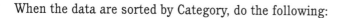

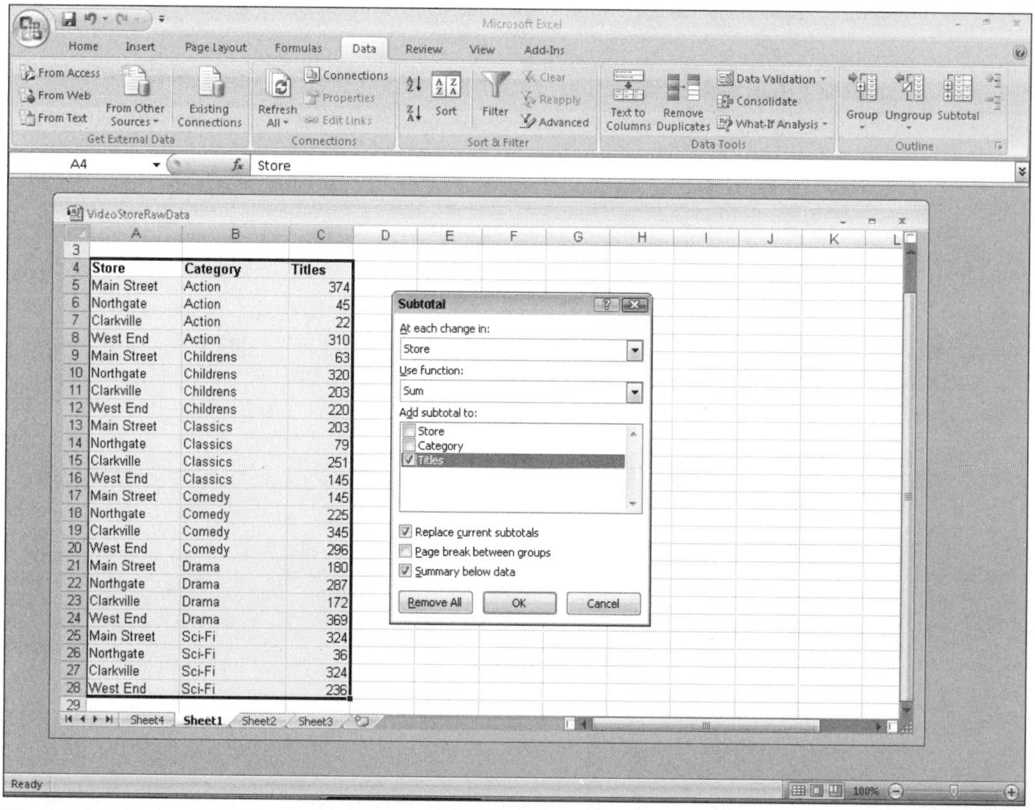

Figure 9-3: You use the Subtotal dialog box to define subtotals.

3. In the At Each Change In list, select the field on which the subtotals will be based; in this example, this field is Category.

4. In the Use Function list, select the function to be used to calculate the subtotals. You can choose between Sum (appropriate for this example) and several other measures (explained in the list following step 6).

5. In the Add Subtotal To list, place a checkmark next to the field or fields you want subtotaled. For this example you will place a check next to Titles.

6. Select the following as desired:

- **Replace current subtotals**—If this option is selected, any subtotals already in the data table will be replaced with the new ones. If it is not selected, the new subtotals will be included in the data table along with any existing ones. If there are no subtotals in the data table, this option has no effect.

- **Page break between groups**—Excel inserts a page break after each group. (This is relevant for printing only.)

- **Summary below data**—If this option is selected, each subtotal will be displayed below the group of records it is subtotaling, and the grand total will be displayed in the last row. If this option is not selected, each subtotal will be displayed above the group of records it is subtotaling, and the grand total will be displayed in the first row.

7. Click OK.

Figure 9-4 shows the data subtotaled by Category. You can see that the same subtotals are calculated as in the PivotTable report shown in Figure 9-2. The arrangement is different, of course, with the analysis results interspersed in the data table rather than in their own separate table.

	A	B	C	D
3				
4	Store	Category	Titles	
5	Main Street	Action	374	
6	Northgate	Action	45	
7	Clarkville	Action	22	
8	West End	Action	310	
9		**Action Total**	751	
10	Main Street	Childrens	63	
11	Northgate	Childrens	320	
12	Clarkville	Childrens	203	
13	West End	Childrens	220	
14		**Childrens Total**	806	
15	Main Street	Classics	203	
16	Northgate	Classics	79	
17	Clarkville	Classics	251	
18	West End	Classics	145	
19		**Classics Total**	678	
20	Main Street	Comedy	145	
21	Northgate	Comedy	225	
22	Clarkville	Comedy	345	
23	West End	Comedy	296	
24		**Comedy Total**	1011	
25	Main Street	Drama	180	
26	Northgate	Drama	287	
27	Clarkville	Drama	172	
28	West End	Drama	369	
29		**Drama Total**	1008	

Figure 9-4: Totals by Category calculated with the Excel subtotal tool.

When defining subtotals, you can choose from the following summary calculations:

- **Average**—The average of the values (sum divided by number of values).
- **Count**—The number of values, not including text data or blank cells.
- **Count Numbers**—The number of non-blank cells, including both text and number data.
- **Max**—The largest value.
- **Min**—The smallest value.
- **Product**—The product of the values.
- **StDev**—The standard deviation of the values, estimated for the sample.
- **StDevP**—The standard deviation of the values, estimated for the population.
- **Sum**—The sum of the values.
- **Var**—The variance of the values, estimated for the sample.
- **VarP**—The variance of the values, estimated for the population.

NOTE

To remove all subtotals from a data range, click the Remove All button in the Subtotal dialog box.

Nesting Subtotals

You are not limited to creating one level of subtotals for your data. You can nest them, subtotaling by one field and then, within those groupings, by another. Look, for example, at Figure 9-5. This is an expansion of the video store data from Figure 9-1, with an additional field that breaks down the titles by rating—G, PG, or R. These data are in the file `VideoDataWithRatings.xls`.

	A	B	C	D	E
1	**Store**	**Category**	**Rating**	**Titles in Stock**	
2	Downtown	Adventure	G	99	
3	North Hills	Adventure	G	109	
4	Southpoint	Adventure	G	102	
5	Downtown	Adventure	PG	78	
6	North Hills	Adventure	PG	45	
7	Southpoint	Adventure	PG	98	
8	Downtown	Adventure	R	89	
9	North Hills	Adventure	R	78	
10	Southpoint	Adventure	R	90	
11	Downtown	Classics	G	123	
12	North Hills	Classics	G	87	
13	Southpoint	Classics	G	99	
14	Downtown	Classics	PG	98	
15	North Hills	Classics	PG	78	
16	Southpoint	Classics	PG	78	
17	Downtown	Classics	R	56	
18	North Hills	Classics	R	65	
19	Southpoint	Classics	R	89	
20	Downtown	Comedy	G	114	
21	North Hills	Comedy	G	123	
22	Southpoint	Comedy	G	79	
23	Downtown	Comedy	PG	90	
24	North Hills	Comedy	PG	45	
25	Southpoint	Comedy	PG	87	
26	Downtown	Comedy	R	101	

Figure 9-5: The video store data with an additional field for rating.

Here are the steps required to create nested subtotals for these data. First, you sort the data on both of the fields that will be subtotaled, and then you create the subtotals:

1. Open the file `VideoDataWithRatings.xlsx` in Excel.

2. Place the cell pointer anywhere in the data table.

3. Select Sort from the Data menu to display the Sort dialog box.

4. Under Column, select Category from the list.

5. Under Sort On, select Values from the list.

6. Under Order, select A-Z from the list.

7. Click the Add Level button to add a second sort level called Then By.

8. For the second sort level, select Rating, Values, and A-Z.

9. Make sure that the My Data Has Header option is selected. The Sort dialog box should now look like Figure 9-6.

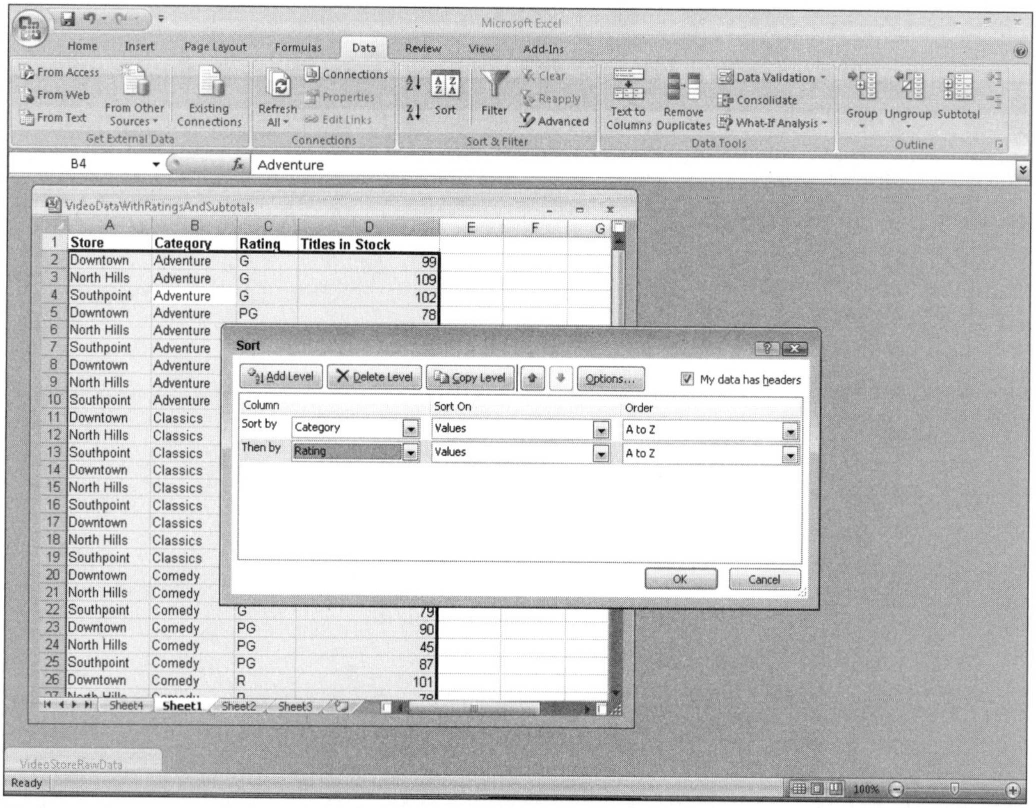

Figure 9-6: Sorting the data before applying subtotals.

10. Click OK to perform the sort.

11. Click Subtotal on the Data ribbon to display the Subtotal dialog box (shown earlier in Figure 9-3).

12. Select Category in the At Each Change In list.

13. Select Sum in the Use Function list.

14. In the Add Subtotal To list, select Titles in Stock and remove any other check marks.

15. Make sure the Page Break Between Groups option is off and the Summary Below Data option is on.

16. Click OK.

At this point the data look like Figure 9-7. You can see that it includes subtotals for Category.

	A	B	C	D	E
1	**Store**	**Category**	**Rating**	**Titles in Stock**	
2	Downtown	Adventure	G	99	
3	North Hills	Adventure	G	109	
4	Southpoint	Adventure	G	102	
5	Downtown	Adventure	PG	78	
6	North Hills	Adventure	PG	45	
7	Southpoint	Adventure	PG	98	
8	Downtown	Adventure	R	89	
9	North Hills	Adventure	R	78	
10	Southpoint	Adventure	R	90	
11		**Adventure Total**		788	
12	Downtown	Classics	G	123	
13	North Hills	Classics	G	87	
14	Southpoint	Classics	G	99	
15	Downtown	Classics	PG	98	
16	North Hills	Classics	PG	78	
17	Southpoint	Classics	PG	78	
18	Downtown	Classics	R	56	
19	North Hills	Classics	R	65	
20	Southpoint	Classics	R	89	
21		**Classics Total**		773	
22	Downtown	Comedy	G	114	
23	North Hills	Comedy	G	123	
24	Southpoint	Comedy	G	79	
25	Downtown	Comedy	PG	90	
26	North Hills	Comedy	PG	45	
27	Southpoint	Comedy	PG	87	
28	Downtown	Comedy	R	101	
29	North Hills	Comedy	R	78	

Figure 9-7: Subtotaling the data by Category.

The next step is to add the nested subtotals for Rating, as follows:

1. Click Subtotal on the Data ribbon to display the Subtotal dialog box again.

2. Select Rating in the At Each Change In list.

3. Select Sum in the Use Function list.

4. In the Add subtotal to list, place a check next to Titles in Stock and remove any other checks.

5. Make sure the Page Break Between Groups option is off and the Summary Below Data option is on. Most important, make sure the Replace Current Subtotals option is off.

6. Click OK.

The new subtotal is added, as shown in Figure 9-8. Now you can see that within each Category group, the data for each rating are broken out and subtotaled separately.

	A	B	C	D	E
1	Store	Category	Rating	Titles in Stock	
2	Downtown	Adventure	G	99	
3	North Hills	Adventure	G	109	
4	Southpoint	Adventure	G	102	
5			G Total	310	
6	Downtown	Adventure	PG	78	
7	North Hills	Adventure	PG	45	
8	Southpoint	Adventure	PG	98	
9			PG Total	221	
10	Downtown	Adventure	R	89	
11	North Hills	Adventure	R	78	
12	Southpoint	Adventure	R	90	
13			R Total	257	
14		Adventure Total		788	
15	Downtown	Classics	G	123	
16	North Hills	Classics	G	87	
17	Southpoint	Classics	G	99	
18			G Total	309	
19	Downtown	Classics	PG	98	
20	North Hills	Classics	PG	78	
21	Southpoint	Classics	PG	78	
22			PG Total	254	
23	Downtown	Classics	R	56	
24	North Hills	Classics	R	65	
25	Southpoint	Classics	R	89	
26			R Total	210	
27		Classics Total		773	
28	Downtown	Comedy	G	114	
29	North Hills	Comedy	G	123	

Figure 9-8: The data are subtotaled at two levels, Category and Rating.

Hiding and Showing Subtotal Detail

When you add subtotals to a data list in Excel, you see a vertical area immediately to the left of the row numbers at the left edge of the worksheet. This is called the *outline section*, and the controls in this area enable you to hide and display different levels of detail. Look at Figure 9-9, which is again the data from the previous section.

Three controls are available in the outline area:

- The Hide Detail button is displayed when the rows in a group are visible. Clicking the Hide Detail button hides the rows.

- The Show Detail button is displayed when the rows in a group are hidden. Clicking the Show Detail button displays the rows.

- The Level buttons each represent a level of organization in the list. Click a Level button to show all the detail for the level of the button and hide all detail below.

Subtotals versus PivotTables

Subtotals are easy to use and the fact that the subtotals are displayed along with the data may be an advantage in some situations. However, the use of subtotals is dependent on the data being organized in a certain way, and restricts the ways in which they can be sorted. Also, there is no reliable way to get data out of a data table that includes subtotals—in other words, there is no equivalent of the GETPIVOTDATA function. Subtotals certainly have their uses but are not capable of performing most of the robust types of analysis for which PivotTables are designed.

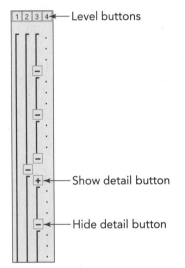

Level buttons

Show detail button

Hide detail button

Figure 9-9: You can use the outline area to control the level of detail displayed.

Working with Database Functions

Excel has a special category of functions intended specifically for working with databases. In this context, a database is any table of data with column headings identifying the fields, just the kind of data that is commonly analyzed with PivotTables. The database functions perform the same calculations as other Excel functions, such as sum, average, and standard deviation. What sets them apart is that they include only values that meet one or more criteria.

To illustrate, look at the video store data presented earlier in Figure 9-5. You have already seen how you can use a PivotTable or subtotals to extract summary data that will answer questions such as "What's the total number of videos in the Drama category?" Database functions can perform much the same task.

The database function names all start with D. The remainder of the name describes the function and is the same as the name of the equivalent non-database function. The following list describes the database functions:

- DAVERAGE returns the average of selected database entries.
- DCOUNT counts the cells that contain numbers in a database.
- DCOUNTA counts nonblank cells in a database.
- DMAX returns the maximum value from selected database entries.
- DMIN returns the minimum value from selected database entries.
- DPRODUCT multiplies the values in a particular field of records that match the criteria in a database.
- DSTDEV estimates the standard deviation based on a sample of selected database entries.
- DSTDEVP calculates the standard deviation based on the entire population of selected database entries.
- DSUM adds the numbers in the field column of records in the database that match the criteria.
- DVAR estimates variance based on a sample from selected database entries.
- DVARP calculates variance based on the entire population of selected database entries.

The functions all take the same arguments:

```
DXXXXX(Database, Field, Criteria)
```

where:

- Database is the worksheet range containing the data, including the first row of column or field names. It can be a range address such as A1:J150 or an assigned range name.
- Field is the name of the field or column whose values will be summarized by the function.
- Criteria is the worksheet range where the criteria for the database function is located.

Defining Criteria

Defining the criteria is the only tricky part of using database functions. The criteria tell the function which rows, or records, to include in its calculation. For example, to calculate the total number of titles for the Drama category, the criteria would in effect tell the DSUM function to include only those records where the Category field contains the value Drama.

At a minimum, the criteria range contains two cells in one column. The top cell contains the name of the field that the criterion applies to, and the lower cell contains the criterion itself. For example, the criterion in Figure 9-10 specifies that only those records which contain Adventure in the Category column will be included in the calculation.

Category
Adventure

Figure 9-10: A simple criterion for a database function.

To see a real example, return to the video store data and calculate the sum of titles in stock for the Adventure category. Assuming that you placed the criterion in cells G2:G3, the database function will be

```
=DSUM(A1:D46, "Titles in Stock", G2:G3)
```

The three arguments are as follows:

- `A1:D46` is the range of cells containing the data, including the row of field names at the top.

- `Titles in Stock` is the name of the column whose values you want to summarize.

- `G2:G3` is the range containing the criterion.

For text criteria, such as in the previous example, simply enter the text you want to match. For numbers, if you want an exact match simply enter the number. For example, the criterion range in Figure 9-11 matches records in which the Age field is equal to 23.

Age
23

Figure 9-11: A numeric criterion for a database function.

Where to Put Your Criteria

You can put your criteria essentially anywhere in the workbook. The only place you should avoid is below the data table. It's a good idea to leave this area blank in case you need to add data to the table.

Numeric criteria that are not exact matches are specified with the symbols in the following table.

Symbol	Meaning	Example	Matches
>	Greater than	>15	Values greater than 15
<	Less than	<0	Values less than 0
>=	Greater than or equal to	>=15	Values of 15 or greater
<=	Less than or equal to	<=0	Values of 0 or less

You can also define a criteria range for more complex criteria. To match more than one value in a field, place the values in two or more cells below the field name. For example, the criterion range shown in Figure 9-12 will match records in which the Category field contains either Adventure or Drama. Of course, the range passed as the criterion argument to the database function must specify all the cells in the criterion range.

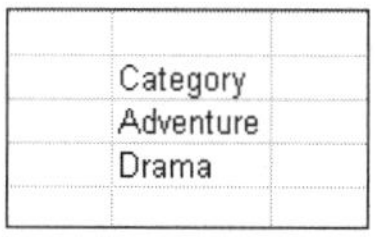

Category
Adventure
Drama

Figure 9-12: A criterion that matches either of two values in the Category field.

To define criteria that include two or more fields, create a criterion range with two or more adjacent columns. Place a field name at the top of each column and the criteria in the cells below. The example shown in Figure 9-13 will match only those records in which the Category field contains Adventure and the Rating field contains PG. As before, the criterion range passed to the database function must include all the rows and columns of the range.

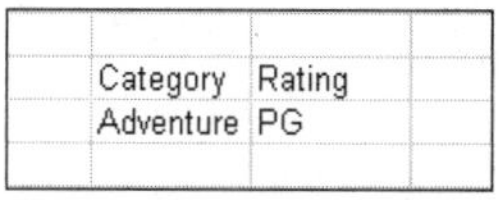

Category	Rating
Adventure	PG

Figure 9-13: A criterion that specifies matches for two database fields.

Database Functions versus PivotTables

Database functions are very powerful, although they can be a little tricky to use. They are at their best when you need to pull specific summary information out of a database without necessarily summarizing all the information. They are also more appropriate when you know in advance the type of analysis you will be performing and know that it will not change down the road. A PivotTable report is a better choice for summarizing an entire database or significant parts of it, or if you want to be able to vary the type of analysis you perform.

Working with Filters

Filters are very useful Excel database tools that enable you to filter your data, showing only those records that meet certain criteria. Other non-matching records are still present in the database, but they are hidden while the filter is applied.

To create a filter, first place the cell pointer anywhere in the database table; then click the Filter button on the Data ribbon. Excel places a drop-down list at the top of each column in the table, as shown for the video store data in Figure 9-14.

Drop-down lists for filtering

	A	B	C	D
1	Store	Category	Rating	Titles in Stock
2	Downtown	Adventure	G	99
3	North Hills	Adventure	G	109
4	Southpoint	Adventure	G	102
5	Downtown	Adventure	PG	78
6	North Hills	Adventure	PG	45

Figure 9-14: When you add filters to a database, each column heading becomes a drop-down list.

Next, use these drop-down lists to define your filter.

You can also sort the database on the field. The drop-down list for the Category field is shown in Figure 9-15. It gives you the following choices:

- **Sort A to Z**—Sorts the database on this field in ascending order (A–Z, 1–10).

- **Sort Z to A**—Sorts the database on this field in descending order (Z–A, 10–1).

- **Sort by Color**—This command is relevant only if you have used conditional formatting to display data in different colors based on the data (please refer to Excel Help for more information on conditional formatting). Selecting the command opens the Sort dialog box where you can define a custom sort that includes color as a criterion.

- **Clear Filter**—Removes any filter that has been applied.

- **Filter by Color**—If you have used conditional formatting to display data in different colors, you can filter the data based on the color.

- **[Individual data values]**—Displays only those records with the selected value.

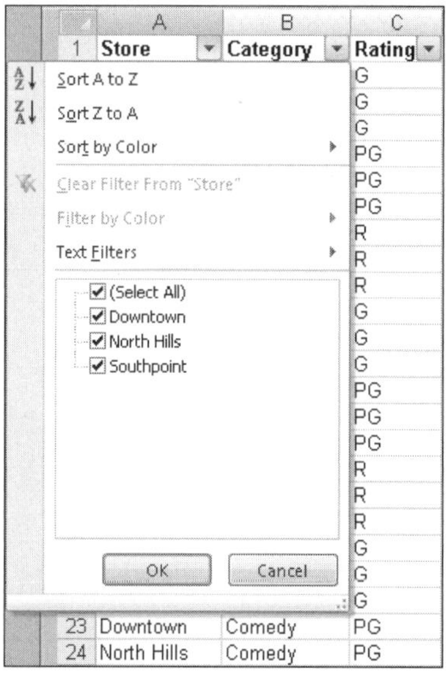

Figure 9-15: A drop-down filter list enables you to define your filter and/or sort the database.

To remove the filter drop-down lists, click the Filter button on the Data ribbon.

Filters versus PivotTables

Filters are not really an alternative to PivotTables. They can be very useful tools for some data-presentation and analysis tasks, but they do not provide the kind of summary analyses that PivotTables, subtotals, and database functions do.

Chapter 10

Programming PivotTables with VBA

Excel includes a powerful programming language called Visual Basic for Applications (VBA). With VBA you can automate essentially any task in Excel, including the creation and manipulation of PivotTable reports. This chapter provides you with the information you need to create VBA procedures (or macros) to work with PivotTables and contains numerous working examples. This chapter does not, however, teach the fundamentals of VBA programming. After all, that is a topic that can fill an entire book. For the purposes of this chapter, I assume you have at least intermediate-level experience working with VBA and the VBA editor.

In This Chapter

- ◆ The PivotTable object model
- ◆ Referencing and creating PivotTables
- ◆ Manipulating PivotTables in code
- ◆ Creating PivotCharts in code

Understanding the PivotTable Object Model

In VBA, PivotTables and all their various parts and components are represented by *object models*. This means that everything is represented by a specific kind of object. For example, the PivotTable itself is represented by a PivotTable object, an individual cell in a PivotTable is represented by a PivotCell object, and so on. Programming PivotTables essentially means manipulating the underlying objects.

The PivotTable object model has two basic features:

- It is hierarchical, meaning that every object except for the Excel application itself has a parent object and most objects also have child objects.

- It uses collections, a special kind of object designed to hold other objects. By convention, a collection object has a name that is the plural of the name of the type of objects it contains. For example, the PivotTables collection contains each PivotTable in a given workbook. There are exceptions to this naming rule, however.

To manipulate an object in code you must first get a reference to it, a variable name that you use in code to refer to the object. If the object already exists, such as a PivotTable already present in a workbook, you retrieve the reference from the appropriate collection. The most important objects and collections in the PivotTable object model are described in Table 10-1. The relationships among these objects and collections are diagrammed in Figure 10-1.

TABLE 10-1 IMPORTANT OBJECTS AND COLLECTIONS IN THE PIVOTTABLE OBJECT MODEL

Object/Collection	Description
PivotTable	This object represents a single PivotTable.
PivotTables	This collection contains all the PivotTables on a single worksheet.
PivotField	This object represents a field in a PivotTable.
PivotFields	This collection contains all the fields in a single PivotTable.
PivotItem	This object represents a single item (an individual data entry) in a field.
PivotItems	This collection contains all the items for a single field.
CalculatedFields	This collection contains all the calculated fields in the PivotTable. Each calculated field is represented by a PivotField object.

Object/Collection	Description
CalculatedMembers	This collection contains all the calculated measures in the PivotTable.
CalculatedMember	Each calculated measure is represented by a CalculatedMember object.
PivotFormula	The PivotFormula object represents each formula used to calculate results (sum, average, and so on) in a PivotTable.
PivotFormulas	The PivotFormulas collection contains all the formulas for a single PivotTable.

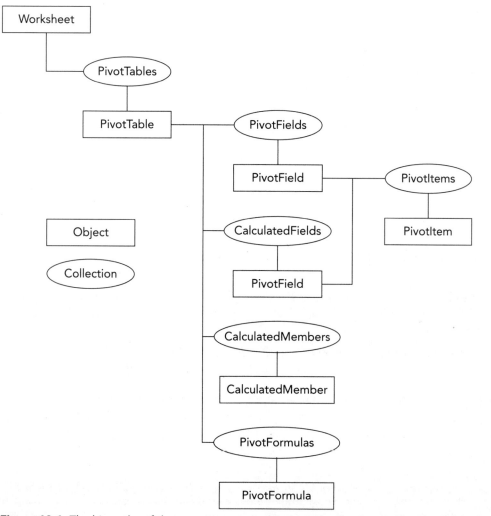

Figure 10-1: The hierarchy of the most important objects and collections in the PivotTable object model.

Macro Security in Excel 2007

Remember that Excel 2007 provides two types of workbooks, a macro-free type that is saved with the `.xslx` extension and a macro-enabled type that is saved with the `.xslm` extension. You must use the latter type if you want to run macros.

Referencing and Creating PivotTables

The first step in manipulating a PivotTable is to obtain a reference to it. How you do this depends on whether the PivotTable already exists. If it does, you obtain a reference to the existing PivotTable. If it doesn't, you create the PivotTable and, in the process, obtain the reference. The following sections explain both techniques.

Referencing an Existing PivotTable

A PivotTable that already exists will be present in the PivotTables collection for the worksheet in which it is located. Assuming that the variable `ws` is a reference to that worksheet, the syntax is as follows. First, declare a variable of the proper type to hold the reference:

```
Dim pt As PivotTable
```

Then retrieve the reference and store it in the variable:

```
Set pt = ws.PivotTables(index)
```

The `index` argument identifies the PivotTable. It can be either of the following:

- **A number that identifies the position of the PivotTable on the worksheet**—The first PivotTable created on a worksheet has `index-1`, the next one created has `index-2`, and so on.

- **A string specifying the name of the PivotTable**—Each PivotTable has a name, either the default name assigned by Excel (PivotTable1, and so on) or the name you specified.

By default PivotTables on a given worksheet are assigned the names PivotTable1, PivotTable2, and so on. You can change the name in the Table Options dialog box. To display this dialog box, right-click the PivotTable and select Table options from the popup menu.

If you specify a PivotTable that does not exist, a runtime error occurs. Listing 10-1 illustrates this technique for obtaining a reference to an existing PivotTable. It opens a workbook and gets a reference to the first PivotTable on Sheet4.

The PivotTables Collection

You might think that all the PivotTables in a workbook would be organized together in a PivotTables collection that belongs to the workbook itself, but that's not the way Excel does things. Instead, each worksheet has its own PivotTables collection.

Listing 10-1: A VBA procedure that opens a workbook and references a PivotTable

```
Sub GetPivotTableReference()

Dim wb As Workbook
Dim pt As PivotTable

On Error GoTo ErrorHandler

' Open the workbook.
Set wb = Workbooks.Open("c:\PivotData\SurveyResults.xlst")
' Get the PivotTable reference.
Set pt = wb.Worksheets("Sheet4").PivotTables(1)

' Code here can use the variable pt to work with the PivotTable

EndOfSub:
Exit Sub

ErrorHandler:

If Err.Number = 5 Or Err.Number = 9 then
    MsgBox "The workbook file could not be found"
ElseIf Err.Number = 1004 Then
    MsgBox "The PivotTable could not be found"
Else
    MsgBox "Error " & Err & " - " & Err.Description
End If

Resume EndOfSub

End Sub
```

Creating a New PivotTable in Code

You can create a new PivotTable using VBA code in two ways. The easiest, and the one you should use whenever possible, involves the PivotTableWizard method. Despite its name, this method doesn't display the PivotTable Wizard, but rather uses it behind the scenes to create a PivotTable based on options that you specify in code. The limitation of this method is that it cannot be used with OLE DB data sources. When you are using such a data source, you must use the second method, which does not involve the `PivotTableWizard` method. These two techniques are explained in the following sections.

Using the PivotTableWizard Method

To create a new PivotTable in a worksheet, call the `PivotTableWizard` method on the `Worksheet` object where you want the PivotTable located. The syntax of this method is quite complex, with numerous optional arguments that are infrequently used. For this exercise, it will be most helpful to look at some examples. (You can also get the full details from the VBA online Help.)

At its simplest, the `PivotTableWizard` method requires that you specify the type of the source data and their location. For data in an Excel list, you use the constant `xlDatabase` to specify the type. For example, this line of code creates a PivotTable based on the data in the range A4:E250 on Sheet1. The PivotTable is placed on Sheet2, by default in the active cell.

```
Worksheets("Sheet2").PivotTableWizard SourceType:=xlDatabase, _
    SourceData:=Range("Sheet1!A4:E250")
```

You can specify a location other than the active cell for the PivotTable, and you can also assign a name to the report when it is created:

```
Worksheets("Sheet2").PivotTableWizard SourceType:=xlDatabase, _
   SourceData:=Range("Sheet1!A4:E250"), _
   TableDestination:=Range("D4"), _
   TableName:="My Pivot Table"
```

Finally, you can specify that the PivotTable include grand totals for the rows or the columns:

```
Worksheets("Sheet2").PivotTableWizard SourceType:=xlDatabase, _
   SourceData:=Range("Sheet1!A4:E250"), _
   TableDestination:=Range("D4"), _
   TableName:="My Pivot Table", _
   RowGrand:=True, ColumnGrand:=True
```

Figure 10-2 shows a data table in Excel on which the example PivotTable report used here is based. This is the video store stock data workbook that has been used in previous examples.

You can create a PivotTable report based on these data with the following VBA code; note the first line which makes Sheet2 active, required for the code to work properly:

```
Worksheets("Sheet2").Activate
Worksheets("Sheet2").PivotTableWizard SourceType:=xlDatabase, _
    SourceData:=Range("Sheet1!A4:C28"), _
    TableDestination:=Range("B2")
```

	A	B	C	D
1				
2	Popcorn Video Rentals			
3				
4	Store	Category	Titles	
5	Main Street	Action	374	
6	Main Street	Drama	180	
7	Main Street	Childrens	63	
8	Main Street	Sci-Fi	324	
9	Main Street	Classics	203	
10	Main Street	Comedy	145	
11	Northgate	Action	45	
12	Northgate	Drama	287	
13	Northgate	Childrens	320	
14	Northgate	Sci-Fi	36	
15	Northgate	Classics	79	
16	Northgate	Comedy	225	
17	Clarkville	Action	22	
18	Clarkville	Drama	172	
19	Clarkville	Childrens	203	
20	Clarkville	Sci-Fi	324	
21	Clarkville	Classics	251	
22	Clarkville	Comedy	345	
23	West End	Action	310	
24	West End	Drama	369	
25	West End	Childrens	220	

Figure 10-2: The video store stock data for the PivotTable report.

Displaying the Developer Ribbon

To work with macros and VBA in Excel you need to display the Developer ribbon. If it is not displayed, here's what to do:

1. Click the Office button.

2. Click the Excel Options button to open the Excel Options window.

3. On the left, select the Popular category.

4. Select the Show Developer Tab in the Ribbon option.

5. Click OK.

The resulting PivotTable is shown in Figure 10-3. But wait; this does not look right. There are two reasons for this.

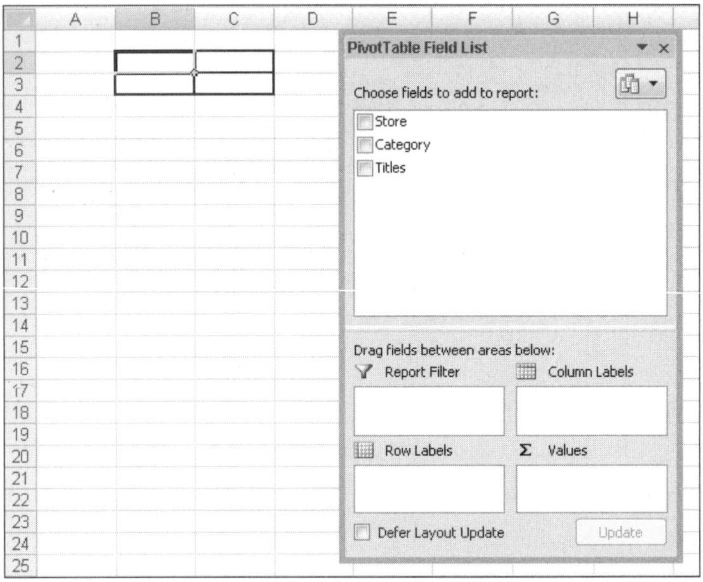

Figure 10-3: The blank PivotTable report created by the VBA code.

A PivotTable created in VBA code using this method is by default in Classic PivotTable view rather than the new Excel 2007 view (you learned about this in Chapter 3). But a PivotTable in Classic view should display drop zones, and this one does not. You can still drag and drop fields onto the PivotTable, although it is difficult because the target regions are not identified. But the main reason is that when you use VBA to create a PivotTable, you will almost always use VBA to place the fields on it as well, so the visual interface of the PivotTable is not that important at this stage of things. Adding fields and other parts of defining a PivotTable in code are covered later in the chapter.

After you have created the PivotTable, you can get a reference to it using the techniques I explained earlier in this part in the section "Referencing an Existing PivotTable." You can also get the reference at the same time that the PivotTable is created, because the `PivotTableWizard` method returns a reference to the newly created PivotTable. For example:

```
Dim pt As PivotTable
Set pt = Worksheets("Sheet3").PivotTableWizard _
  (SourceType:=xlDatabase, _
  SourceData:=Range("Sheet1!A4:C28"), _
  TableDestination:=Range("B2"))
```

Note that when you use the return value of the method, its arguments must be enclosed in parentheses. This is required by VBA syntax rules.

Creating a New PivotTable Without the PivotTableWizard Method

Creating a new PivotTable using VBA code without the `PivotTableWizard` method is a bit more complicated than you might think at first glance. This is because an object called `PivotCache` is involved. When you create a PivotTable manually in a worksheet or in code using the `PivotTableWizard`, the `PivotCache` object is created automatically. It exists behind the scenes and the user never has to be concerned with it. When you are working in VBA and not using the `PivotTableWizard` method, however, you must attend to these details.

The memory dedicated to a PivotTable report is represented by a `PivotCache` object, and each PivotTable has its own `PivotCache` (although in certain situations you can have two or more PivotTables based on a single `PivotCache`). All `PivotCache` objects in a workbook are represented in the `PivotCaches` collection. Thus, there are two steps in creating a new PivotTable:

1. Create a new `PivotCache` object by calling the `Add` method of the `PivotCaches` collection. At this time you specify the data source for the PivotTable.

2. Create the new PivotTable by calling the `CreatePivotTable` method of the `PivotCache` object that you created in Step 1. In this step you specify the location for the new PivotTable and, optionally, assign a name to it.

The VBA example in Listing 10-2 shows you how to create a PivotTable from data in a list in an Excel workbook. You can also create a PivotTable from external data (including OLE DB data), from another PivotTable report, and from multiple consolidation ranges. (You can find detailed descriptions of these techniques in the VBA online documentation.)

This example uses the video store data you used in Chapter 9 and saw earlier in Figure 10-2. The code opens the workbook with the data and then creates the PivotTable on Sheet2. It's important to note the location of the source data—cells A4:C28 on Sheet1—because you need this information when creating the `PivotCache` object.

Listing 10-2: A VBA procedure that opens a workbook and creates a new PivotTable based on data in an Excel list

```
Public Sub CreatePivotTable()

Dim wb As Workbook
Dim pt As PivotTable
Dim pc As PivotCache

On Error GoTo ErrorHandler

' Open the workbook.
```

```
Set wb = Workbooks.Open("c:\PivotData\VideoStoreRawData.xlsx")


' Create the PivotCache.
Set pc = wb.PivotCaches.Add(SourceType:=xlDatabase, _
    SourceData:="[VideoStoreRawData.xlsx]Sheet1!A4:C28")


' Create the PivotTable on Sheet 2 of the same workbook.

Set pt = pc.CreatePivotTable _
  (TableDestination:=wb.Worksheets("Sheet2").Range("A1"), _
    TableName:="Video Data")


' At this point the variable pt refers to the new PivotTable and
' can be used to manipulate it.


' Activate the worksheet containing the PivotTable.
wb.Worksheets("Sheet2").Activate


EndOfSub:


Exit Sub


ErrorHandler:


If Err.Number = 5 Or Err.Number = 9 Then
    MsgBox "The file could not be found"
ElseIf Err.Number = 1004 Then
    MsgBox "There is already a PivotTable at that location"
Else
    MsgBox "Error " & Err & " - " & Err.Description
End If


Resume EndOfSub



End Sub
```

When you run this VBA procedure, it creates a new blank PivotTable, similar to what you see at the completion of the PivotTable Wizard when you are creating a PivotTable manually. As when you use the PivotTable Wizard, the new PivotTable doesn't have the Drop Here labels. Users can still drop fields on the PivotTable, but as I mentioned before, you will most often be completing the PivotTable layout in code rather than letting the user do it manually. Or, you can switch from Classic PivotTable view to the default view and use the Field List as usual.

Working with the PivotTable Object

Manipulating the `PivotTable` object is, as you might expect, at the heart of working with PivotTables in code. Given the power and flexibility of PivotTables, it is not too surprising that the PivotTable object is quite complex. It has over a dozen methods and several dozen properties with which you can work. Some of these are essential and are used almost every time you need to manipulate a PivotTable in VBA code. Others are relatively obscure and are rarely used. Tables 10-2 and 10-3 list the more important properties and methods of this object with a brief description of each. Then, the following sections show you how to perform real-world tasks with PivotTables using VBA code. Properties marked Read Only can be read but not set in code. Properties marked Read/Write can be read and set.

TABLE 10-2   IMPORTANT PROPERTIES OF THE PIVOTTABLE OBJECT

Property	Read Only (R) or Read/Write (R/W)	Description
CalculatedMembers	R	Returns a `CalculatedMembers` collection representing all the calculated members and measures for an OLAP-based PivotTable.
ColumnFields	R	If the PivotTable has only one column field, returns a `PivotField` object representing the field. If the PivotTable has more than one column field, returns a `PivotFields` collection containing one `PivotField` object for each column field.
ColumnGrand	R/W	Returns `True` if the PivotTable displays column grand totals, `False` if not.
DataFields	R	If the PivotTable has only one data field, returns a `PivotField` object representing the field. If the PivotTable has more than one data field, returns a `PivotFields` collection that contains one `PivotField` object for each data field.
EnableDrillDown	R/W	Returns `True` (the default) if drill-down is enabled, `False` if not.

continued

Part III

TABLE 10-2   IMPORTANT PROPERTIES OF THE PIVOTTABLE OBJECT *(continued)*

Property	Read Only (R) or Read/Write (R/W)	Description
GrandTotalName	R/W	Specifies the heading label for grand total rows and columns. The default is "Grand Total."
Name	R/W	The name of the PivotTable.
PageFields	R	If the PivotTable has only one visible page field, returns a PivotField object representing the field. If the PivotTable has more than one visible page field, returns a PivotFields collection that contains one PivotField object for each page field.
PivotFormulas	R	Returns a PivotFormulas object that represents the collection of formulas for the PivotTable.
PreserveFormatting	R/W	Returns True if the table's formatting is preserved when refreshed or recalculated, False if it is not.
RowFields	R	If the PivotTable has only one row field, returns a PivotField object representing the field. If the PivotTable has more than one row field, returns a PivotFields collection containing one PivotField object for each row field.
RowGrand	R/W	Returns True if the PivotTable displays row grand totals, False if it does not.

TABLE 10-3   IMPORTANT METHODS OF THE PIVOTTABLE OBJECT

Method	Description	Return Value
AddDataField	Adds a data field to the PivotTable report.	A reference to the PivotField object for the added field.
AddFields	Adds row, column, or page fields successfully. (Not available for OLAP data sources.)	True if the field was added to the PivotTable report; False otherwise.
Format	Applies one of several predefined formats to the PivotTable.	N/A
GetData	Returns data from a specified cell in the PivotTable report.	The returned data as a double.
GetPivotData	Returns a range object representing specified data in the PivotTable report.	A range object.
ListFormulas	Creates a new worksheet containing a list of all calculated PivotTable items and fields. (Not available for OLAP data sources.)	N/A
PivotFields	Returns visible and hidden PivotTable fields (all in the Field List).	A PivotField object representing a single PivotTable field or a PivotFields collection of multiple visible and hidden fields.
PivotSelect	Selects part of a PivotTable report.	N/A
RefreshTable	Refreshes the PivotTable report.	True if successful, False if not.
ShowPages	Creates a new PivotTable report, on a new worksheet, for each item in the page field	True if successful, False if not.

Part III

Adding and Removing Row, Column, and Filter Fields

A PivotTable report is largely defined by its row, column, and filter fields. When you first create a PivotTable report using the methods described earlier in this chapter, it has no fields at all and you must add them. After a report has been defined, you may want to remove certain fields and add others, or move a field from the Row Labels area to the Column Labels area. You can do all this with the `AddFields` method.

```
AddFields(RowFields, ColumnFields, PageFields, AddToTable)
```

The first three arguments specify the fields to be added to the row, column, or filter areas respectively (filter fields were called page fields in earlier versions of Excel, hence the name of the third argument). You must specify at least one of these arguments, and you can also specify two or three of them in a single call. The argument takes one of two forms:

- If you are adding a single field to an area, it is the field name.
- If you are adding more then one field to an area, it is an array containing the field names.

The `AddToTable` argument determines whether existing fields in the PivotTable are replaced. If this argument is `True`, the specified fields are added to the report without any existing fields being deleted. If this argument is `False` or is omitted, existing fields are deleted and replaced with the new ones.

The following code adds the field named Region to the Column area of the first PivotTable on Sheet1, adding it to any existing column fields:

```
Worksheets("Sheet1").PivotTables(1).AddFields _
    (ColumnFields:="Region", AddToTable:=True)
```

This code adds the fields named Status and DueDate to the Row area of the PivotTable referenced by the variable myPivotTable, replacing any existing row fields:

```
myPivotTable.AddFields(RowFields:=Array("Status", "DueDate"))
```

This final example adds two page fields, one row field, and one column field to a PivotTable report, replacing any existing fields:

```
myPivotTable.AddFields(RowFields:="Region", _
    ColumnFields:="Quarter", _
    PageFields:=Array("Status", "DueDate"))
```

After you learn how to add value fields to a PivotTable, I will put everything together in a real-world example.

Adding and Removing Value Fields

In addition to row, column, and page fields, a PivotTable report needs one or more value fields. You add a value field to a PivotTable report with the `AddDataField` method (so named because in earlier versions of Excel value fields were called data fields). It has the following syntax:

```
AddDataField(Field, Caption, Function)
```

where:

- The `Field` argument specifies the field to add. You might think you could just specify the field name, but you cannot; you must pass a reference to the field. I'll show you how later in this section.

- The `Caption` argument specifies the caption that will be used for the field—in other words the label displayed in the PivotTable report.

- The `Function` argument specifies the function that the added field uses. The default is `Sum`.

The `AddDataField` function returns a reference to the added field.

The first argument specifies the field to add, but it must be a reference to a `PivotField` object for that field and not just the field name. This seems like an unnecessary complication, but that's the way it works. You can get this reference from the PivotTable's `PivotFields` method as follows, where `Name` is the name of the field:

```
PivotFields(Name)
```

Here's an example of adding a value field to a PivotTable report. This code first gets a reference to the PivotTable named PivotTable1 on Sheet1. Then it adds the field named Sales with the caption Total Sales. The field uses the default `Sum` function:

```
Dim pt As PivotTable
Set pt = Worksheets("Sheet1").PivotTables("PivotTable1")
pt.AddDataField pt.PivotFields("Sales"), "Total Sales"
```

Creating a PivotTable Using VBA Code

The code presented in this section builds on the code examples presented earlier that show you how to create a PivotTable using the PivotTable Wizard. Listing 10-3 contains a complete VBA procedure that creates a PivotTable and populates it with row, column, and value fields. The code creates a PivotTable from the data shown in Figure 10-2.

Let Excel Find the Data Range

Suppose you know where the data are located but not the precise number of rows they contain. Can you still create a PivotTable in code? You bet, using the `CurrentRegion` property. All you need to know is the address of any single cell in the data range: then this property returns the range of surrounding cells that contain data. Specifically, it returns the range of data bounded by empty rows, empty columns, or the edges of the worksheet. For example, the expression

```
Range("Sheet1!A4").CurrentRegion,
```

returns the range of data surrounding cell A4 on Sheet1—in this case A4:C28.

The code performs the following steps:

1. Opens the worksheet `c:\PivotData\VideoStoreRawData.xlsx`. (You'll need to change this if you have placed the file in a different location.)
2. Creates the PivotTable report at cell B2 in Sheet 2.
3. Adds Store as a row field and Category as a column field.
4. Adds Titles as the value field with the caption Total Titles.

The resulting PivotTable report is shown in Figure 10-4. You can see that this is a complete PivotTable, with all required fields in place. With code such as this you can automate the procedure of creating a PivotTable, letting users create a PivotTable with the least effort. Of course, you need to know something about the data, specifically their location and the field names.

Listing 10-3: A VBA procedure that creates a PivotTable and adds all required fields to it

```
Public Sub CreateCompletePivotTable()

Dim wb As Workbook
Dim pt As PivotTable

On Error GoTo ErrorHandler

' Open the workbook.
Set wb = Workbooks.Open("c:\PivotData\VideoStoreRawData.xlsx")

' Create the PivotTable and get a reference to it.
Set pt = Worksheets("Sheet2").PivotTableWizard _
  (SourceType:=xlDatabase, _
  SourceData:=Range("Sheet1!A4:C28"), _
```

```
            TableDestination:=Range("Sheet2!B2"))


    ' Add row and column fields.
    pt.AddFields RowFields:="Store", ColumnFields:="Category"


    ' Add value field.
    pt.AddDataField pt.PivotFields("Titles"), "Total Titles"


EndOfSub:
    Exit Sub


ErrorHandler:


    If Err.Number = 5 Or Err.Number = 9 Then
        MsgBox "The file could not be found"
    ElseIf Err.Number = 1004 Then
        MsgBox "There is already a PivotTable at that location"
    Else
        MsgBox "Error " & Err & " - " & Err.Description
    End If


    Resume EndOfSub


End Sub
```

	A	B	C	D	E	F	G	H	I
1									
2		Total Titles	Category						
3		Store	Action	Childrens	Classics	Comedy	Drama	Sci-Fi	Grand Total
4		Clarkville	22	203	251	345	172	324	1317
5		Main Street	374	63	203	145	180	324	1289
6		Northgate	45	320	79	225	287	36	992
7		West End	310	220	145	296	369	236	1576
8		Grand Total	751	806	678	1011	1008	920	5174
9									

Figure 10-4: The PivotTable report created by the VBA procedure in Listing 10-3.

Working with PivotTable Fields

All of the fields in a PivotTable report, both visible and not visible, are represented by the `PivotField` object. If you want to write code to manipulate fields, performing actions such as changing the display format and changing position, you will need to use the `PivotField` object in code. This object has a large number of properties and methods, most of which are rarely needed. Rather than presenting a long table of details I will present some real-world examples of how you use the `PivotField` object to accomplish certain tasks.

Creating and Changing Filters

As you learned in Chapters 3 and 4, a filter enables you specify that only some of a field's items are to be displayed in the PivotTable report. To review briefly, an item is an individual data value in a field. For example, the Month field would contain the items Jan, Feb, and so on. To create a filter you are actually hiding or showing individual items by setting the `Visible` property to `False` or `True`. The procedure involves simply setting the individual item's `Visible` property to `True` or `False` as desired:

```
Dim pt As PivotTable

Set pt = Worksheets(1).PivotTables(1)

With pt.PivotFields("Month")
    .PivotItems("Jan").Visible = True
    .PivotItems("Feb").Visible = False
    .PivotItems("Mar").Visible = True
  End With
```

Changing a Field's Position

A field's position—whether it is a row, column, filter, or value field—is controlled by the `PivotField` object's `Orientation` property. A field can also be hidden, meaning that it is not part of the PivotTable report but is available to be added to the report. These settings are represented by the defined constants `xlHidden`, `xlRowField`, `xlColumnField`, `xlPageField`, `xlDataField`, and `xlHidden`.

To change a field's position, you need to get a reference to the field and then set its `Orientation` property as desired. The following code assumes that the variable `pt` has been set to refer to the PivotTable report of interest. It then sets the field named Color to be a row field:

```
Dim pf As PivotField
Set pf =pt.PivotFields("Color")
pf.Orientation=xlRowField
```

When a PivotTable report has more than one field in the row or column area, the fields have a hierarchy beginning with the outermost field. In the row area, for example, the outer field is displayed at the far left and provides the top level of organization of the PivotTable's rows, while the inner field is displayed at the right and provides the lowest level of organization. To change a field's inner/outer position, you set its `Position` property. A value of 1 specifies the outer field, 2 is the next level, and so on. This addition to the previous example sets the Color field to be the outer row field:

```
Dim pf As PivotField
Set pf =pt.PivotFields("Color")
pf.Orientation=xlRowField
pf.Position=1
```

Creating Calculated Fields and Items

A PivotTable report can contain calculated fields and calculated items. To review briefly, a calculated field is a data field whose value is based upon a calculation performed on one or more other fields in the PivotTable report. A calculated item is similar to a calculated field in that it is based on a calculation using an existing data field, but it is not a field; rather, it is an independent item in the report.

Calculated fields are maintained in the PivotTable object's `CalculatedFields` collection. To create a new calculated field, you call the collection's `Add` method and pass it the name of the new field as well as the calculation formula. The calculation formula consists of the following parts:

- A leading equals sign

- The name or names of one or more existing fields, including other calculated fields

- The mathematical operators + (addition), - (subtraction), / (division), * (multiplication), and ^ (exponentiation)

- Numerical values

For example, the formula `=Amount*0.07` creates a calculated field that displays 7 percent of the value in the Amount field. Likewise the formula `=Commission*Sale` creates a calculated field that displays the product of the Commission and Sale fields.

Here is a code snippet that creates a calculated field named Sales Tax that is equal to 5 percent of the Amount field. Assume that `pt` is a reference to the PivotTable report of interest:

```
Dim pf As PivotField
Set pf = pt.CalculatedFields.Add(Name:="=Sales Tax", _
        Formula:="Amount*0.05")
pf.Orientation=xlDataField
```

Note the last line of this code, which sets the field to be a value field. This is required if you want the calculated field to be displayed. If you do not do this, the field will be created and will be available for use in the PivotTable report, but it will remain hidden.

A calculated item is associated with an existing field, and you create it by adding to the field's `CalculatedItems` collection. The syntax for the calculation formula is the same as described for calculated fields. You also specify a caption for the calculated item when you create it. This code adds a calculated item named Next Quarter to the Quarter field, displaying the calculation of 0.9 times the value of the Qtr1 item. Assume that the variable `pt` is a reference to the PivotTable report:

```
Dim pf As PivotField
Set pf = pt.PivotFields(Index:="Quarter")
pf.CalculatedItems.Add Name:="Next Quarter", Formula:="=Qtr1*0.9"
```

Part III

Hide and Show Field Items

Hiding and showing fields is actually a matter of changing their positions. A field is *hidden* when it is not a row, column, value, or filter field. You saw how to do this in the section "Changing a Field's Position" earlier in this chapter. To hide a field, set its position to `xlHidden`. To show a field, set its position to `xlPageField`, `xlRowField`, `xlColumnField`, or `xlDataField`.

Using AutoShow and AutoSort

You learned in Chapter 4 how to use the sort feature to sort data in a PivotTable report, and also how to use a Top 10 filter to display only certain values such as the 10 highest. You can also use these features from VBA code.

To sort the report on a field you use the `PivotField` object's `AutoSort` method. This method has the following syntax:

```
AutoSort(Order, Field)
```

where:

- `Order` determines the sort order, either `xlAscending`, `xlDescending`, or `xlManual`.
- `Field` is the name of the field on which to sort. This must be the unique field name (as returned from the `SourceName` property) and not the displayed name, which may be different.

The following code sets the field Salesman to sort in ascending order based on the data in the Sales Total field:

```
ActiveSheet.PivotTables(1).PivotField("Salesman") _
    .AutoSort xlAscending, "Sales Total"
```

To enable a Top 10 filter, you call the field's `AutoShow` method. The syntax is as follows:

```
AutoShow(Type, Range, Count, Field)
```

where:

- `Type` is either `xlAutomatic` to enable a Top 10 filter for the field or `xlManual` to disable it.
- `Range` specifies whether top or bottom items are shown using the constants `xlTop` and `xlBottom`.

- `Count` specifies how many items to show.

- `Field` is the name of the field to use for determinations. It must be the unique field name (as returned from the `SourceName` property) and not the displayed name, which may be different.

This example enables `AutoShow` for the Salesperson field, assuming the PivotTable is named PivotTable1, displaying the top four records based on the value in the Total Sales field.

```
ActiveSheet.PivotTables("PivotTable1").PivotFields("Salesperson").AutoShow
xlAutomatic, xlTop, 4, "Total Sales"
```

Changing a Field's Summary Calculation

PivotTable reports enable you to specify various calculations to be performed by a data field, such as sum and average. You can change a field's calculation using VBA code by setting the field's `Calculation` property and sometimes the `BaseField` and `BaseItem` properties as well.

The Calculation field is set to a defined constant that specifies the calculation. The permitted values are:

- `xlDifferenceFrom`

- `xlIndex`

- `xlNoAdditionalCalculation`

- `xlPercentDifferenceFrom`

- `xlPercentOf`

- `xlPercentOfColumn`

- `xlPercentOfRow`

- `xlPercentOfTotal`

- `xlRunningTotal`

The `BaseField` property specifies the field that will be used as the base for the calculation.

The `BaseItem` property specifies the item in the `BaseField` property that will be used for the calculation.

What About OLAP Data?

Because field calculations for OLAP-based PivotTable reports are defined in the OLAP cube and not in the PivotTable itself, you cannot change the calculation displayed by data fields, either manually or in VBA code. You must modify the OLAP cube itself in order to change a field calculation.

The following code sets the calculation for the field referenced by the variable pf to be the difference from the Jun item in the Month field:

```
With pf
    .Calculation = xlDifferenceFrom
    .BaseField = "Month"
    .BaseItem = "Jun"
End With
```

Changing the Display Format of a Field

The display format used for numbers in a field is controlled by the field's `NumberFormat` property. To change the format you must generate a format string that defines the format. These strings use specific characters, as explained in the Table 10-4. (You can find complete details in the Excel online Help.)

TABLE 10-4   CHARACTERS USED IN STRINGS TO DEFINE FORMATTING

Character	Function
#	Defines a character-display position; insignificant zeros are not displayed.
0 (zero)	Defines a character-display position; insignificant zeros are displayed.
. (period)	Indicates the position of the decimal point.
, (comma)	Indicates a thousands separator.
$	Includes a leading dollar sign.
%	Displays number as a percent (for example, 0.08 as 8%).

Character	Function
[xxx] where xxx is Black, Green, White, Blue, Magenta, Yellow, Cyan, or Red	Specifies the text color.
; (semicolon)	Separates sections of the format string. The format specified before the separator is used for values 0 and greater; the format specified after the separator is used for values less than 0.
Other characters	As themselves, such as (and).

Some examples of format strings and the resulting displays are given in Table 10-5.

TABLE 10-5   EXAMPLE TABLE STRINGS AND RESULTS

Value	Format string	Displayed
123.4	0.00	123.40
123.4	0	123
123.4	0000	0123
123456	#,##0	123,456
123456	#,##0.00	123,456.00
123456	$#,###	$123,456
0.095	#.0%	9.5%
0.095	#.000%	9.500%
100000	$#,###.00;	$100,000.00
-100000	$(#,###.00)	$(100,000.00)

You can also control the display format of dates that are part of a PivotTable report. Certain characters in the format string determine how days, months, and years are displayed. These are described in Table 10-6.

Part III

TABLE 10-6   STRINGS THAT DETERMINE HOW DAYS, MONTHS, AND YEARS DISPLAY

To display	Use this code
Months as 1–12	m
Months as 01–12	mm
Months as Jan–Dec	mmm
Months as January–December	mmmm
Months as J–D	mmmmm
Days as 1–31	d
Days as 01–31	dd
Days as Sun–Sat	ddd
Days as Sunday–Saturday	dddd
Years as 00–99	yy
Years as 1900–1999	yyyy

Creating a PivotChart in Code

Creating a PivotChart in VBA code is surprisingly simple. Because a PivotChart is always based on a PivotTable report, all that is required is to create a new chart and then specify the PivotTable as its data source. More specifically, you need to specify the section of the PivotTable report that excludes the page fields, if there are any. The PivotTable object has the `TableRange1` property that returns this range. (The `TableRange2` property returns the range of the entire PivotTable report, including page fields.)

The procedure is as follows:

1. Call the `Charts` collection's `Add` method to create a new chart.

2. Call the chart's `Location` method to specify where the chart will be placed (see the following for details).

3. Call the chart's `SetSourceData` method, passing the `TableRange1` property of the PivotTable report as an argument.

The Location method has the following syntax:

```
Location(Where, Name)
```

where:

- Where is the constant xlLocationAsNewSheet, to put the chart on a new worksheet, or xlLocationAsObject, to embed the chart as an object on an existing worksheet.

- Name is optional if you are placing the chart on a new worksheet and specifies the name of the new sheet. If the Name argument is omitted, Excel assigns the default name to the worksheet (Chart1, Chart2, and so on). Name is required if you are embedding the chart on an existing worksheet and specifies the name of the worksheet where you want the chart placed.

Here's an example. This code creates a PivotChart and places it on a new worksheet named Sales Data Chart, basing the PivotChart on a PivotTable that is located on Sheet2 and is named PivotTable2:

```
Charts.Add
With ActiveChart
    .Location Where:=xlLocationAsNewSheet, Name:="Sales Data Chart" _
    .SetSourceData _
        Source:=Worksheets("Sheet2").PivotTables("PivotTable2").TableRange1
End With
```

Can't Create Embedded PivotCharts?

The VBA documentation says that you should be able to create a PivotChart embedded on an existing worksheet using the techniques described here. However, when you attempt to do so an Automation Error occurs, at least in my experience, it's not clear whether this is a bug or an error with the documentation.

Part III

Appendix A

Troubleshooting PivotTables and PivotCharts

PivotTables are powerful tools and with that power comes some unavoidable complexity. This section covers the more common problems that users encounter when creating and using PivotTables and suggests solutions.

Problems When Using External Data

This section covers problems that you may encounter when a PivotTable is based on external data.

Slow Responses or Error Messages

When you are creating a PivotTable based on external data, you may run into problems such as slow response and error messages. Some of these problems cannot be avoided because they are caused by problems with the external database itself or with your network connection to the data. You can, however, avoid or minimize these difficulties.

When your PivotTable report is based on a large amount of external data, laying the report out in the worksheet after completing the PivotTable wizard can be slow and can sometimes cause error messages to display. Specifically, when

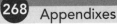

you add a field to an area of the PivotTable report there may be a delay before the data are retrieved and displayed. To prevent this, turn on the Defer Layout Update option at the bottom of the Field List. You can then make all the changes to the layout without any delays and then click the Update button to retrieve and display the data.

Problems Creating PivotTable Reports

This section covers common problems that you may encounter when creating a PivotTable report.

The Desired Source Report Is Not Listed in the Wizard

When you are creating a PivotTable report from an existing PivotTable report, the desired source PivotTable report may not be listed in Step 2 of the PivotTable and PivotChart Wizard. This is usually because the report is in a different workbook; the wizard lists only the PivotTable reports in the workbook that was active when the wizard was started. You can get around this problem by copying the desired source PivotTable report into the current workbook.

Problems with PivotTable Report Layout and Formatting

This section covers frequently encountered problems with PivotTable formatting and layout.

My Formatting Disappears

Some Excel users are dismayed to see their carefully applied formatting disappear when they refresh the table or change its layout. This can be avoided for most formatting by making sure that the Preserve Cell Formatting on Update option is selected in the PivotTable options dialog box.

I Cannot Pivot the Report

If you cannot move certain fields to pivot the report, there are several possible causes.

- If the PivotTable is based on OLAP data, certain fields may be restricted as to where in the report they can be placed. For example, a field may be usable only as a report filter field or a value field.

- The workbook may contain a VBA macro that disables the ability to drag fields.

- If the worksheet has protection turned on, and the Use PivotTable Reports option was not selected when the protection was enabled, you will not be able to modify the report layout.

Problems When Using OLAP Data

This section deals with problems frequently encountered with OLAP data.

The Summary Function I Want Is Not Available

A PivotTable report based on OLAP data is limited to the summary functions defined in the cube file. The OLAP Cube Wizard has a limited number of summary functions, namely Sum, Count, Min, and Max. It does not support the other summary functions such as StdDev and Product. There are two possible solutions:

- If the amount of data is such that your system can handle a standard query (that is, non-OLAP), then create the PivotTable report directly from the external data source rather than from an OLAP cube. You will then have the full range of summary functions available.

- Set up an OLAP server using Microsoft SQL Server OLAP Services. This product offers a much wider range of summary functions than the OLAP Cube Wizard that is part of Office.

Data Present in the Data Source Are Not Available for My PivotTable Report

An OLAP cube does not necessarily contain all of the data in the data source, and a PivotTable based on an OLAP cube is limited to the data in the cube. Depending on how the cube was created, you may be able to modify it to contain the needed data. If, however, the cube was created with the OLAP Cube Wizard in Microsoft Query, you will not be able to add data but will have to redefine a new cube that contains the data.

Appendix B

Excel Version Differences for PivotTables

The PivotTable capabilities of Excel have evolved over the years as new versions of Office were introduced. PivotTables and PivotCharts have undergone significant changes in Excel 2007, the latest version of the program and the one covered in this book. These changes primarily affect the way that you create and work with PivotTables and not the capabilities of the reports or charts themselves.

Perhaps the most obvious change is that the PivotTable and PivotChart Wizard has been replaced by a new Create PivotTable dialog box. This interface is much simpler and easier to use than the wizard, and much less prone to confusion and errors. The wizard is still available using the classic Excel keyboard commands, for those who prefer to use it.

Another major change is in how you lay out and pivot the table. Rather than dragging and dropping fields within the report itself, you use the redesigned field list which displays containers for the four areas of the report: row, column, value, and report filter. Note that what used to be called the data area is not the values area, and what used to be called a page field is now termed a report filter field. Note that the classic PivotTable layout is still available as an option, allowing you to drag and drop fields within the report itself.

PivotCharts have been streamlined as well. In older versions of Excel, many changes could be made to either the PivotTable or the PivotChart. Now, almost all modifications must be done with the underlying PivotTable to be reflected in the PivotChart.

Other PivotTable changes include the following:

- Improved persistence of formatting in PivotTables based on OLAP data.

- Improvements in table sorting to better meet user expectations.

- New table filters permitting filters to be defined on values, text, and dates.

- New expand/collapse indicators make the table structure clearer.

- Availability of three basic report layout options: compact, outline, and tabular.

- Table autoformat has been replaced with the more flexible and easier-to-use table styles.

- No more PivotTable toolbar. PivotTable commands are accessed via the Options and Design ribbons and context menus.

- In VBA, changes to the way you define filters for the PivotField object. There is no more PivotItems collection; rather, you use the PivotFilters property.

- When you add a second field to the Values area, PivotTables now default to putting the labels on columns and not rows.

- Connections to external data are easier to manage. You can see a list of the connections that are used in your workbook.

- If you choose format as table from the Home ribbon, you can format a range as an Excel table (used to be a list). If you then create a PivotTable based on this table, the input range is dynamic, that is any additions to the table (such as new rows) will show up in the PivotTable without having to redefine the input range.

Finally, some of the limitations as to the size and content of PivotTables have been increased:

- Maximum number of rows in a PivotTable increased from 64k to 1 million.

- Maximum number of columns in a PivotTable increased from 255 to 16k.

- Maximum number of unique items within a single PivotField increased from 32k to 1 million.

- The length at which fields' labels are truncated when added to PivotTable; this also includes caption length limitations: increased from 255 characters to 32k.

- The number of fields (as seen in the field list) that a single PivotTable can have increased from 255 to 16k.

Appendix C

An Excel Chart Primer

The charting abilities of Excel are extensive and powerful. When you combine Excel charts with PivotTables, you get PivotCharts, a means by which you can graphically display the data in a PivotTable report. You learned about the PivotChart-specific aspects in Chapter 6, which assumed that you had some basic knowledge of Excel charts in general. This appendix is provided for those readers whose experience with Excel charts is limited or who want to brush up on the basics. With this information, you will be able to format and customize your PivotCharts exactly as desired.

This appendix does not cover the steps required to create a chart but assumes that you have already created your PivotChart. Nor does it cover changing chart type, which was covered in Chapter 6.

Formatting Data Series

A data series in a chart represents a related set of values. Usually the values that make up a data series are in a row in the underlying table, although it is possible to have columns of values as data series as well. In a column or bar chart, a data series is represented by a set of columns/bars (or parts of columns/bars) with the same color or pattern. In a line chart, it is represented by a line with the same color and symbols. These two types of charts are illustrated in Figures C-1 and C-2.

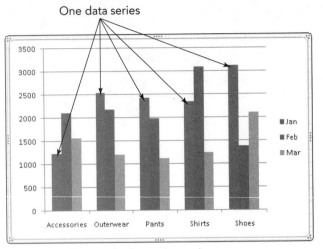

Figure C-1: Data series in a column chart.

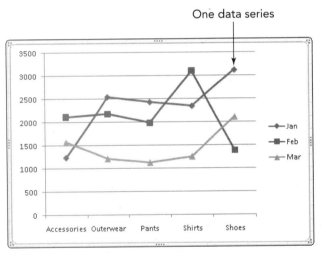

Figure C-2: Data series in a line chart.

You can change the format of a data series in a chart by right-clicking the data series and selecting Format Data Series from the popup menu. In the Format Data Series dialog box, the options available to you depend on whether you are working with a column chart or a line chart.

For a column chart, the data series format options are divided into several categories as listed on the left side of the Format Data Series dialog box (see Figure C-3). Select the desired category and the dialog box will display the available options on the right (as shown for the Fill options in the figure). The categories of options are:

- **Series Options**—Specify whether individual columns are overlapped or separated.

- **Fill**—Defines patterns and/or colors used to fill the columns.

- **Border Color**—Defines the color of the border around each column.

- **Border Styles**—Defines the style of the border around each column (width, solid/dashed, and so on).

- **Shadow**—Specifies shadow effects for the columns.

- **3-D Format**—Defines aspects of appearance for 3-D style charts.

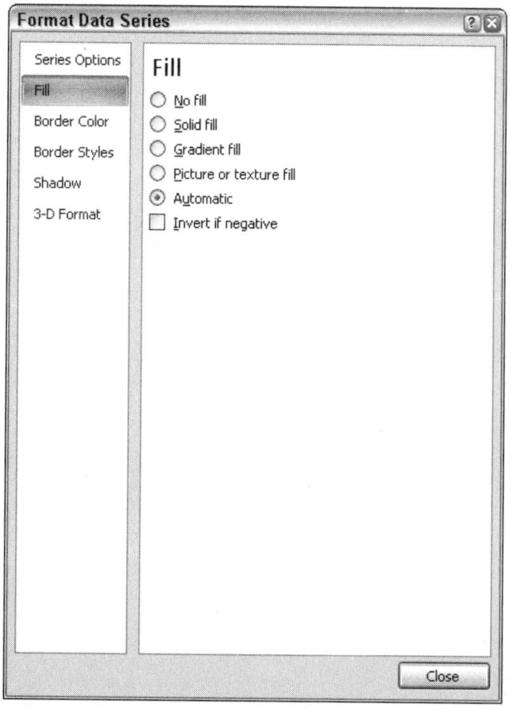

Figure C-3: Formatting options for a data series in a column chart.

If you are working with a line chart, the formatting options for a data series organized as shown in Figure C-4. The categories are:

- **Series Options**—Specify whether the series is plotted on the chart's main Y axis or on a secondary Y axis.

- **Marker Options**—Specifies the shape and size of the markers (symbols) displayed at each data point.

- **Marker Fill**—Defines the fill pattern for the series markers.

- **Line Color**—Defines the color of the series lines.

- **Line Style**—Defines the style (width, solid, dashed, and so on) for the series lines.

- **Marker Line Color**—Defines the color of the line around each marker.

- **Marker Line Style**—Defines the style (width, solid, dashed, and so on) for the line around each marker.

- **Shadow**—Defines shadow effects for the data series line and markers.

- **3-D Format**—Defines aspects of appearance for 3-D style charts.

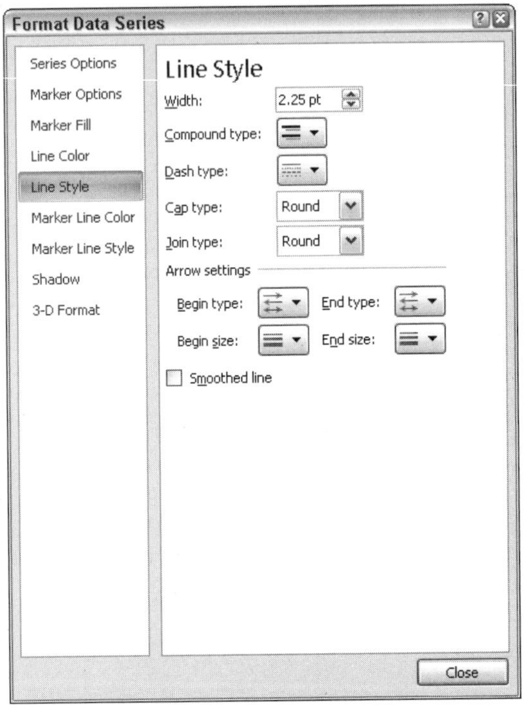

Figure C-4: Formatting options for a data series in a line chart.

Formatting Chart Axes

Most Excel charts have two axes. The vertical axis is called the *value axis* while the horizontal axis is called the *category axis*. Three-dimensional charts have three axes, the *series axis* as well as the other two. These axes are illustrated in Figures C-5 and C-6.

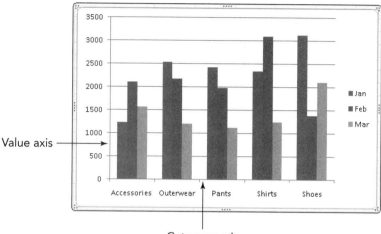

Value axis

Category axis

Figure C-5: Most line and column charts have two axes.

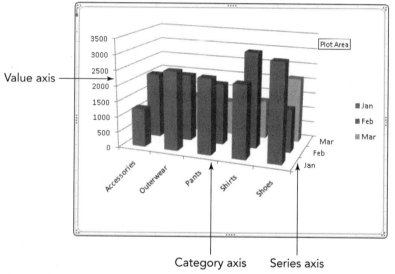

Value axis

Category axis   Series axis

Figure C-6: 3-D charts have three axes.

To change the format of an axis, right-click it and select Format Axis from the popup menu. The Format Axis dialog box has several categories that give you great flexibility in changing the appearance of an axis. The options that are available will differ somewhat depending on whether you are working with the value axis or the category or series axis. Let's look at some of the more important options.

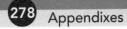

Axis Options

The Axis Options category for a value axis is shown in Figure C-7. The most important options in this category have to do with the axis scale. The axis scale is normally set by Excel to values based on the nature of the data. You can set these values manually by selecting the Fixed option next to a setting and then entering the desired value manually. The available settings are:

- **Minimum**—The lowest value on the value axis.

- **Maximum**—The highest value on the value axis.

- **Major unit**—The distance between major tick marks and labels.

- **Minor unit**—The distance between minor tick marks.

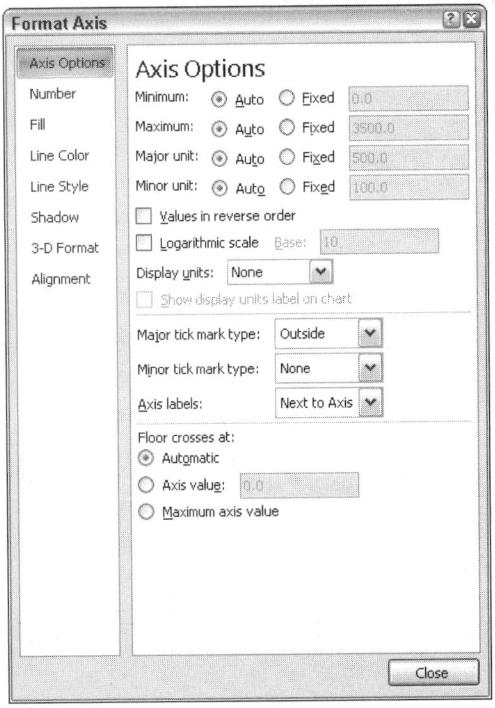

Figure C-7: Axis options for a value axis.

The Axis Options category for a category axis is shown in Figure C-8. Because numbers are not involved, there is no axis scale to worry about. You can specify the interval between category labels, the distance of the labels from the axis, the appearance of the tick marks, and whether the axis plot text or dates.

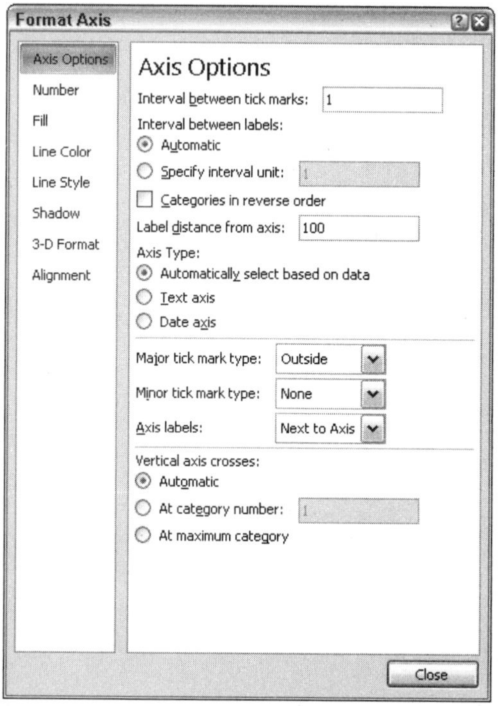

Figure C-8: Axis options for a category axis.

Number

The Number category is available in the Format Axis dialog box as shown in Figure C-9. It lets you specify the display format for axis numbers. The number formats are the same as those for formatted numerical values in a worksheet—Currency, Percent, General, and so on.

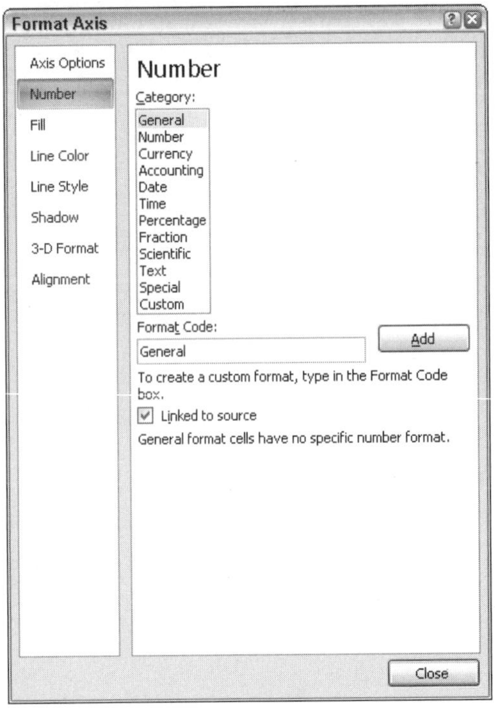

Figure C-9: The Number category in the Format Axis dialog box controls the display format of numbers on the axis.

Alignment

The Alignment category in the Format Axis dialog box, shown in Figure C-10, controls the text direction at which axis labels are displayed. By default the text direction is usually horizontal. In the Text Direction list you can choose to rotate the labels 90 degrees either to the left or right, or to stack the text. You can also use the Custom Angle field to specify another angle such as 45 degrees from the horizontal axis.

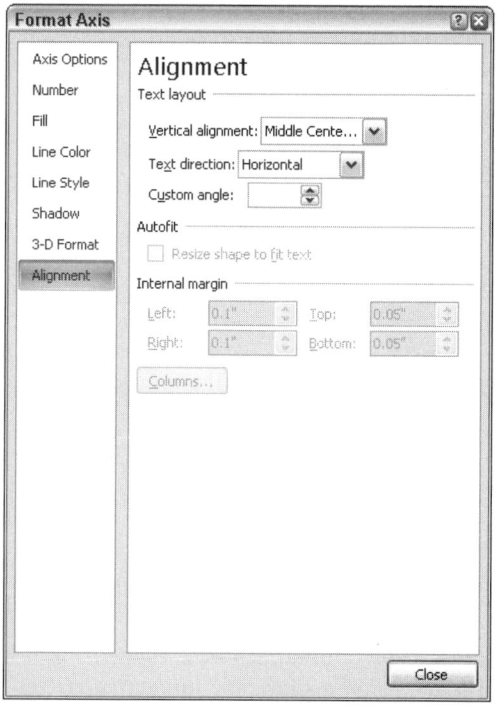

Figure C-10: The Alignment category in the Format Axis dialog box controls the display angle for axis labels.

Rotating the labels on the category axis can be useful when there are too many labels to display in the horizontal orientation.

Changing Font

To change the font used for axis labels, right-click the axis. Excel will display a popup menu and a formatting toolbar as shown in Figure C-11. You then have two choices.

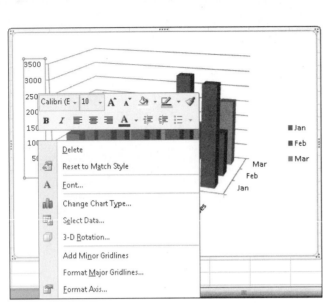

Figure C-11: Right-click an axis to display a popup menu and a formatting toolbar.

You can use the commands on the formatting toolbar to change the font, its size, the background and foreground colors, apply boldface and italics, change alignment, and so on. Or you can select the Font command on the popup menu to open the Font dialog box, which is shown in Figure C-12. This dialog box provides you with some font options that are not available on the formatting toolbar, such as underlining, strikethrough, and character spacing.

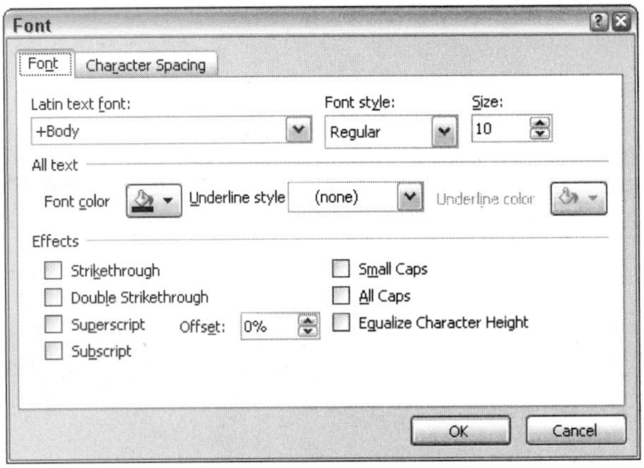

Figure C-12: Changing the axis font with the Font dialog box.

Changing Chart and Axis Titles

With a chart you have the option of displaying a title for the chart itself and for each axis in the chart. An axis title is distinct from the axis labels, as shown in Figure C-13.

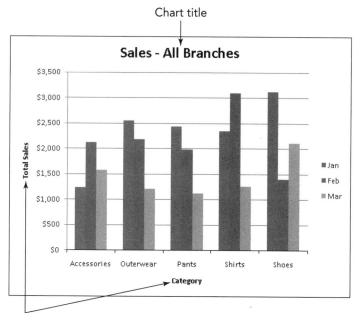

Figure C-13: A chart can display chart and/or axis titles.

To work with titles, make sure the chart is active, and then display the Layout ribbon. To add a chart title, click the Chart Title button, and then select one of the following:

- **None**—Removes an existing chart title.
- **Centered Overlay Title**—The chart remains the same size and the title is placed on top of the chart.
- **Above Chart**—The chart is made smaller vertically to make room for the title above the chart.

When you add a chart title it appears in position on the chart with the default text Chart Title. Click anywhere in the title to edit it.

> ## Linking Chart Titles to Worksheet Data
>
> You can link a chart title to a worksheet cell so that the title displays whatever is in the cell. Select the title in the chart, enter = in the formula bar, and then enter the cell address (or click the cell). Press Enter to complete the entry.

To add an axis title, click the Axis Titles button on the ribbon and select one of the following:

- **Primary Horizontal Axis Title**—Select None or place a horizontal title below the axis.
- **Primary Vertical Axis Title**—Select None, Rotated Title, Vertical Title, or Horizontal Title.

When you add an axis title, it will appear in the chart. Click it to edit the text.

To modify a title, right-click it to display the popup menu. Then select one of the following commands from the menu:

- **Delete**—Remove the title from the chart.
- **Edit Text**—Change the title text.
- **Font**—Change the font of the title.
- **Format**—Specify fill, borders, shadows, and other aspects of the title.

The Chart Legend

Excel creates a legend automatically for most charts. The legend, illustrated in Figure C-14, identifies the data series in the chart by color or symbol, depending on the chart type.

Some charts, such as those with only one data series, may not need a legend. You can remove it by right-clicking the legend and selecting Delete from the popup menu. You can also change the font of the legend by selecting Font from the popup menu.

Other aspects of the legend can be modified by selecting Format Legend from the popup menu to display the Format Legend dialog box, shown in Figure C-15. This dialog box has several categories, most of which are self-explanatory. The Legend Options category, shown in Figure C-15, lets you specify the location of the legend on the chart and whether it overlaps the chart.

Note that you can also set the position of the legend by clicking the Legend button on the Layout ribbon.

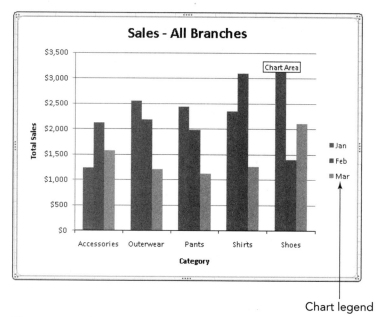

Chart legend

Figure C-14: The chart legend identifies the data series in the chart.

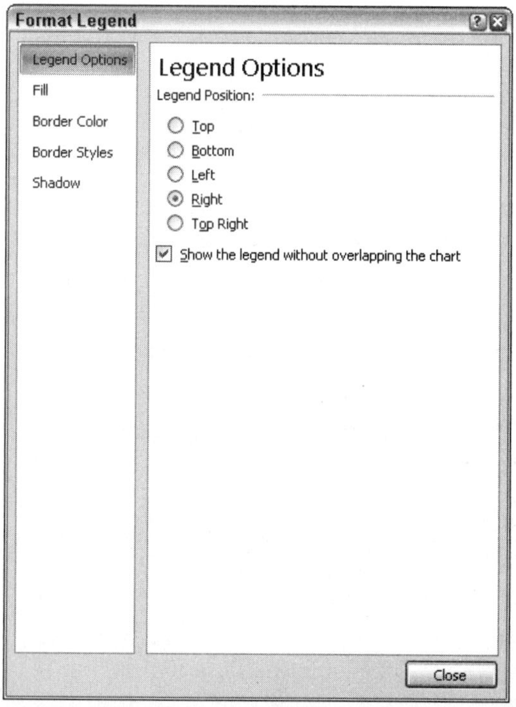

Figure C-15: The Format Legend dialog box lets you change the position of the legend.

Using Data Labels

Data labels provide a way for you to display text information directly on the chart. Figure C-16 shows an example in which the numerical values of two data points are displayed as a data label.

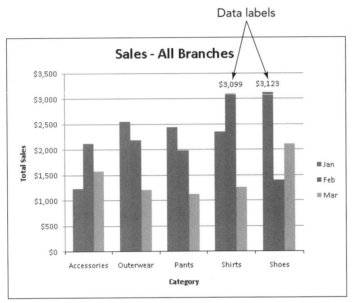

Figure C-16: Data labels let you display text information directly on the chart.

You can display data labels for all data series in the chart, for one or more individual data series, or for individual data points within a data series. Where data labels are displayed is controlled by what is selected:

- If no data series is selected in the chart, data labels are added to all data series.

- If a data series is selected, data labels are added to all data points in that series. To select a data series, click it. A selected data series is indicated by small handles displayed on each data point, as shown in Figure C-17.

- If a single data point is selected, a data label will be added for just that data point. To select a single data point, click it once to select the series and then click again to select just that data point.

To add data labels, first select the data point/series where you want the labels (or select nothing if you want the data labels on all data points). Then click the Data Labels button on the Layout ribbon. This menu, shown in Figure C-18, gives you several options as to how the data labels are positioned with respect to the data points and also lets you remove existing data labels.

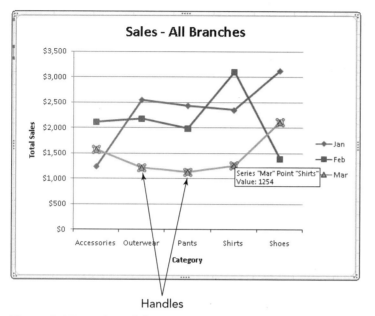

Handles

Figure C-17: A selected data series is indicated by handles on the data points.

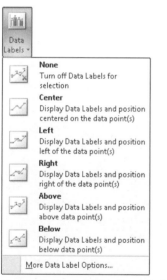

Figure C-18: Adding data labels to a chart.

After you have added your data labels, you can format them by right-clicking a label and selecting Format Data Labels from the popup menu. The dialog box that appears lets you select font, background, number format, and alignment for the labels. Note that a format applies only to labels for a single data series.

Other Chart Options

In this final section I will mention briefly some other chart options that you may find useful.

Gridlines

A chart can display vertical or horizontal gridlines in the background of the chart to provide visual organization and a scale for interpreting the chart data. Many of the Excel chart types display horizontal gridlines by default, but you also can customize gridlines to suit your needs. You can display gridlines at major tick intervals, minor tick intervals, or both.

To control gridlines, click the Gridlines button on the Layout ribbon. You can control horizontal and vertical gridlines separately, choosing to display gridlines at major tick intervals, minor tick intervals, or both—and of course you can turn gridlines off.

Displaying a Data Table

A data table displays a table of the chart's numerical data under the chart itself, as shown in Figure C-19. You can use a data table when you want to display precise number values as well as the overall trend. Data labels, covered earlier in this appendix, are another way to do this.

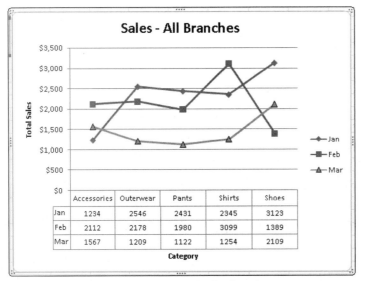

Figure C-19: A chart with a data table displayed.

To display a data table, click the Data Table button on the Layout ribbon. You can display the data table with or without a legend key, and of course you can remove an existing data table from a chart.

Index

Symbols

continued

continued